NEW
ENGLISH DRAMATISTS

6

INTRODUCED BY HAROLD HOBSON
EDITED BY TOM MASCHLER

A MAN FOR ALL SEASONS
Robert Bolt

THE DEVILS
John Whiting

NIL CARBORUNDUM
Henry Livings

PENGUIN BOOKS

Penguin Books Ltd, Harmondsworth, Middlesex
AUSTRALIA: Penguin Books Pty Ltd, 762 Whitehorse Road,
Mitcham, Victoria

—

A Man for All Seasons
First published by Heinemann 1960
Published in Penguin Books 1963
Copyright © Robert Bolt, 1961

—

The Devils
First published by Heinemann 1961
Published in Penguin Books 1963
Copyright © John Whiting, 1961

—

Nil Carborundum
First published in Penguin Books 1963
Copyright © Henry Livings, 1963

—

Made and printed in Great Britain
by Hazell Watson & Viney Ltd
Aylesbury, Bucks
Set in Monotype Bembo

CONTENTS

INTRODUCTION

EACH of the three plays included in this volume of Penguin Plays has been presented with considerable success in the West End of London; and one of them later obtained in the United States as great a triumph as has been achieved by any British production in recent years. But, although all three plays were seen and in varying degrees appreciated by London audiences, they differed a good deal in their methods of presentation. Robert Bolt's A MAN FOR ALL SEASONS was put on at the Globe Theatre in the summer of 1960 by H. M. Tennent, the most glittering of commercial managements, in the expectation of the long run which in actual fact it successfully accomplished. In the spring of 1962 the Arts Theatre, appealing to a small club audience of more than averagely intelligent playgoers, offered, under the aegis of the Royal Shakespeare Company, Henry Livings's NIL CARBOR-UNDUM. Between these dates the same Royal Shakespeare Company presented John Whiting's THE DEVILS at the Aldwych to audiences which, whilst less selective than those at the Arts, may be considered, because of the aesthetic prestige of Peter Hall's Company, to be on the whole less glossy and more serious-minded than the hundreds of pleasure-seekers who nightly crowded the Globe Theatre for several months on end.

All this is very curious. One would expect from these facts that the most severely intellectual of these dramas would be NIL CARBOR-UNDUM, and A MAN FOR ALL SEASONS the least. But exactly the opposite is the case. The liveliest, funniest, wildest, and most ribald of the three pieces in this book is in fact that written by Mr Livings, the one which was presented to the bulging brains of the Arts Theatre; whilst the prosperity of A MAN FOR ALL SEASONS was due to audiences which are popularly supposed to be both fashionable and stupid.

Superficially there is little resemblance between the work of Mr Bolt, Mr Whiting, and Mr Livings. Mr Livings's play is contemporary. Both the others are historical. But they deal with different countries and different periods of history. A MAN FOR ALL SEASONS had in it Paul Scofield, a star of the first magnitude. THE DEVILS included in its cast, if no one of the stature and fame of Mr Scofield, such well-known and admired players as Dorothy Tutin and Richard

7

Johnson; but NIL CARBORUNDUM was decorated by no eminent name, though James Booth gave in it an admirable performance in the part of the R.A.F. cook, Neville Harrison.

Fundamentally, however, they have a great deal in common. It is generally accepted nowadays that men and women are much more political animals than even Aristotle supposed them to be. Until our own lifetime it was more or less possible for private people to live private lives. I do not mean by this that they could carry on their daily affairs without risk of being harried by the gossip writers of the daily Press. I mean rather that if they wished they could ignore the sweep and nature of public developments. Napoleon rose and fell, George Osborne lay dead upon the field of Waterloo, and another George, considerably more illustrious, went mad without in the least interfering with the quiet, sarcastic lives of Jane Austen's heroes and heroines. Fielding wrote a long novel about the year 1745 without ever mentioning war seriously: and this at a time when Britain was actually being invaded.

Such detachment is no longer possible. A slight miscalculation in places as widely separated from each other and as far from us as Cuba, Berlin, or Laos could at any moment result in our own personal annihilation. We cannot therefore divorce our attention from world affairs: however insignificant we may be, they concern us vitally. The continuance of our existence depends on them.

This consciousness is bred into the bone of all serious writers today. It is certainly realized by Mr Bolt, Mr Whiting, and Mr Livings. It underlies uneasily these plays of theirs which appear to be so different from each other. The problem facing Neville Harrison, Sir Thomas More, and Urbain Grandier is essentially the same problem. They are at grips with a force infinitely greater than themselves: with the R.A.F., with the State, with the Church. They exist, in the twentieth century, in the sixteenth century, in the seventeenth century, in the impossibility of leading private lives. And they resent it.

Of the three dramatists Mr Livings is the only one who can propose a remedy for the ills that beset his hero. This does not mean that Mr Livings is a better dramatist than the other two. It is the business of the drama to ask questions rather than to answer them, to provoke deep and disquieting emotions and thoughts more than to offer slick panaceas. Nevertheless, Mr Livings does know, if not all the answers, at least one of them. But it will be time for that in a moment.

Mr Livings has no formal style. He does not bother about syntax. He writes as a man talks who is lounging over a pub counter. He is not pretentious, he is not difficult, but easy and colloquial. He does not shy away from clichés: he sees no shame in describing Warrant Officer McKendrick, the Catering Officer, as 'a tough old bird'. Of Taffy (A/C/2 Jones) he says, 'He is nearly illiterate, reads American funnies with hypnotized concentration and loves the sound and roll of the spoken word. He's a monumental mason by trade and it's a bloody shame he ever joined.' 'A bloody shame he ever joined': this is not one of Mr Livings's characters speaking: it is Mr Livings himself, in a serious piece of description. It amply demonstrates the unbuttoned, uninhibited nature of his way of writing. Yet now and again he catches a vivid, even memorable, phrase which contrasts with his normal informality, as when he writes of Margit ('grossly fat, and about fifty'), ' "Have your fun while you're young" she was telling herself fuzzily as a succession of airmen looted her last traces of bloom.'

There is some affection in these small sketches. Though he has never been produced at the Royal Court Theatre, Mr Livings is part of the social drama movement which started there with John Osborne's LOOK BACK IN ANGER. Like Arnold Wesker he finds most of his characters among the working class. These are the people that he likes. Mr Wesker in CHIPS WITH EVERYTHING is awed by the public-school boy Pip; Mr Osborne admires the Anglo-Indian colonel in LOOK BACK IN ANGER, and in his skit on royalty, THE BLOOD OF THE BAMBERGS, gives all the panache and quickness of decision to upper-class characters.

Mr Livings has none of this instinctive respect for authority. He is angry about the Commanding Officer of the R.A.F. Station he writes of in NIL CARBORUNDUM. 'Wing Commander Howard was a bomber hero during the war. He is now nothing but mis-spent aggression: a louring unhappy man, blackavised and a heavy drinker.' When he is not angry with this class of man, he is contemptuous. Thus, though he says of the Adjutant that he is earnest and intelligent, it is with a visible effort, and he immediately adds, 'If he were in his father's business or a bank he would not be an ass, but he isn't and here he seems an ass.' He is equally supercilious about Groupie (Group Captain Lyons). 'He sold vacuum cleaners door to door in 1939, and suddenly somebody made him a gentleman.'

But Mr Livings's ruling class do not have a monopoly of the disagreeable. John, the blind man, is malicious, the life of Sergeant Bull has been a 'tragic waste', and Mr Higgins, the civilian steward, is a phoney. The workers are not, in Mr Livings's eyes, all heroes. But they have their Taffys and Harrisons, and the upper classes, as represented in Mr Livings's R.A.F., do not. Still, in the main, it would appear to be Mr Livings's considered judgement that all classes of society are bad, but that some are worse than others.

Yet, when the play is performed, things do not work out at all like this. It is not the pessimistic view of human beings that strikes the audience so much as the high spirits of a rip-roaring farce. Perhaps when we saw the play at the Arts a good deal of this effect was due to the speed, precision, and gaiety of Anthony Page's brilliantly composed production. However this may be, the principal emotion that NIL CARBORUNDUM creates in performance is one of immense exhilaration. It is true that Mr Livings, beneath all the jokes and the horse-play, has a serious purpose. His R.A.F. camp caught up in a mock invasion exercise is deliberately of an unparalleled inefficiency. The home counties are supposed to have been devastated, and the umpires wear yellow arm-bands. This ludicrous contrast is emphasized by Mr Livings in order to embody the (for him) enormous and portentous futility of military activity.

One recognizes that easily enough. But there is something else that one recognizes even more easily. It is that this futility does not at all depress Mr Livings. He remains throughout in the most outrageous spirits. It would take more than a mock war to depress Mr Livings. He has what is one of the most vital elements of success in any activity: vitality. And out of his vitality springs something one would never guess from his cold, considered descriptions of his people. When he looks at them in dispassionate assessment he has a poor view of them. But in the heat of dramatic creation affection and love are generated in him. One of the best things in NIL CARBORUNDUM is the bitter fatuity of the Commanding Officer's speech to the camp at the start of the exercise. Anyone who saw the Arts production will remember how striking was the sardonic, rasping, self-hating performance of Graham Crowden at this point. One suddenly felt pity for this disappointed man.

Human beings in this play engage in ridiculous and useless and highly dangerous enterprises; but when he is feeling rather than thinking Mr Livings likes them. Officers roar orders; lights flash on when the camp is supposed to be in darkness; privates filch the camp's supplies and sell them in a clandestine market; spies walk in with broad grins on their faces, and, of course, such is the absurdity of the military mind, they are immediately mistaken for people of superior authority; yet for all these idiotic creatures Mr Livings proves to have an amiable affection.

Neville Harrison, the cook, is in the middle of all this muddle, but he is not of it. This is what I mean when I say that Mr Livings has an answer to man's present involvement with dangerous and interfering forces that are greater than himself. Through all the bustle and confusion, thieving, shouting, and folly which make up the action of this uproariously funny yet tragic play, Neville Harrison moves in and out of his kitchen, resolutely aloof and separate from everything that is going on around him. He is uninvolved, uncompromised, uncommitted, and alone. He is, in Mr Livings's opinion, a wise man.

This is a remarkable statement. For years now, advanced dramatists have been telling us that the world is ill, and it is our duty to find a medicine: Marx, Christianity, or even, with Ibsen, an unpolluted municipal water supply. Nonsense, maintains Mr Livings, in this, the first drama of disengagement. Take no notice of the patient. His delirium has by now become so violent that the sane man knows there is nothing to be done about it. In the midst of the rushing, the panic, the inefficiency, the petty larceny, the stupidity of the camp under mock attack, he bids us watch his National Service cook, the man who notices nothing; at the Arts Theatre Mr Booth showed us sardonically what resolution of negation this requires. And Mr Crowden, the Commanding Officer barking his futile orders, the aftermath of not having it.

Is this disturbing? Does Mr Livings really think that England –

humanity – is not worth saving? Is it really every man for himself? Perhaps it is his version of work out your own salvation. Has he no fear and trembling? No thumping heart? No heart at all? He does not give that impression. As I say, he seems (in the play) to like his people. Yet he dispatches them to their folly, without compunction and without regret. His laugh is untroubled, but dismissive.

Neville Harrison is not a complex character. One cannot imagine him singing madrigals, examining the theoretical bases of the *nouveau roman*, arguing the merits of Sartre against those of Camus as a revolutionary writer, speculating whether, when Simone de Beauvoir says that for years Sartre believed he was followed everywhere by a *langouste*, she means a tart or a crayfish, or even having a spirited evening of social protest at the Royal Court Theatre or the Establishment. He is simple and uncultivated. He may have heard of Winterbottom and Real Madrid, but not of Marguerite Duras. He can therefore cut himself off from society, with all its risks and madnesses, without personal deprivation. Mr Bolt's hero, Sir Thomas More, is a man of a different sort.

More loved God, but he loved the world also. His subtle intellect rejoiced in his being Lord Chancellor. He was skilled in words, and enjoyed the society of able and wealthy men. He wished to do the State service, and thought this service would be rendered best if he occupied an exalted position in the realm. His imagination could be touched by colour and pageantry, and he enjoyed the company of the King, as can be seen in the rhythms and mood of Mr Bolt's play. His problem therefore was not as simple as that of Harrison. He did not want to go out of the world and be separate. He had the more difficult desire of being separate and at the same time of remaining in the world. Harrison asks only to be left alone. More demands to be given everything but to be excused paying the last few pennies of the price. He reserves a part of himself from the domination of the State. He thinks that he can participate in all the glories of an earthly kingdom whilst keeping a part of the heavenly kingdom unsullied to himself. He wishes to be involved and disinvolved at the same time.

It is to be noted that he has a conscience, even a scrupulous conscience. There have been sincerely religious men who have not hesitated to tell lies, and even blaspheme in order to preserve their lives, and by preserving their lives to carry on the work with which they thought that God had entrusted them. Pascal talks of them in his *Lettres provinciales*. He attacks the Jesuits for their persecution of the suspectedly Jansenist convent of Port Royal, and reflects upon the conduct of their missionaries to the Far East. The courage of these missionaries cannot be questioned. They faced appalling dangers in order to spread the doctrines of their Church. But they were subtle men, and did not pursue a straight path. They would bow down before idols whilst holding a Cross up their sleeves. Pascal did not approve of this: nor would More. More was a less brave man than these Jesuits, for he was afraid of the stake, and they were not. But with steady nerves and casuistical reasoning they were determined to avoid the stake: and in the last resort More, a timider man, was not.

Mr Bolt dramatically shows his timidity. When Henry visits him the king and he talk of the king's desire for divorce from his wife Catherine of Aragon, who had been his sister-in-law. Mr Bolt's dialogue is vigorous and full of personality.

HENRY: ... You must consider, Thomas, that I stand in peril of my soul. It was no marriage; she was my brother's widow. Leviticus: 'Thou shalt not uncover the nakedness of thy brother's wife.' Leviticus, Chapter 18, Verse 16.

MORE: Yes, Your Grace. But Deuteronomy –

HENRY [*triumphant*]: Deuteronomy's ambiguous!

MORE [*bursting out*]: Your Grace, I'm not fit to meddle in these matters – to me it seems a matter for the Holy See –

HENRY [*reproving*]: Thomas, Thomas, does a man need a Pope to tell him when he's sinned? It was a sin, Thomas; I admit it; I repent. And God has punished me; I have no son. ... Son after son she's borne me, Thomas, all dead at birth, or dead within the month; I never saw the hand of God so clear in anything. ... I have a daughter, she's a good child, a well-set child – But I have no son. [*Flares up.*] It is my bounden *duty* to put away the Queen and all the Popes back to St Peter shall not come between me and my duty! How is it that you cannot see? Everyone else does.

MORE [*eagerly*]: Then why does Your Grace need my poor support?

HENRY: Because you are honest. What's more to the purpose, you're

13

known to be honest. . . . There are those like Norfolk who follow
me because I wear the Crown, and there are those like Master Cromwell who follow me because they are jackals with sharp teeth and I
am their lion, and there is a mass that follows me because it follows
anything that moves – and there is you.

MORE: I am sick to think how much I must displease Your Grace.

HENRY: No, Thomas, I respect your sincerity. Respect? Oh, man it's
water in the desert. . . . How did you like our music? That air
they played, it had a certain – well, tell me what you thought
of it.

MORE [relieved at this turn; smiling]: Could it have been Your Grace's
own?

HENRY [smiles back]: Discovered! Now I'll never know your true
opinion. And that's irksome, Thomas, for we artists, though we love
praise, yet we love truth better.

MORE [mildly]: Then I will tell Your Grace truly what I thought of it.

HENRY [a little disconcerted]: Speak then.

MORE: To me it seemed – delightful.

HENRY: Thomas – I chose the right man for Chancellor.

MORE: I must in fairness add that my taste in music is reputedly
deplorable.

HENRY: Your taste in music is excellent. It exactly coincides with my
own. . . .

But a moment later the King's preoccupation asserts itself, and
More betrays his weakness of nerve;

HENRY: No opposition I say! No opposition! Your conscience is your
own affair; but you are my Chancellor! There, you have my word –
I'll leave you out of it. But I don't take it kindly, Thomas, and I'll
have no opposition! I see how it will be; the Bishops will oppose me.
The full-fed, hypocritical, 'Princes of the *Church*'! Ha! As for the
Pope! Am I to burn in Hell because the Bishop of Rome, with the
Emperor's knife to his throat, mouths me Deuteronomy? Hypocrites! They're all hypocrites! Mind they do not take you in,
Thomas! Lie low if you will, but I'll brook no opposition – no words,
no signs, no letters, no pamphlets – mind that, Thomas, no writings
against me!

MORE: Your Grace is unjust. I am Your Grace's loyal minister. If I
cannot serve Your Grace in this great matter of the Queen –

HENRY: I have no Queen! Catherine is not my wife and no priest can

make her so, and they that say she is my wife are not only liars . . .
but Traitors! Mind it, Thomas!

MORE: Am I a babbler, Your Grace? [*But his voice is unsteady.*]

Now this dialogue illustrates one of Mr Bolt's weaknesses. He does
not seem to trust his actors. Why all those brackets? Why those
incessant instructions on how the words are to be spoken? They are
surely expressive enough in themselves. But it shows Mr Bolt's
strength also. There is no fustian here. He adapts himself naturally to
the speech of the eminent and royal. And subtly and slightly he
reveals the two traits of More's character which are the foundation
of his play.

The first is his unreadiness of courage, and the other his quickness
in wit. No man is more difficult to deal with than an author who asks
one to one's face what one thinks of his work. But on this point
More handles Henry with consummate skill. It is this skill, applied to
his knowledge of the law, in which he puts his trust. 'And whoever
hunts for me, Roper, God, or Devil, will find me hiding in the
thickets of the law! And I'll hide my daughter with me! Not hoist
her up the mainmast of your seagoing principles! They put about so
nimbly!' He believes that he can avoid committing himself. As I said
when the play was first produced in London, so long as More has
not been condemned to the last penalty, he answers no question
straightly, reveals, even to his wife or daughter, no opinion on any
question that shook England at the time of Henry VIII's desire for
divorce from Catherine of Aragon, takes no stand on any issue. If he
makes no statement of any kind, he believes that the impenetrable
thickets of the law will protect him from danger. If he says nothing,
he cannot be proved wrong. He is not, as he himself says, the stuff of
which martyrs are made.

The dramatic interest of Mr Bolt's play, therefore, is that of a
prolonged cross-examination. The King, the Duke of Norfolk, above
all, Thomas Cromwell, appeal to his affection, or to his fear, to make
him declare on which side of the quarrel between State and Pope he
stands. His eyes peering dimly, watching the consequences and
implications of every question that is proposed to him, his face lined
deep with the anxiety of a man who knows that everything that is
said to him is a trap that may prove deadly, his voice dry so that

what cannot be divined from words spoken shall not be revealed in an intonation, Paul Scofield's More was an infinitely instructed lawyer resolved to preserve, in spite of all the speeches he makes, what is, in effect, a silence.

More will not utter a lie. He is not like those Jesuit missionaries, though he is less brave than they. But he uses constantly all the resources of an unsleeping and at times even devious intellect to avoid, till faced with the last compulsion, telling the truth. When that compulsion comes, when nothing can be saved by evasion, he does indeed say what he thinks in words that still ring down the ages. Much of More's speech in this play is made up of his actual words, and this gives the script an unusual distinction which Mr Bolt has spoilt only occasionally with such uncouth observations as, 'The case rests.'

The play is an intellectual feat of a high order, displaying the intricacies of an acute and cultivated mind. After its long London run it went to New York, and there it made one of the biggest successes ever achieved by an English play. Mr Bolt's previous drama, FLOWERING CHERRY, a frankly theatrical piece, had not pleased American audiences at all, but A MAN FOR ALL SEASONS gave them that delightful sense of participating in an elevated cultural exercise which they value highly.

Mr Scofield's performance too was enormously regarded in the United States. For myself I found him a trifle grey. I saw in his performance the unwearied mind and the unflagging caution, but not till the end the blaze of excitement. But in the last moments of the play he was very fine. Till then he had offered us a bowed and stooping man. For the first time, when hope is finally lost, and no means exist any longer for escaping the declaration of what truly is in him, he straightened his back and lifted his voice. I am bound to say that the effect was very great.

The play in London had the advantage of a strong supporting company, who brought out its compelling qualities both as a police story, in that it deals with the trapping of a clever man, and as a tale of heroism. The figure of Henry is particularly interesting. Richard Leech, carefully following Mr Bolt's intentions, did not give the audience a replica of the gross Holbein portrait as Charles Laughton had done in the film *The Private Life of Henry VIII* twenty years earlier, but offered instead a sketch of the king, who was after all a highly cultured man, as a forerunner of the Roi Soleil. In performance Cromwell becomes a dominating character in the play, though at the Globe Theatre Alexander Keir hardly made him subtle enough to look like the first man in England to have read Machiavelli. But the most curious character of all is the Common Man.

About this repellent being, who was powerfully played by Leo McKern, Mr Bolt seems in the process of time to have changed his mind; and not only to have changed his mind, but to have changed it quickly. Writing in September 1960 Mr Bolt says,

He is called 'The Common Man' (just as there is a character called 'The King') and the word 'common' was intended primarily to indicate 'that which is common to us all'. But he was taken instead as a portrayal of that mythical beast 'The Man In The Street'. This in itself was not so bad; after all he was intended to be something with which everyone would be able to identify. But once he was identified as common in that sense, my character was by one party accepted as a properly belittling account of that vulgar person, and by another party bitterly resented on his behalf.

This is clear and convincing, and marks down two foreseeable reactions of the public. It is what Mr Bolt goes on to say that is surprising, surprising, that is, in view of his instructions in the play. For in September 1960, in the Preface to the published text, he not only comes down strongly on the side of the Common Man, but claims that he has been on his side from the beginning. 'Myself I had meant him to be attractive, and his philosophy impregnable.' These words are unequivocal. Yet in his description of characters in the play Mr Bolt says, 'THE COMMON MAN: Late middle age. He wears from head to foot black tights which delineate his pot-bellied figure. His face is crafty, loosely benevolent, its best expression that of base humour.' Can one really suppose that Mr Bolt admires pot bellies or sees in base humour impregnable philosophy? I incline rather to think that Mr Bolt, seeing in performance what he had done to democracy's impressions of itself, regretted the effect of a too-emphatic performance, and convinced himself that his original intention had been something wholly different.

In John Whiting's THE DEVILS, presented in London for the first time in February 1961, it is a priest, Urbain Grandier, Vicar of St Peter's Church in Loudun, who finds himself inextricably caught in conflict, not with the State, but with the Church. He is a less mentally resourceful man than More, though infinitely suppler than Harrison; and like More, he does not escape. The theme of the play is taken from Aldous Huxley's *The Devils of Loudun*. This book was brought to Mr Whiting's attention by Peter Hall with the suggestion that he should make a play out of it. Mr Whiting had not written for the stage for several years before Mr Hall came to him with this request. His previous pieces, especially SAINT'S DAY, had been so savagely received by critics, and so neglected by the public, that he may well have felt discouraged. If so, the welcome given to THE DEVILS has probably done a great deal to encourage him. For it was immediately recognized as a work of distinction.

Mr Whiting has conceived a wonderfully complex method through which his story of lust and hysteria and salvation is unfolded in a narrative that, in spite of constant changes of character and setting, preserves an absolutely uninterrupted progression from the beginning to the end. The play is written in a multiplicity of brief scenes, yet its continuity is unbroken. THE DEVILS is a marvel of organization, a mosaic so finely put together that it has the effect of a living picture.

Its central theme is that of a man who searches for God through many different ways: first through lust, then through human affection, then through martyrdom, and at last through disciplined thought. Even from the beginning this capacity for controlled thinking is apparent in Grandier. There is a very fine scene in which Grandier preaches from his pulpit against the accusations of demonic possession which have been brought against him.

GRANDIER: ... For some lewd fellows go about the town and speak against me. I know them. And you will know them when I say that Surgery and Chemistry go hand in hand, vermination against the wall. They have borne false witness. They spy. They sneak. They snigger. And the first sinful man was called Adam, and he begot murder. Why do they pursue me? I am not sick!

If they be here, in this holy place, let them stand before me and

18

declare their hatred, and give the reason for it. I am not afraid to speak openly of what they attempt to discover secretly. If they be in this church let them stand before me. [*Silence.*] No, they are in some hole in the ground, scratching, so that more venom may come to the surface, and infect us all; distilling bile in retorts; revealing lust, envy, and blight with the turn of a scalpel. . . .

O my dear children, I should not speak to you so from this place. And I should not speak to you in bitterness as your pastor.

Do they provoke me to anger? saith the Lord: do they not provoke themselves to the confusion of their own faces?

The man who, even in his lust, is capable of this controlled and memorable speech, these brief, incisive phrases, is already more than half prepared for the growing steadfastness of his resolution when the day of his trial comes. At the Aldwych Richard Johnson was an exceedingly handsome Grandier, a smooth, proud figure who might well make the hearts of the girls in his congregation beat faster. But he seemed to play Grandier from the outside. I never quite believed that any fire, of lust or religion or intellect, was burning within him. Patrick Wymark, on the other hand, as Laubardemont, pressed his questions with a grinding and perverse joy that made the last scenes in the play more memorable than any of the others.

LAUBARDEMONT: I fear for you, Grandier. I fear for you very much. I have seen men before you take this brave standing in the shadow of the Question. It was unwise. Grandier. Think again.

GRANDIER: No.

LAUBARDEMONT: You will go into the darkness before your death. Let me talk to you a moment about pain. It is very difficult for us standing here, both healthy men, to imagine the shattering effect of agony. The sun's warm on your face at the moment, isn't it? And you can curl your toes if you want in your slippers. You are alive, and you know it. But when you are stretched out in that little room, with the pain screaming through you like a voice, let me tell you what you will think. First: how can man do this to man? Then: how can God allow it? Then: there can be no God. Then: there is no God. The voice of pain will grow stronger, and your resolution weaker. Despair, Grandier. You used the word yourself. You called it the gravest sin. Don't reject God at this moment. Reconcile yourself. For you have bitterly offended Him. Confess.

GRANDIER: No.

D'ARMAGNAC: Are those tears on De Laubardemont's face?

DE CERISAY: I'm afraid so.

D'ARMAGNAC: Does he believe what he's saying?

DE CERISAY: Yes. Touching, isn't it?

LAUBARDEMONT [*to Grandier*]: Very well, I ask you once more. Once more! Will you sign?

    [GRANDIER *shakes his head.*]

LAUBARDEMONT: Take him away.

    [*The guard surrounds Grandier.*]

This, then, after the hilarity and outrageousness of NIL CARBORUNDUM, is the gloom to which we have come. Or rather this is the gloom from which we have come away. It is the men of the sixteenth and seventeenth centuries who are destroyed, and the man of our own day who escapes. There may be comfort and hope for us yet.

HAROLD HOBSON

ROBERT BOLT

A Man for All Seasons

More is a man of an angel's wit and singular learning; I know not this fellow. For where is the man of that gentleness, lowliness, and affability? And as time requireth a man of marvellous mirth and pastimes; and sometimes of a sad gravity: a man for all seasons.

ROBERT WHITTINGTON

He was the person of the greatest virtue these islands ever produced.

SAMUEL JOHNSON

First presented in London at the Globe Theatre on 1 July 1960 by
H. M. Tennent Ltd, with the following cast:

THE COMMON MAN	Leo McKern
THOMAS MORE	Paul Scofield
RICHARD RICH	John Brown
THE DUKE	Alexander Gauge
ALICE MORE	Wynne Clark
MARGARET MORE	Pat Keen
THE CARDINAL	Willoughby Goddard
THOMAS CROMWELL	Andrew Keir
THE AMBASSADOR	Geoffrey Dunn
HIS ATTENDANT	Brian Harrison
WILLIAM ROPER	John Carson
THE KING	Richard Leech
A WOMAN	Beryl Andrews
THE ARCHBISHOP	William Roderick

Directed by Noël Willman
Scenery and costumes by Motley

CHARACTERS

THE COMMON MAN: Late middle age. He wears from head to foot black tights which delineate his pot-bellied figure. His face is crafty, loosely benevolent, its best expression that of base humour.

SIR THOMAS MORE: Late forties. Pale, middle-sized, not robust. But the life of the mind in him is so abundant and debonair that it illuminates the body. His movements are open and swift but never wild, having a natural moderation. The face is intellectual and quickly delighted, the norm to which it returns serious and compassionate. Only in moments of high crisis does it become ascetic – though then freezingly.

RICHARD RICH: Early thirties. A good body unexercised. A studious unhappy face lit by the fire of banked down appetite. He is an academic hounded by self-doubt to be in the world of affairs and longing to be rescued from himself.

DUKE OF NORFOLK: Late forties. Heavy, active, a sportsman and soldier held together by rigid adherence to the minimal code of conventional duty. Attractively aware of his moral and intellectual insignificance, but also a great nobleman, untouchably convinced that his acts and ideas are important because they are his.

ALICE MORE: Late forties. Born into the merchant class, now a great lady, she is absurd at a distance, impressive close to. Overdressed, coarsely fashioned, she worships society; brave, hot-hearted, she worships her husband. In consequence, troubled by and defiant towards both.

MARGARET MORE: Middle twenties. A beautiful girl of ardent moral fineness; she both suffers and shelters behind a reserved stillness which it is her father's care to mitigate.

CARDINAL WOLSEY: Old. A big decayed body in scarlet. An almost megalomaniac ambition unhappily matched by an excelling intellect, he now inhabits a lonely den of self-indulgence and contempt.

THOMAS CROMWELL: Late thirties. Subtle and serious; the face expressing not inner tension but the tremendous outgoing will of the renaissance. A self-conceit that can cradle gross crimes in the name of effective action. In short an intellectual bully.

23

CHAPUYS: Sixties. A professional diplomat and lay ecclesiastic dressed in black. Much on his dignity as a man of the world, he in fact trots happily along a mental footpath as narrow as a peasant's.

CHAPUYS'S ATTENDANT: An apprentice diplomat of good family.

WILLIAM ROPER: Early thirties; a stiff body and an immobile face. Little imagination, moderate brain, but an all-consuming rectitude which is his cross, his solace, and his hobby.

THE KING: *Not* the Holbein Henry, but a much younger man, clean-shaven, bright-eyed, graceful, and athletic. The Golden Hope of the New Learning throughout Europe. Only the levity with which he handles his absolute power foreshadows his future corruption.

A WOMAN: Middle fifties. Self-opinionated, self-righteous, selfish, indignant.

CRANMER: Late forties. Sharp-minded, sharp-faced. He treats the Church as a job of administration and theology as a set of devices, for he lacks personal religiosity.

ACT ONE

[*When the curtain rises, the set is in darkness but for a single spot which descends vertically upon the* COMMON MAN, *who stands in front of a big property basket.*]

COMMON MAN: It is perverse! To start a play made up of Kings and Cardinals in speaking costumes and intellectuals with embroidered mouths, with me.

If a King or a Cardinal had done the prologue he'd have had the right materials. And an intellectual would have shown enough majestic meanings, coloured propositions, and closely woven liturgical stuff to dress the House of Lords! But this!

Is this a costume? Does this say anything? It barely covers one man's nakedness! A bit of black material to reduce Old Adam to the Common Man.

Oh, if they'd let me come on naked, I could have shown you something of my own. Which would have told you without words –! . . . Something I've forgotten . . . Old Adam's muffled up. [*Backing towards basket*] Well, for a proposition of my own, I need a costume. [*Takes out and puts on the coat and hat of* STEWARD.] Matthew! The Household Steward of Sir Thomas More! [*Lights come up swiftly on set. He takes from the basket five silver goblets, one larger than the others, and a jug with a lid, with which he furnishes the table. A burst of conversational merriment off; he pauses and indicates head of stairs.*] There's company to dinner. [*Finishes business at table.*] All right! A Common Man! A sixteenth-century Butler! [*He drinks from the jug.*] All right – the six – [*Breaks off, agreeably surprised by the quality of the liquor, regards the jug respectfully, and drinks again.*] The sixteenth century is the Century of the Common Man. [*Puts down the jug.*] Like all the other centuries. [*Crossing right*] And that's my proposition.

[*During the last part of the speech, voices off. Now, enter, at head of stairs,* SIR THOMAS MORE.]

STEWARD: That's Sir Thomas More.

MORE: The wine please, Matthew?

STEWARD: It's there, Sir Thomas.

MORE [looking into jug]: Is it good?

STEWARD: Bless you, sir! *I* don't know.

MORE [mildly]: Bless you too, Matthew.

[Enter RICH at head of stairs.]

RICH [enthusiastically pursuing an argument]: But every man has his price!

STEWARD [contemptuous]: Master Richard Rich.

RICH: But yes! In money too.

MORE [gentle impatience]: No no no.

RICH: Or pleasure. Titles, women, bricks-and-mortar, there's always something.

MORE: Childish.

RICH: Well, in suffering, certainly.

MORE [interested]: Buy a man with suffering?

RICH: Impose suffering, and offer him – escape.

MORE: Oh. For a moment I thought you were being profound.

[Gives cup to Rich.]

RICH [to Steward]: Good evening, Matthew.

STEWARD [snubbing]: 'Evening, sir.

RICH: No, not a bit profound; it then becomes a purely practical question of how to make him suffer sufficiently.

MORE: Mm . . . [Takes him by the arm and walks with him.] And . . . who recommended you to read Signor Machiavelli?

[RICH breaks away laughing; a fraction too long. MORE smiles.]

No, who? [More laughter.] . . . Mm?

RICH: Master Cromwell.

MORE: Oh . . . [Back to the wine jug and cups.] He's a very able man.

RICH: And so he is!

MORE: Yes, I say he is. He's very able.

RICH: And he will do something for me, he says.

MORE: I didn't know you knew him.

RICH: Pardon me, Sir Thomas, but how much do you know about me?

MORE: Whatever you've let me know.

RICH: I've let you know everything!

MORE: Richard, you should go back to Cambridge; you're deteriorating.

RICH: Well, I'm not used! ... D'you know how much I have to show for seven months' work –

MORE: – Work?

RICH: – Work! Waiting's work when you wait as I wait, hard! ... For seven months, that's two hundred days, I have to show: the acquaintance of the Cardinal's outer doorman, the indifference of the Cardinal's inner doorman, and the Cardinal's chamberlain's hand in my chest! ... Oh – also one half of a Good Morning delivered at fifty paces by the Duke of Norfolk. Doubtless he mistook me for someone.

MORE: He was very affable at dinner.

RICH: Oh, everyone's affable *here*. . . .

   [MORE *is pleased*.]

Also of course, the friendship of Sir Thomas More. Or should I say acquaintance?

MORE: Say friendship.

RICH: Well, there! 'A friend of Sir Thomas and still no office? There must be something wrong with him.'

MORE: I thought we said friendship. . . . [*Considers; then*] The Dean of St Paul's offers you a post; with a house, a servant, and fifty pounds a year.

RICH: What? What post?

MORE: At the new school.

RICH [*bitterly disappointed*]: A teacher!

MORE: A man should go where he won't be tempted. Look Richard, see this. [*Hands a silver cup.*] Look . . . Look . . .

RICH: Beautiful.

MORE: Italian . . . Do you want it?

RICH: Why – ?

MORE: No joke; keep it; or sell it.

RICH: Well I – Thank you of course – Thank you! Thank you! But –?

MORE: You'll sell it, won't you?

RICH: Yes, I think so. Yes, I will.

MORE: And buy, what?

RICH [*sudden ferocity*]: Some decent clothes!

MORE [*with sympathy*]: Ah.

RICH: I want a gown like yours.

MORE: You'll get several gowns for that I should think. It was sent to me a little while ago by some woman. Now she's put a lawsuit into the Court of Requests. It's a bribe, Richard.

RICH: Oh . . . [*Chagrined*] So you give it away of course.

MORE: Yes!

RICH: To me?

MORE: Well, I'm not going to keep it, and you need it. Of course – if you feel it's contaminated . . .

RICH: No, no. I'll risk it.

[*Both smile.*]

MORE: But, Richard, in office they offer you all sorts of things. I was once offered a whole village, with a mill, and a manor house, and heaven knows what else – a coat of arms I shouldn't be surprised. Why not be a teacher? You'd be a fine teacher. Perhaps, a great one.

RICH: And if I was who would know it?

MORE: You, your pupils, your friends, God. Not a bad public, that. . . . Oh, and a *quiet* life.

RICH [*laughing*]: *You* say that!

MORE: Richard, I was commanded into office; it was inflicted on me. . . .

[RICH *regards him.*]

Can't you believe that?

RICH: It's hard.

MORE [*grimly*]: Be a teacher.

[*Enter at head of stairs* NORFOLK.]

STEWARD [*to audience*]: The Duke of Norfolk. A lord.

NORFOLK: I tell you he stooped from the clouds! [*Breaks off, irritable.*] Alice!

[*Enter instantly at head of stairs* ALICE.]

ALICE [*irritable*]: Here!

STEWARD [*to audience*]: Lady Alice. My master's wife.

NORFOLK: I tell you he stooped –

ALICE: – He didn't –

NORFOLK: – Goddammit he did –

28

ALICE: – Couldn't –

NORFOLK: – He *does* –

ALICE: – Not possible –

NORFOLK: – But *often* –

ALICE: – Never.

NORFOLK: Well, damn my soul. [*Takes wine.*] Thank you, Thomas.

MORE [*to* MARGARET, *having appeared on gallery*]: Come down, Meg.

STEWARD [*to audience, soapy*]: Lady Margaret, my master's daughter, lovely; really lovely.

ALICE (*glances suspiciously at Steward*): Matthew, get about your business.

[*Exit* STEWARD.]

We'll settle this, my lord, we'll put it to Thomas. Thomas, no falcon could stoop from a cloud, could it?

MORE: I don't know, my dear; it sounds unlikely. I have seen falcons do some very splendid things.

ALICE: But how could he stoop from a cloud? He couldn't see where he was going.

NORFOLK: You see, Alice – you're ignorant of the subject; a real falcon don't *care* where he's going! Anyway, I'm talking to Meg. [*A sportsman's story.*] 'Twas the very first cast of the day, Meg; the sun was behind us. And from side to side of the valley like the roof of a tent, was solid mist –

ALICE: Oh, mist.

NORFOLK: Well, mist is cloud isn't it?

ALICE: No.

RICH: The opinion of Aristotle is that mists are an exhalation of the earth whereas clouds –

NORFOLK: He stooped five hundred feet! Like *that*! Like an Act of God isn't he, Thomas?

MORE: He's tremendous.

NORFOLK [*to Alice*]: Tremendous.

MARGARET: Did he kill the heron?

NORFOLK: Oh, the *heron* was *clever*. [*Very discreditable evidently.*] It was a royal stoop though. [*Sly*] If you could ride, Alice, I'd show you.

ALICE [*hotly*]: I can ride, my lord!

MORE: No, no, you'll make yourself ill.

ALICE: And I'll bet – twenty-five – no thirty shillings I see no falcon stoop from no cloud!

NORFOLK: Done.

MORE: Alice – you can't ride with *them*.

ALICE: God's body, Thomas, remember who you are. Am I a City Wife?

MORE: No indeed, you've just lost thirty shillings I think; there *are* such birds. And the heron got home to his chicks, Meg, so everything was satisfactory.

MARGARET [*smiling*]: Yes.

MORE: What was that of Aristotle's, Richard?

RICHARD: Nothing, Sir Thomas – 'twas out of place.

NORFOLK [*to Rich*]: I've never found much use in Aristotle myself, not practically. Great philosopher of course. Wonderful mind.

RICH: Exactly, Your Grace!

NORFOLK [*suspicious*]: Eh?

MORE: Master Rich is newly converted to the doctrines of Machiavelli.

RICH: Oh *no*. . . !

NORFOLK: Oh, the Italian. Nasty book, from what I hear.

MARGARET: Very practical, Your Grace.

NORFOLK: You read it? Amazing girl, Thomas, but where are you going to find a husband for her?

[MORE *and* MEG *exchange a glance.*]

MORE: Where indeed?

RICH: The doctrines of Machiavelli have been largely mistaken I think; indeed properly apprehended he has no doctrine. Master Cromwell has the sense of it I think when he says –

NORFOLK: You know Cromwell?

RICH: . . . Slightly, Your Grace. . . .

NORFOLK: The Cardinal's Secretary.

[*Exclamations of shock from* MORE, MARGARET, *and* ALICE.]
It's a fact.

MORE: When, Howard?

NORFOLK: Two, three days.

[*They move about uneasily.*]

ALICE: A *farrier's* son?

NORFOLK: Well, the Cardinal's a butcher's son, isn't he?

ALICE: It'll be up quick and down quick with Master Cromwell.
  [NORFOLK *grunts.*]

MORE [*quietly*]: Did you know this?

RICH: No!

MARGARET: Do you *like* Master Cromwell, Master Rich?

ALICE: He's the only man in London if he does!

RICH: I think I do, Lady Alice!

MORE [*pleased*]: Good. . . Well, you don't need *my* help now.

RICH: Sir Thomas, if only you knew how much, much rather I'd
  yours than his!
  [*Enter* STEWARD *at head of stairs. Descends and gives letter to
  More who opens it and reads.*]

MORE: Talk of the Cardinal's Secretary and the Cardinal appears.
  He wants me. Now.

ALICE: At this time of the night?

MORE [*mildly*]: The King's business.

ALICE: The Queen's business.

NORFOLK: More than likely, Alice, more than likely.

MORE [*cuts in sharply*]: What's the time?

STEWARD: Eleven o'clock, sir.

MORE: Is there a boat?

STEWARD: Waiting, sir.

MORE [*to Alice and Margaret*]: Go to bed. You'll excuse me, Your
  Grace? Richard? [*Kisses wife and daughter.*] Now you'll go to bed.
  . . . [*The More family, as a matter of routine, put their hands together
  and:*]

MORE } Dear Lord give us rest tonight, or if we must be
ALICE } wakeful, cheerful. Careful only for our soul's salva-
MARGARET } tion. For Christ's sake. Amen.

MORE: And Bless our Lord the King.

ALICE } And Bless our Lord the King.
MARGARET }

ALL: Amen.
  [*And then immediately a brisk leave-taking,* MORE *moving off below,
  the others mounting the stairs.*]

MORE: Howard, are *you* at Richmond?

NORFOLK: No, down the river.

MORE: Then good night! [*Sees Rich disconsolate.*] Oh, Your Grace, here's a young man desperate for employment. Something in the clerical line.

NORFOLK: Well, if you recommend him.

MORE: No, I don't recommend him; but I point him out. [*Moving off*] He's at the New Inn. You could take him there.

NORFOLK [*to Rich, mounting stairs*]: All right, come on.

RICH: My Lord.

NORFOLK: We'll hawk at Hounslow, Alice.

ALICE: Wherever you like.

   [ALICE *and* MARGARET *follow Norfolk.*]

RICH [*at foot of stairs*]: Sir Thomas! . . .

   [MORE *turns.*]

   Thank you.

MORE: Be a teacher. [*Moving off again*] Oh – The ground's hard at Hounslow, Alice!

NORFOLK: Eh? [*Delighted roar.*] That's where the Cardinal crushed his bum!

MORE
NORFOLK
ALICE } Good night! Good night!
RICH

   [*They process off along the gallery.*]

MORE [*softly*]: Margaret!

MARGARET: Yes?

MORE: Go to bed.

   [MARGARET *exits above,* MORE *exits below. After a moment* RICH *walks swiftly back down stage, picks up the goblet, and is going off with it.*]

STEWARD: Eh!

RICH: What – ! Oh. . . It's a gift, Matthew. Sir Thomas gave it to me.

   [STEWARD *takes it and regards it silently.*]

   He gave it to me.

STEWARD [*returns it*]: Very nice present, sir.

RICH [*backing away with it.*]: Yes. Good night, Matthew.

STEWARD: Sir Thomas has taken quite a fancy to you, sir.

RICH: Er, here – [*Gives money and goes.*]

STEWARD: Thank you, sir. . . . [*To audience*] That one'll come to nothing. [*Begins packing props into basket. Pauses with cup in hand.*] My master Thomas More would give anything to anyone. Some say that's good and some say that's bad, but I say he can't help it – and that's bad . . . because some day someone's going to ask him for something that he wants to keep; and he'll be out of practice. [*Puts cloth with papers, ink, etc., on table.*] There must be something that he wants to keep. That's only Common Sense.

[*Enter* WOLSEY. *He sits at table and immediately commences writing, watched by* COMMON MAN *who then exits. Enter* MORE.]

WOLSEY [*writing*]: It's half past one. Where've you been?

[*Bell strikes one.*]

MORE: One o'clock, Your Grace. I've been on the river.

[WOLSEY *writes in silence, while* MORE *waits standing.*]

WOLSEY [*still writing, pushes paper across table*]: Since you seemed so violently opposed to the Latin dispatch, I thought you'd like to look it over.

MORE [*touched*]: Thank you, Your Grace.

WOLSEY: Before it goes.

MORE [*smiles*]: Your Grace is very kind. [*Takes and reads.*] Thank you.

WOLSEY: Well, what d'you think of it? [*He is still writing.*]

MORE: It seems very well phrased, Your Grace.

WOLSEY [*permits himself a chuckle*]: The devil it does! [*Sits back.*] And apart from the style, Sir Thomas?

MORE: I think the Council should be told before that goes to Italy.

WOLSEY: Would you tell the Council? Yes, I believe you would. You're a constant regret to me, Thomas. If you could just see facts flat on, without that moral squint; with just a little common sense, you could have been a statesman.

MORE [*little pause*]: Oh, Your Grace flatters me.

WOLSEY: Don't frivel. . . Thomas, are you going to help me?

MORE [*hesitates, looks away*]: If Your Grace will be specific.

WOLSEY: Ach, you're a plodder! Take you altogether, Thomas, your scholarship, your experience, what are you?

[*A single trumpet calls, distant, frosty, and clear.* WOLSEY *gets up and goes and looks from window.*]

Come here.

[MORE *joins him.*]

The King.

MORE: Yes.

WOLSEY: Where has he been? D'you know?

MORE: I, Your Grace?

WOLSEY: Oh, spare me your discretion. He's been to play in the muck again.

MORE [*coldly*]: Indeed.

WOLSEY: Indeed! Indeed! Are you going to oppose me?

[*Trumpet again,* WOLSEY *visibly relaxes.*]

He's gone in. . . . [*Leaves window.*] All right, we'll plod. The King wants a son; what are you going to do about it?

MORE [*dry murmur*]: I'm very sure the King needs no advice from me on what to do about it.

WOLSEY [*from behind grips his shoulder fiercely*]: Thomas, we're alone. I give you my word. There's no one here.

MORE: I didn't suppose there was, Your Grace.

WOLSEY: Oh.

[*Goes to table, sits, signs More to sit.* MORE *unsuspectingly obeys. Then, deliberately loud*]

Do you favour a change of dynasty, Sir Thomas? D'you think two Tudors is sufficient?

MORE [*starting up in horrified alarm*]: – For God's sake, Your Grace – !

WOLSEY: Then the King needs a son; I repeat what are you going to do about it?

MORE [*steadily*]: I pray for it daily.

[WOLSEY *snatches up candle and holds to More's face.*]

WOLSEY [*softly*]: God's death, he means it. . . . That thing out there's at least fertile, Thomas.

MORE: But she's not his wife.

WOLSEY: No, Catherine's his wife and she's as barren as brick. Are you going to pray for a miracle?

MORE: There *are* precedents.

WOLSEY: Yes. All right. Good. Pray. Pray by all means. But in addition to Prayer there is Effort. My effort's to secure a divorce. Have I your support or have I not?

MORE [*sits*]: A dispensation was given so that the King might marry Queen Catherine, for state reasons. Now we are to ask the Pope to – dispense with his dispensation, also for state reasons?

WOLSEY: – I don't *like* plodding, Thomas, don't make me plod longer than I have to – Well?

MORE: Then clearly all we have to do is approach His Holiness and ask him.

[*The pace becomes rapid.*]

WOLSEY: – I think we might influence His Holiness' answer –

MORE: – Like this? – [*The dispatch.*]

WOLSEY: – Like that and in other ways –

MORE: – I've already expressed my opinion on this –

WOLSEY: – Then, good night! Oh, your conscience is your own affair; but you're a statesman! Do you *remember* the Yorkist Wars?

MORE: Very clearly.

WOLSEY: Let him die without an heir and we'll have them back again. Let him die without an heir and this 'peace' you think so much of will go out like that! [*Extinguishes candle.*] Very well, then England needs an heir; certain measures, perhaps regrettable, perhaps not – [*pompous*] there is much in the Church that *needs* reformation, Thomas –

[MORE *smiles.*]

All right, regrettable! But necessary, to get us an heir! Now explain how you as Councillor of England can obstruct those measures for the sake of your own, private, conscience.

MORE: Well . . . I believe, when statesmen forsake their own private conscience for the sake of their public duties . . . they lead their country by a short route to chaos. [*During this speech he relights the candle with another.*] And we shall have my prayers to fall back on.

WOLSEY: You'd like that, wouldn't you? To govern the country by prayers?

MORE: Yes, I should.

WOLSEY: I'd like to be there when you try. Who *will* deal with all this – paper, after me? You? Fisher? Suffolk?

MORE: Fisher for me.

WOLSEY: Aye, but for the King. What about my Secretary, Master Cromwell?

MORE: Cromwell!

WOLSEY: You'd rather do it yourself?

MORE: Me rather than Cromwell.

WOLSEY: Then come down to earth. . . . And until then, allow for an enemy, here!

MORE: As Your Grace pleases.

WOLSEY: As God wills!

MORE: Perhaps, Your Grace. [*Mounting stairs.*]

WOLSEY: More! You should have been a cleric!

MORE [*amused, looking down from gallery*]: Like yourself, Your Grace? [*Exit* MORE. WOLSEY *is left staring, then exits through the lower arches with candle, taking most of the light from the stage as he does so. But the whole rear of the stage now patterns with webbed reflections thrown from brightly moonlit water, so that the structure is thrown into black relief, while a strip of light descends along the front of the stage, which is to be the acting area for the next scene.*]

[*An oar and a bundle of clothing are lowered into this area from above. Enter* COMMON MAN; *he unties the bundle and dons the coat and hat of* BOATMAN.]

MORE [*off*]: Boat! [*Approaching*] Boat!

BOATMAN [*donning coat and hat*]: Here, sir!

MORE [*off*]: A boatman please!

BOATMAN: Boat here, sir! [*He seizes the oar.*]
    [*Enter* MORE.]

MORE [*peering*]: Boatman?

BOATMAN: Yes, sir. [*To audience, indicating oar*] A boatman.

MORE: Take me home.

BOATMAN [*pleasantly*]: I was just going home myself, sir.

MORE: Then find me another boat.

BOATMAN: Bless you, sir – that's all right! [*Comfortably*] I expect you'll make it worth my while, sir.
    [CROMWELL *steps from behind arch, left.*]

CROMWELL: Boatman, have you a licence?

BOATMAN: Eh? Bless you, sir, yes; I've got a licence.

CROMWELL: Then you know that the fares are fixed – [*Turns to More. With exaggerated pleasure*] Why, it's Sir Thomas!

MORE: Good morning, Master Cromwell. You work very late.

CROMWELL: I'm on my way to the Cardinal. [*He expects an answer.*]

MORE: Ah.

CROMWELL: You have just left him I think.

MORE: Yes, I have.

CROMWELL: You left him ... in his laughing mood, I hope?

MORE: On the whole I would say, not. No, not laughing.

CROMWELL: Oh, I'm sorry. [*Backing to exit*] I am one of your *multitudinous* admirers, Sir Thomas. A penny ha'penny to Chelsea, Boatman.

[*Exit* CROMWELL.]

BOATMAN: The coming man they say, sir.

MORE: Do they? Well, where's your boat?

BOATMAN: Just along the wharf, sir.

[*They are going, when enter* CHAPUYS *and* ATTENDANT *from archway, right.*]

CHAPUYS: Sir Thomas More!

MORE: Signor Chapuys? You're up very late, Your Excellency.

CHAPUYS [*significantly*]: So is the Cardinal, Sir Thomas.

MORE [*closing up*]: He sleeps very little.

CHAPUYS: You have just left him, I think.

MORE: You are correctly informed. As always.

CHAPUYS: I will not ask you the subject of your conversation. ... [*He waits.*]

MORE: No, of course not.

CHAPUYS: Sir Thomas, I will be plain with you ... plain, that is, so far as the diplomatic decencies permit. [*Loudly*] My master Charles, the King of Spain! [*Pulls More aside, discreet.*] My master Charles, the King of Spain, feels himself concerned in anything concerning his blood relation! He would feel himself insulted by any insult offered to his father's sister! I refer of course to Queen Catherine. [*Regards More, keenly.*] The King of Spain would feel himself insulted by any insult offered to Queen Catherine.

MORE: His feeling would be natural.

CHAPUYS [*consciously sly*]: Sir Thomas, may I ask if you and the Cardinal parted, how shall I say, amicably?

MORE: Amicably... Yes.

CHAPUYS [*a shade indignant*]: In agreement?

MORE: Amicably.

CHAPUYS [*warmly*]: Say no more, Sir Thomas; I understand.

MORE [*a shade worried*]: I hope you do, Your Excellency.

CHAPUYS: You are a good man.

MORE: I don't see how you deduce that from what I've told you.

CHAPUYS [*holds up hand*]: A nod is as good as a wink to a blind horse. I understand. You are a good man. [*Turns to exit.*] Dominus vobiscum.

[*Exit* CHAPUYS. MORE *looks after him. Then:*]

MORE [*abstracted*]: ...`spiritu tuo ...

BOATMAN [*mournful; he is squatting on the ground*]: People seem to thinks boats stay afloat on their own, sir, but they don't; they cost money.

[MORE *is abstractedly gazing over the audience.*]

Take anchor rope, sir, you may not believe me for a little skiff like mine, but it's a penny a fathom.

[MORE *is still abstracted.*]

And with a young wife, sir, as you know...

MORE [*abstracted*]: I'll pay what I always pay you. ... The river looks very black tonight. They say it's silting up, is that so?

BOATMAN [*joining him*]: Not in the middle, sir. There's a channel there getting deeper all the time.

MORE: How is your wife?

BOATMAN: She's losing her shape, sir, losing it fast.

MORE: Well, so are we all.

BOATMAN: Oh yes, sir; it's common.

MORE [*going*]: Well, take me home.

[*Exit* MORE.]

BOATMAN: That I will, sir! [*Crossing to basket and pulling it out*] From Richmond to Chelsea, downstream, a penny halfpenny ... coat, hat ... coat, hat [*goes for table-cloth*] from Chelsea to Richmond, upstream, a penny halfpenny. Whoever makes the regulations doesn't row a boat. Cloth. . . . [*Puts cloth in basket, takes out slippers.*] Home again.

[*Lighting changes to More's house interior.*

Enter MORE *on stairs. Sits wearily. Takes off hat, half takes off coat, but is too tired. It chimes three.* STEWARD *kneels to put on his slippers for him.*]

MORE: Ah, Matthew. . . Thank you. Is Lady Alice in bed?

STEWARD: Yes, sir.

MORE: Lady Margaret?

STEWARD: No, sir. Master Roper's here.

MORE [*surprised*]: At this hour? . . . Who let him in?

STEWARD: He's a hard man to keep out, sir.

MORE: Where are they?

[*Enter* MARGARET *and* ROPER.]

MARGARET: Here, Father.

MORE [*regarding them, resignedly*]: Good morning, William. It's a little early for breakfast.

ROPER [*solidly*]: I haven't come for breakfast, sir.

[MORE *looks at him and sighs.*]

MARGARET: Will wants to marry me, Father.

MORE: Well, he can't marry you.

ROPER: Sir Thomas, I'm to be called to the Bar.

MORE [*warmly*]: Oh, congratulations, Roper!

ROPER: My family may not be at the palace, sir, but in the City –

MORE: The Ropers were advocates when the Mores were selling pewter; there's nothing wrong with your family. There's nothing wrong with your fortune – there's nothing wrong with you – [*sourly*] except you need a clock –

ROPER: I can buy a clock, sir.

MORE: Roper, the answer's 'no'. [*Firmly*] And will be 'no' so long as you're a heretic.

ROPER [*firing*]: That's a word I don't like, Sir Thomas!

MORE: It's not a likeable word. [*Coming to life*] It's not a likeable thing!

[MARGARET *is alarmed, and from behind More tries to silence Roper.*]

ROPER: The Church is heretical! Doctor Luther's proved that to my satisfaction!

MORE: Luther's an excommunicate.

ROPER: From a heretic Church! Church? It's a shop – Forgiveness by the florin! Joblots now in Germany! . . . Mmm, and divorces.

MORE [*expressionless*]: Divorces?

ROPER: Oh, half England's buzzing with that.

MORE: 'Half England.' The Inns of Court may be buzzing, England doesn't buzz so easily.

ROPER: It will. And is that a Church? Is that a Cardinal? Is that a Pope? Or Antichrist!

[MORE *looks up angrily.* MARGARET *signals frantically*.]

Look, what I know I'll say!

MARGARET: You've no sense of the *place*!

MORE [*rueful*]: He's no sense of the time.

ROPER: I –

[*But* MORE *gently holds up his hand and he stops*.]

MORE: Listen, Roper. Two years ago you were a passionate Churchman; now you're a passionate – Lutheran. We must just pray, that when your head's finished turning your face is to the front again.

ROPER: Don't lengthen your prayers with *me*, sir!

MORE: Oh, one more or less. . . . Is your horse here?

ROPER: No, I walked.

MORE: Well, take a horse from the stables and get back home.

[ROPER *hesitates*.]

Go along.

ROPER: May I come again?

[MORE *indicates* MARGARET.]

MARGARET: Yes, soon.

ROPER: Good night, sir.

[*Exit* ROPER.]

MARGARET: Is that final, Father?

MORE: As long as he's a heretic, Meg, that's absolute. [*Warmly*] Nice boy. . . Terribly strong principles though. I told you to go to bed.

MARGARET: Yes, why?

MORE [*lightly*]: Because I intended you to *go* to bed. You're very pensive?

MARGARET: You're very gay. Did he talk about the divorce?

MORE: Mm? You know I think we've been on the wrong track with Will – It's no good arguing with a Roper –

MARGARET: Father, did he?

MORE: *Old* Roper was just the same. Now let him think he's going *with* the current and he'll turn round and start swimming in the opposite direction. What we want is a really substantial attack on the Church.

MARGARET: We're going to get it, aren't we?

MORE: Margaret, I'll not have you talk treason. . . . And I'll not have you repeat lawyer's gossip. I'm a lawyer myself and I know what it's worth.

ALICE [*off, indignant and excited*]: Thomas – !

MORE: Now look what you've done.

[*Enter* ALICE *at head of stairs in nightgown.*]

ALICE: Young Roper! I've just seen young Roper! On *my* horse.

MORE: He'll bring it back, dear. He's been to see Margaret.

ALICE: Oh – why you don't beat that girl!

MORE: No no, she's full of education – and it's a delicate commodity.

ALICE: Mm! And more's the pity!

MORE: Yes, but it's there now and think what it cost. [*He sneezes.*]

ALICE [*pouncing*]: Ah! Margaret – hot water.

[*Exit* MARGARET.]

MORE: I'm sorry you were awakened, chick.

ALICE: I wasn't sleeping very deeply, Thomas – what did Wolsey want?

MORE [*innocent*]: Young Roper asked for Margaret.

ALICE: What! Impudence!

MORE: Yes, wasn't it?

ALICE: Old fox! What did he want, Thomas?

MORE: He wanted me to read a dispatch.

ALICE: Was that all?

MORE: A Latin dispatch.

ALICE: Oh! Won't you talk about it?

MORE [*gently*]: No.

[*Enter* MARGARET *with cup which she takes to More.*]

ALICE: Norfolk was speaking for you as Chancellor before he left.

MORE: He's a dangerous friend then. Wolsey's Chancellor, God help him. We don't want another.

[MARGARET *takes cup to him; he sniffs it.*]

I don't want this.

ALICE: Drink it. Great men get colds in the head just the same as commoners.

MORE: That's dangerous, levelling talk, Alice. Beware of the Tower. [*Rises.*] I will, I'll drink it in bed.

[*All move to stairs and ascend, talking.*]

MARGARET: Would you want to be Chancellor?

MORE: No.

MARGARET: That's what I said. But Norfolk said if Wolsey fell –

MORE [*no longer flippant*]: If Wolsey fell, the splash would swamp a few small boats like ours. There will be no new Chancellors while Wolsey lives.

[*Exit above.*

The light is dimmed there and a bright spot descends below. Into this bright circle from the wings is thrown the great red robe and the Cardinal's hat. The COMMON MAN *enters from the opposite wing and roughly piles them into his basket. He then takes from his pocket a pair of spectacles and from the basket a book. He reads.*]

COMMON MAN [*reading*]: 'Whether we follow tradition in ascribing Wolsey's death to a broken heart, or accept Professor Larcomb's less feeling diagnosis of pulmonary pneumonia, its effective cause was the King's displeasure. He died at Leicester on 29 November 1530 while on his way to the Tower under charge of High Treason. England's next Lord Chancellor was Sir Thomas More, a scholar and, by popular repute, a saint. His scholarship is supported by his writings; saintliness is a quality less easy to establish. But from his wilful indifference to realities which were obvious to quite ordinary contemporaries, it seems all too probable that he had it.'

[*Exit* COMMON MAN. *As he goes, lights come up and a screen is lowered depicting Hampton Court.* CROMWELL *is sitting half-way up the stairs.*

Enter RICH, *crossing.*]

CROMWELL: Rich!

[RICH *stops, sees him, and smiles willingly.*]

What brings you to Hampton?

RICH: I came with the Duke last night, Master Cromwell. They're hunting again.

CROMWELL: It's a kingly pastime, Master Rich. [*Both smile.*] I'm glad you found employment. You're the Duke's Secretary are you not?

RICH [*flustered*]: My work *is* mostly secretarial.

CROMWELL [*as one making an effort of memory*]: Or is it his librarian you are?

RICH: I do look after His Grace's library, yes.

CROMWELL: Oh. Well, that's something. And I don't suppose you're bothered much by His Grace – in the library? [RICH *smiles uncertainly.*] It's odd how differently men's fortunes flow. My late master died in disgrace, and here I am in the King's own service. There you are in a *comparative* backwater – yet the new Lord Chancellor's an old friend of yours. [*He looks at him directly.*]

RICH [*uncertainly*]: He isn't really my *friend*. . . .

CROMWELL: Oh, I thought he was. [*Gets up, prepares to go.*]

RICH: – In a sense he is.

CROMWELL [*reproachful*]: Well, I always understood he set you up in life.

RICH: Master Cromwell – what *is* it that you do for the King?
[*Enter* CHAPUYS.]

CHAPUYS [*roguish*]: Yes, *I* should like to know that, Master Cromwell.

CROMWELL: Ah, Signor Chapuys. You've met His Excellency Rich? [*Indicates Chapuys.*] The Spanish Ambassador. [*Indicates Rich.*] The Duke of Norfolk's librarian.

CHAPUYS: But how should we introduce *you*, Master Cromwell, if we had the happiness?

CROMWELL: Oh sly! Do you notice how sly he is, Rich? [*Walks away.*] Well, I suppose you would call me [*suddenly turns*] 'The King's Ear'. . . . [*Deprecating shrug*] It's a useful organ, the ear. But in fact it's even simpler than that. When the King wants something done, I do it.

CHAPUYS: Ah. [*With mock interest*] But then why these Justices, Chancellors, Admirals?

CROMWELL: Oh, *they* are the constitution. Our ancient, English constitution. I merely do things.

CHAPUYS: For example, Master Cromwell. . . .

CROMWELL [*admiring*]: Oho – beware these professional diplomats. Well now, for example; next week at Deptford we are launching the *Great Harry* – one thousand tons, four masts, sixty-six guns, an overall length of one hundred and seventy-five feet, it's expected to be very effective – all this you probably know. However you may not know that the King himself will guide her down the river; yes, the King himself will be her pilot. He will have assistance of course but he himself will be her pilot. He will have a pilot's whistle upon which he will blow, and he will wear in every respect a common pilot's uniform. Except for the material, which will be cloth of gold. These innocent fancies require more preparation than you might suppose and someone has to do it. [*He spreads his hands.*] Meanwhile, I do prepare myself for, higher things. I stock my mind.

CHAPUYS: Alas, Master Cromwell, don't we all? This ship for instance – it has fifty-six guns by the way, not sixty-six and only forty of them heavy – After the launching I understand, the King will take his barge to Chelsea.

[CROMWELL'S *face darkens during this speech.*]

CROMWELL [*sharply*]: Yes –

CHAPUYS: – To –

CROMWELL
CHAPUYS } [*together*]: Sir Thomas More's.

CHAPUYS [*sweetly*]: Will you be there?

CROMWELL: Oh no – they'll talk about the divorce.

[*It is* CHAPUYS'S *turn to be shocked:* RICH *draws away uneasily.*] The King will ask him for an answer.

CHAPUYS [*ruffled*]: He has given his answer!

CROMWELL: The King will ask him for another.

CHAPUYS: Sir Thomas is a good son of the Church!

CROMWELL: Sir Thomas is a man.

[*Enter* STEWARD. *Both* CROMWELL *and* CHAPUYS *look towards him sharply, then back at one another.*]

CHAPUYS [*innocently*]: Isn't that his Steward now?

CROMWELL: I believe it is. Well, good day, Your Excellency.

CHAPUYS [*eager*]: Good day, Master Cromwell. [*He expects him to go.*]

CROMWELL [*standing firm*]: Good day.

> [*And* CHAPUYS *has to go.*
>
> CROMWELL *walks to the side of the stage, with furtive and urgent beckonings to Steward to follow.* RICH *follows but hangs off. Meanwhile* CHAPUYS *and his* ATTENDANT *have gone behind the screen, beneath which their legs protrude clearly.*]

STEWARD [*conspiratorial*]: Sir, Sir Thomas doesn't talk about it. [*He waits but* CROMWELL *remains stony.*] He doesn't talk about it, to his wife, sir. [*He waits again.*]

CROMWELL: This is worth nothing.

STEWARD [*significant*]: But he doesn't talk about it to Lady Margaret – that's his daughter, sir.

CROMWELL: So?

STEWARD: So he's worried, sir. . . .

> [CROMWELL *is interested.*]

Frightened. . . .

> [CROMWELL *takes out a coin but pauses suspiciously.*]

Sir, he goes *white* when it's mentioned!

CROMWELL [*hands coin*]: All right.

STEWARD [*looks at coin; reproachful*]: Oh, sir – !

CROMWELL [*waves him away*]: Are you coming in my direction, Rich?

RICH [*still hanging off*]: No no.

CROMWELL: I think you should, you know.

RICH: *I* can't tell you anything!

> [*Exit* RICH *and* CROMWELL *left and right.* CHAPUYS *and* ATTENDANT *come from behind screen.*]

CHAPUYS [*beckons Steward*]: Well?

STEWARD: Sir Thomas rises at six, sir, and prays for an hour and a half.

CHAPUYS: Yes?

STEWARD: During Lent, sir, he lived entirely on bread and water.

CHAPUYS: Yes?

STEWARD: He goes to confession twice a week, sir. Parish priest. Dominican.

CHAPUYS: Ah. He is a true son of the Church.

STEWARD: [*soapy*]: That he is, sir.

CHAPUYS: What did Master Cromwell want?

STEWARD: Same as you, sir.

CHAPUYS: No man can serve two masters, Steward.

STEWARD: No indeed, sir; I serve one. [*He pulls to the front an enormous cross until then hanging at his back on a length of string – a caricature of the ebony cross worn by Chapuys.*]

CHAPUYS: Good, simple man. Here. [*Gives coin. Going*] Peace be with you.

STEWARD: And with you, sir.

CHAPUYS: Our Lord watch you.

STEWARD: You too, sir.

[*Exit* CHAPUYS.]

That's a very religious man.

[*Enter* RICH.]

RICH: What does Signor Chapuys want, Matthew?

STEWARD: I've no idea, sir.

RICH [*gives coin*]: What did you tell him?

STEWARD: I told him that Sir Thomas says his prayers and goes to confession.

RICH: Why that?

STEWARD: That's what he wanted to know, sir. I mean I could have told him any number of things about Sir Thomas – that he has rheumatism, prefers red wine to white, is easily sea-sick, fond of kippers, afraid of drowning. But that's what he wanted to know, sir.

RICH: What did he say?

STEWARD: He said that Sir Thomas is a good churchman, sir.

RICH [*going*]: Well, that's true, isn't it?

STEWARD: I'm just telling you what he said, sir. Master Cromwell went that way, sir.

RICH [*furious*]: Did I ask you which way Master Cromwell went?

[*Exit* RICH *opposite.*]

STEWARD [*to audience, thoughtfully*]: The great thing's not to get out of your depth. . . . What I can tell them's common knowledge! But now they've given money for it and everyone wants value for his money. They'll make a secret of it now to prove they've not been bilked. . . . They'll make it a secret by making it dangerous. . . . Mm. . . Oh, when I can't touch the bottom I'll go deaf blind and dumb. [*Holds out coins.*] And that's more than I *earn* in a fortnight!

[*On this; a fanfare of trumpets; plainsong; the rear of the stage becomes a source of glittering blue light; Hampton Court is hoisted out of sight, and other screens are lowered one after the other, each masking the rest, bearing respectively sunflowers, hollyhocks, roses, magnolias. When the fanfare ceases the plainsong goes on quietly, and the screens throw long shadows like the shadows of trees, and* NORFOLK, ALICE, MARGARET, *erupt on to the stage.*]

ALICE [*distressed*]: No sign of him, my lord!

NORFOLK: God's body, Alice, he must be found!

ALICE [*to Meg*]: He *must* be in the house!

MARGARET: He's *not* in the house, Mother!

ALICE: Then he must be here in the garden!

[*They search among the screens.*]

NORFOLK: He takes things too far, Alice.

ALICE: Do I not know it?

NORFOLK: It will end badly for him!

ALICE: I know that too!

[*They notice the Steward.*]

MARGARET ⎫   ⎧ Matthew! Where's my father?
ALICE   ⎬ [*together*]:   ⎨ Where is Sir Thomas?
NORFOLK ⎭   ⎩ Where's your master?

[*Fanfare, shorter but nearer.*]

NORFOLK [*despairing*]: Oh my God.

ALICE: Oh Jesus!

STEWARD: My lady – the King?

NORFOLK: Yes, fool! [*Threatening*] And if the King arrives and the Chancellor's not here –

STEWARD: Sir, my lady, it's not *my* fault!

NORFOLK [*quietly displeased*]: Lady Alice, Thomas'll get no good of it. This is not how Wolsey made himself great.

ALICE [*stiffly*]: Thomas has his own way of doing things, my lord!

NORFOLK [*testy*]: Yes yes, Thomas is unique; but where *is* Thomas?

[STEWARD *swings onstage small gothic door. Plainsong. All run to the door.* NORFOLK *opens it.*]

ALICE: Thomas!

STEWARD: Sir!

MARGARET: Father!

NORFOLK [*indignant*]: My Lord Chancellor!

[*Enter* MORE *through the doorway. He blinks in the light. He is wearing a cassock. Shuts door behind him.*]

What sort of fooling is this? Does the King visit you every day.

MORE: No, but I go to Vespers most days.

NORFOLK: He's here!

MORE: But isn't this visit *meant* to be a surprise?

NORFOLK [*grimly*]: For you, yes, not for him.

MARGARET: Father. . . [*Indicates cassock.*]

NORFOLK: Yes – d'you propose to meet the King disguised as a parish clerk? [*They fall upon him and drag the cassock over his head.*] A parish clerk, my lord Chancellor! You dishonour the King and his office!

MORE [*appearing momentarily in the folds of the cassock*]: The service of God is not a dishonour to any office. [*The cassock is pulled off.*] Believe me, my friend, I do not belittle the honour His Majesty is doing me. [*Briskly*] Well! That's a lovely dress, Alice; so's that, Margaret. [*Looks at Norfolk.*] I'm a dowdy bird, aren't I? [*Looks at Alice.*] Calm yourself, Alice, we're all ready now.

[*He turns about and we see that his gown is caught up behind him revealing his spindly legs in long hose laced up at the thighs.*]

ALICE: Thomas!

[MARGARET *laughs.*]

MORE: What's the matter?

[*He turns round again and his womenfolk pursue him to pull down the gown while* NORFOLK *throws his hands in the air. Expostulation, explanation, exclamation, overlapping in a babble.*]

NORFOLK: By God you can be hare-brained – !

MARGARET: – Be still – !

ALICE: – Oh, Thomas! Thomas! –

NORFOLK: – What whim possessed you –

MORE: – 'Twas not a whim – !

ALICE: – Your second-best stockings – !

MARGARET: – Father, be still – !

NORFOLK: – Oh, enough's enough – !

MORE: – Haven't you done – !

[HENRY, *in a cloth of gold, runs out of the sunlight half-way down the steps, and blows a blast on his pilot's whistle. All kneel. In the silence, he descends slowly to their level, blowing softly. . . .*]

MORE: Your Majesty does my house more honour than I fear my household can bear.

HENRY: No ceremony, Thomas! No ceremony! [*They rise.*] A passing fancy – I happened to be on the river. [*Holds out shoe, proudly.*] Look, mud.

MORE: We do it in better style, Your Grace, when we come by the road.

HENRY: Oh, the road! There's the road for me, Thomas, the river; *my* river. . . . By heaven what an evening! I fear we come upon you unexpectedly, Lady Alice.

ALICE [*shocked*]: Oh no, Your Grace – [*remembering*] that is yes, but we are ready for you – ready to entertain Your Grace that is.

MORE: This is my daughter Margaret, sir. She has not had the honour to meet Your Grace. [*She curtseys low.*]

HENRY [*looks her over, then*]: Why, Margaret, they told me you were a scholar.

[MARGARET *is confused.*]

MORE: Answer, Margaret.

MARGARET: Among women I pass for one Your Grace.

[NORFOLK *and* ALICE *exchange approving glances.*]

HENRY: Antiquone modo Latine loqueris, an Oxoniensi? [Is your Latin the old Latin, or Oxford Latin?]

MARGARET: Quem me docuit pater, Domine.
[My father's Latin, Sire.]

HENRY: Bene. Optimus est. Graecamne linguam quoque te docuit? [Good. That is the best. And has he taught you Greek too?]

MARGARET: Graecam me docuit non pater meus sed mei patris amicus, Johannes Coletus, Sancti Pauli Decanus. In litteris Graecis tamen, non minus quam Latinis, ars magistri minuitur discipuli stultitia.
[Not my father, Sire, but my father's friend, John Colet, Dean of

St Paul's. But it is with the Greek as it is with the Latin; the skill of the master is lost in the pupil's lack of it.]

[*Her Latin is better than his; he is not altogether pleased.*]

HENRY: Ho! [*He walks away from her, talking; she begins to rise from her curtsey,* MORE *gently presses her down again before the King turns.*] Take care, Thomas: 'There is no end to the making of books and too much reading is a weariness of the flesh.' [*Back to Margaret.*] Can you dance, too?

MARGARET: Not well, Your Grace.

HENRY: Well, *I* dance superlatively! [*Plants his leg before her face.*] That's a dancer's *leg*, Margaret!

[*She has the wit to look straight up and smile at him. All good humour, he pulls her to her feet; sees* NORFOLK *grinning the grin of a comrade.*] Hey, Norfolk? [*Indicates Norfolk's leg with much distaste.*] Now *that's* a wrestler's leg. But I can throw him.

[*Seizes Norfolk.*]

Shall I show them, Howard?

[NORFOLK *is alarmed for his dignity. To Margaret*]

Shall I?

MARGARET [*looking at Norfolk, gently*]: No, Your Grace.

HENRY [*releases Norfolk, seriously*]: You are gentle. [*To* MORE, *approving*] That's good. [*To Margaret*] You shall read to me. [MARGARET *is about to demur.*] No no, you shall read to me. Lady Alice, the river's given me an appetite.

ALICE: If Your Grace would share a very simple supper.

HENRY: It would please me to. [*Preparing to lead off, sees Margaret again.*] I'm something of a scholar too; did you know?

MARGARET: All the world knows Your Grace's Book, asserting the seven sacraments of the Church.

HENRY: Ah yes. Between ourselves, your father had a hand in that; eh, Thomas?

MORE: Here and there, Your Grace. In a minor capacity.

HENRY [*looking at him*]: He seeks to shame me with his modesty. . . . [*Turns to Alice.*] On second thoughts we'll follow, Lady Alice, Thomas and I will follow. [*He waves them off. They bow, withdraw, prepare for second bow.*] Wait! [*Raises whistle to lips; then:*] Margaret, are you fond of music?

MARGARET: Yes, Your Grace.

HENRY [*beckons her to him; holds out whistle*]: Blow.

[*She is uncertain.*]

Blow.

[*She does.*]

Louder!

[*She does and at once music without, stately and oversweet. Expressions of pleasure all round.*]

I brought them with me, Lady Alice; take them in!

[*Exit all but More and Henry. The music continues receding.*]

Listen to this, Thomas. [*He walks about, the auditor, beating time.*] Do you know it?

MORE: No, Your Grace, I –

HENRY: Sh! [MORE *is silent;* HENRY *goes on with his listening.*] . . . I launched a ship today, Thomas.

MORE Yes, Your Grace, I –

HENRY: *Listen*, man, listen. . . . [*A silence.*] . . . The *Great Harry* . . . I steered her, Thomas, under sail.

MORE: You have many accomplishments, Your Grace.

[HENRY *holds up a finger for silence. . . . A silence.*]

HENRY: A great experience. [MORE *keeps silent.*] . . . A great experience, Thomas.

MORE: Yes, Your Grace.

[*The music is growing fainter.*]

HENRY: I am a fool.

MORE: How so, Your Grace?

[*A silence, during which the music fades to silence.*]

HENRY: . . . What else but a fool to live in a Court, in a licentious mob – when I have friends, with gardens.

MORE: Your Grace –

HENRY: No courtship, no ceremony, Thomas. Be seated. You *are* my friend are you not?

[MORE *sits.*]

MORE: Your Majesty.

HENRY: And thank God I have a friend for my Chancellor. [*Laughing*] Readier to be friends I trust than he was to be Chancellor.

MORE: My own knowledge of my poor abilities –

HENRY: I will judge of your abilities, Thomas. . . . Did you know that Wolsey named you for Chancellor?

MORE: Wolsey!

HENRY: Aye; before he died. Wolsey named you and Wolsey was no fool.

MORE: He was a statesman of incomparable ability, Your Grace.

HENRY: Was he? Was he so? [*Rises.*] Then why did he fail me? Be seated – it was villainy then! Yes villainy. I was right to break him; he was all pride, Thomas; a proud man; pride right through. And he failed me!

[MORE *opens his mouth.*]

He failed me in the one thing that mattered! The one thing that matters, Thomas, then or now. And why? He wanted to be Pope! Yes, he wanted to be the Bishop of Rome. I'll tell you something, Thomas, and you can check this for yourself – it was never merry in England while we had Cardinals amongst us.

[*He nods significantly at More who lowers his eyes.*]

But look now – [*walking away*] – I shall forget the feel of that . . . great tiller under my hands . . . I took her down to Dogget's Bank, went about and brought her up in Tilbury Roads. A man could sail clean round the world in that ship.

MORE [*affectionate admiration*]: Some men could, Your Grace.

HENRY [*off-hand*]: Touching this matter of my divorce, Thomas; have you thought of it since we last talked?

MORE: Of little else.

HENRY: Then you see your way clear to me?

MORE: That you should put away Queen Catherine, sire? Oh, alas [*thumps table in distress*] as I think of it I see so clearly that I can *not* come with Your Grace that my endeavour is not to think of it at all.

HENRY: Then you have not thought enough! . . . [*With real appeal*] Great God, Thomas, why do you hold out against me in the desire of my heart – the very wick of my heart? –

MORE [*draws up sleeve, baring his arm*]: There is my right arm. [*A practical proposition*] Take your dagger and saw it from my shoulder, and I will laugh and be thankful, if by that means I can come with Your Grace with a clear conscience.

HENRY [*uncomfortably pulls at the sleeve*]: I know it, Thomas, I know. . . .

MORE [*rises, formally*]: I crave pardon if I offend.

HENRY [*suspiciously*]: Speak then.

MORE: When I took the Great Seal your Majesty promised not to pursue me on this matter.

HENRY: Ha! So I break my word, Master More! No no, I'm joking . . . I joke roughly. . . . [*Wanders away.*] I often think I'm a rough fellow. . . . Yes, a rough young fellow. [*Shakes his head indulgently.*] Be seated. . . . That's a magnolia. We have one like it at Hampton – not so red as that though. Ha – I'm in an excellent frame of mind. [*Glances at the magnolia.*] Beautiful. [*Reasonably, pleasantly.*] You must consider, Thomas, that I stand in peril of my soul. It was no marriage; she was my brother's widow. Leviticus: 'Thou shalt not uncover the nakedness of thy brother's wife.' Leviticus, Chapter 18, Verse 16.

MORE: Yes, Your Grace. But Deuteronomy –

HENRY [*triumphant*]: Deuteronomy's ambiguous!

MORE [*bursting out*]: Your Grace, I'm not fit to meddle in these matters – to me it seems a matter for the Holy See –

HENRY [*reproving*]: Thomas, Thomas, does a man need a Pope to tell him when he's sinned? It was a sin, Thomas; I admit it; I repent. And God has punished me; I have no son. . . . Son after son she's borne me, Thomas, all dead at birth, or dead within the month; I never saw the hand of God so clear in anything. . . . I have a daughter, she's a good child, a well-set child – But I have no son. [*Flares up*] It is my bounden *duty* to put away the Queen and all the Popes back to St Peter shall not come between me and my duty! How is it that you cannot see? Everyone else does.

MORE [*eagerly*]: Then why does Your Grace need my poor support?

HENRY: Because you are honest. What's more to the purpose, you're known to be honest. . . . There are those like Norfolk who follow me because I wear the crown, and there are those like Master Cromwell who follow me because they are jackals with sharp teeth and I am their lion, and there is a mass that follows me because it follows anything that moves – and there is you.

MORE: I am sick to think how much I must displease Your Grace.

HENRY: No, Thomas, I respect your sincerity. Respect? Oh, man, it's water in the desert. . . . How did you like our music? That air they played, it had a certain – well, tell me what you thought of it.

MORE [*relieved at this turn; smiling*]: Could it have been Your Grace's own?

HENRY [*smiles back*]: Discovered! Now I'll never know your true opinion. And that's irksome, Thomas, for we artists, though we love praise, yet we love truth better.

MORE [*mildly*]: Then I will tell Your Grace truly what I thought of it.

HENRY [*a little disconcerted*]: Speak then.

MORE: To me it seemed – delightful.

HENRY: Thomas – I chose the right man for Chancellor.

MORE: I must in fairness add that my taste in music is reputedly deplorable.

HENRY: Your taste in music is excellent. It exactly coincides with my own. Ah music! Music! Send them back without me, Thomas; I will live here in Chelsea and make music.

MORE: My house is at Your Grace's disposal.

HENRY: Thomas, you understand me; we will stay here together and make music.

MORE: Will your Grace honour my roof at dinner?

[HENRY *has walked away, blowing moodily on his whistle.*]

HENRY: Mm? Yes; I expect I'll bellow for you. . . .

MORE: My wife will be more –

HENRY: Yes, yes. [*He turns, his face set.*] Touching this other business, mark you, Thomas, I'll have no opposition.

MORE [*sadly*]: Your Grace?

HENRY: No opposition I say! No opposition! Your conscience is your own affair; but you are my Chancellor! There, you have my word – I'll leave you out of it. But I don't take it kindly, Thomas, and I'll have no opposition! I see how it will be; the Bishops will oppose me. The full-fed, hypocritical, 'Princes of the *Church*'! Ha! As for the Pope! – Am I to burn in Hell because the Bishop of Rome, with the Emperor's knife to his throat, mouths me Deuteronomy? Hypocrites! They're all hypocrites! Mind they do not

54

take you in, Thomas! Lie low if you will, but I'll brook no opposition – no words, no signs, no letters, no pamphlets – mind that, Thomas – no writings against me!

MORE: Your Grace is unjust. I am Your Grace's loyal minister. If I cannot serve Your Grace in this great matter of the Queen –

HENRY: I have no Queen! Catherine is not my wife and no priest can make her so, and they that say she is my wife are not only liars ... but Traitors! Mind it, Thomas!

MORE: Am I a babbler, Your Grace? [*But his voice is unsteady.*]

HENRY: You are stubborn. .... [*Wooingly*] If you could come with me, you are the man I would soonest raise – yes, with my own hand.

MORE [*covers his face*]: Oh, Your Grace overwhelms me!

[*A complicated chiming of little bells is heard.*]

HENRY: What's that?

MORE: Eight o'clock, Your Grace.

HENRY [*uneasily eyeing More*]: Oh, lift yourself up, man – have I not promised?

[MORE *braces.*]

Shall we eat?

MORE: If Your Grace pleases. [*Recovering*] What will Your Grace sing for us? [*They approach the stairs.*]

HENRY: Eight o'clock you said? Thomas, the tide will be changing. I was forgetting the tide. I'd better go.

MORE [*gravely*]: I'm sorry, Your Grace.

HENRY: I must catch the tide or I'll not get back to Richmond till ... No, don't come. Tell Norfolk.

[*He has his foot on the bottom stair when enter* ALICE *and* STEWARD *above.*]

Oh, Lady Alice, I must go.

[ALICE *descends, her face serious.*]

I want to catch the tide. To tell the truth, Lady Alice, I have forgotten in your haven here how time flows past outside. Affairs call me to court and so I give you my thanks and say Good night.

[*He mounts.*]

MORE ⎫
ALICE ⎭ [*bowing*]: Good night, Your Grace.

[*Exit* HENRY, *above.*]

ALICE: What's this? You crossed him.

MORE: Somewhat.

ALICE: Why?

MORE [*apologetic*]: I couldn't find the other way.

ALICE [*angrily*]: You're too nice altogether, Thomas!

MORE: Woman, mind your house.

ALICE: I *am* minding my house!

    [MORE *takes in her anxiety.*]

MORE: Well, Alice. What would you *want* me to do?

ALICE: Be ruled! If you won't rule him, be ruled!

MORE [*quietly*]: I neither could nor would rule my King. [*Pleasantly*] But there's a little . . . little, area . . . where I must rule myself. It's very little – less to him than a tennis court. [*Her face is still full of foreboding: he sighs.*] Look; it was eight o'clock. At eight o'clock, Lady Anne likes to dance.

ALICE [*relieved*]: Oh?

MORE: I think so.

ALICE [*irritation*]: And *you* stand between them!

MORE: I? What stands between them is a sacrament of the Church. I'm less important than you think, Alice.

ALICE [*appealing*]: Thomas, stay friends with him.

MORE: Whatever can be done by smiling, you may rely on me to do.

ALICE: You don't know *how* to flatter.

MORE: I flatter very well! My recipe's beginning to be widely copied. It's the basic syrup with just a soupçon of discreet impudence. . . .

ALICE [*still uneasy*]: I wish he'd eaten here. . . .

MORE: Yes – we shall be living on that 'simple supper' of yours for a fortnight.

    [*She won't laugh.*]

Alice. . .

    [*She won't turn.*]

Alice. . .

    [*She turns.*]

Set your mind at rest – this [*tapping himself*] is not the stuff of which martyrs are made.

[*Enter above, quickly,* ROPER.]

ROPER: Sir Thomas!

MORE [*winces*]: Oh, no... !

ALICE: Will Roper, what d'you want?

[*Enter, after* ROPER, MARGARET.]

MARGARET: William, I told you not to!

ROPER: I'm not easily 'told', Meg.

MARGARET: I *asked* you not to.

ROPER: Meg, I'm full to here! [*Indicates throat.*]

MARGARET: It's not convenient!

ROPER: Must everything be made convenient? I'm not a convenient man, Meg – I've got an inconvenient conscience!

[MARGARET *gestures helplessly to More.*]

MORE [*laughs*]: Joshua's trumpet. One note on that brass conscience of yours and my daughter's walls are down.

ROPER [*descending*]: You raised her, sir.

MORE [*a bit puzzled*]: How long have you been here? Are you in the King's party?

ROPER: No, sir, I am *not* in the King's party! [*Advancing*] It's of that I wish to speak to you. My spirit is perturbed.

MORE [*suppressing a grin*]: Is it, Will, Why?

ROPER: I've been offered a seat in the next Parliament.

[MORE *looks up sharply.*]

Ought I to take it?

MORE: No ... Well that depends. With your views on Church Reformation I should have thought you could do yourself a lot of good in the next Parliament.

ROPER: My views on the Church – I must confess – Since last we met my views have somewhat modified.

[MORE *and* MARGARET *exchange a smile.*]

I modify nothing concerning the *body* of the Church – the money-changers in the temple must be scourged from thence – with a scourge of fire if that is needed! ... But an attack on the Church herself! No, I see behind that an attack on God –

MORE: – Roper –

ROPER: The Devil's work!

MORE: – Roper – !

ROPER: To be done by the Devil's ministers!

MORE: For heaven's sake remember my office!

ROPER: Oh, if you stand on your office –

MORE: I don't stand on it, but there are certain things I may not hear!

ROPER: Sophistication. It is what I was told. The Court has corrupted you, Sir Thomas; you are not the man you were; you have learnt to study your 'convenience'; you have learnt to flatter!

MORE: There, Alice; you see? I have a reputation for it.

ALICE: God's Body, young man, if I was the Chancellor I'd have you whipped!

[*Enter* STEWARD.]

STEWARD: Master Rich is here, Sir Thomas.

[RICH *follows him closely.*]

RICH: Good evening, sir.

MORE: Ah, Richard?

RICH: Good evening, Lady Alice.

[ALICE *nods, noncommittal.*]

Lady Margaret.

MARGARET [*quite friendly but very clear*]: Good evening, Master Rich.
[*A pause.*]

MORE: Do you know – ? [*Indicates Roper.*] William Roper, the younger.

RICH: By reputation, of course.

ROPER: Good evening, Master ...

RICH: Rich.

ROPER: Oh. [*Recollecting something*] Oh.

RICH [*quick and hostile*]: You have heard of me?

ROPER [*shortly*]: Yes.

RICH [*excitedly*]: In what connexion? I don't know what you can have heard –[*Looks about; hotly*] I sense that I'm not welcome here!
[*He has jumped the gun; they are startled.*]

MORE[*gently*]: Why, Richard, have you done something that should make you not welcome?

RICH: Why, do you suspect me of it?

MORE: I shall begin to.

RICH [*drawing closer to him and speaking hurriedly*]: Cromwell is asking questions. About you. About you particularly.

[MORE *is unmoved.*]

He is continually collecting information about you!

MORE: I know it.

[STEWARD *begins to slide out.*]

Stay a minute, Matthew.

RICH [*pointing*]: That's one of his sources!

MORE: Of course; that's one of my servants.

RICH [*hurried, low voice again*]: Signor Chapuys, the Imperial Ambassador –

MORE – Collects information too. That's one of his functions. [*He looks at Rich very gravely.*]

RICH [*voice cracking*]: You look at me as though I were an enemy!

MORE [*putting out a hand to steady him*]: Why, Richard, you're shaking.

RICH: I'm adrift. Help me.

MORE: How?

RICH: Employ me.

MORE: No.

RICH [*desperately*]: Employ me!

MORE: No!

[RICH *moves swiftly to exit: turns there.*]

RICH: I would be steadfast!

MORE: Richard, you couldn't answer for yourself even so far as tonight.

[*Exit* RICH. *All watch him; the others turn to More, their faces alert.*]

ROPER: Arrest him.

ALICE: Yes!

MORE: For what?

ALICE: He's dangerous!

ROPER: For libel; he's a spy.

ALICE: He is! Arrest him!

MARGARET: Father, that man's bad.

MORE: There is no law against that.

ROPER: There is! God's law!

MORE: Then God can arrest him.

ROPER: Sophistication upon sophistication!

MORE: No, sheer simplicity. The law, Roper, the law. I know what's legal, not what's right. And I'll stick to what's legal.

ROPER: Then you set Man's law above God's!

MORE: No, far below; but let me draw your attention to a fact – I'm *not* God. The currents and eddies of right and wrong, which you find such plain-sailing, I can't navigate, I'm no voyager. But in the thickets of the law, oh there I'm a forester. I doubt if there's a man alive who could follow me there, thank God. . . . [*He says this to himself.*]

ALICE [*exasperated, pointing after Rich*]: While you talk, he's gone?

MORE: And go he should if he was the devil himself until he broke the law!

ROPER: So now you'd give the Devil benefit of law!

MORE: Yes. What would you do? Cut a great road through the law to get after the Devil?

ROPER: I'd cut down every law in England to do that!

MORE [*roused and excited*]: Oh? [*Advances on Roper.*] And when the last law was down, and the Devil turned round on you – where would you hide, Roper, the laws all being flat? [*Leaves him.*] This country's planted thick with laws from coast to coast – Man's laws, not God's – and if you cut them down – and you're just the man to do it – d'you really think you could stand upright in the winds that would blow then? [*Quietly*] Yes, I'd give the Devil benefit of law, for my own safety's sake.

ROPER: I have long suspected this; this is the golden calf; the law's your god.

MORE [*wearily*]: Oh, Roper, you're a fool, God's my god. . . . [*Rather bitter*] But I find him rather too [*very bitter*] subtle. . . . I don't know where he is nor what he wants.

ROPER: My god wants service, to the end and unremitting; nothing else!

MORE [*dry*]: Are you sure that's God? – He sounds like Moloch. But indeed it may be God – And whoever hunts for me, Roper, God, or Devil, will find me hiding in the thickets of the law! And I'll hide my daughter with me! Not hoist her up the mainmast of your seagoing principles! They put about too nimbly!

[*Exit* MORE. *They all look after him.* MARGARET *touches Roper's hand.*]

MARGARET: Oh, that was harsh.

ROPER [*turning to her, serious*]: What's happened here?

ALICE [*still with her back to them, her voice strained*]: He can't abide a fool, that's all! Be off!

ROPER [*to Margaret*]: Hide you. Hide you from what?

ALICE [*turning, near to tears*]: He said nothing about hiding me you noticed! I've got too fat to hide I suppose!

MARGARET: You know he meant us both.

ROPER: But from what?

ALICE: I don't know. I don't know if he knows. He's not said one simple, direct word to me since this divorce came up. It's not God who's gone subtle! It's him!

[*Enter* MORE, *a little sheepish. Goes to Roper.*]

MORE [*kindly*]: Roper, that was harsh: your principles are – [*can't resist sending him up*] excellent – the very best quality. [*As* ROPER *bridles, contritely*] No truly now, your principles are fine. [*Indicating stairs, to all*] Look, we must make a start on all that food.

MARGARET: Father, can't you be plain with us?

MORE [*looks quickly from daughter to wife. Takes Alice's hand.*] I stand on the wrong side of no statute, and no common law. [*Takes Meg's hand too.*] I have not disobeyed my sovereign. I truly believe no man in England is safer than myself. And I want my supper. [*He starts them up the stairs and goes to Roper.*] We shall need your assistance, Will. There's an excellent Burgundy – if your principles permit.

ROPER: They don't, sir.

MORE: Well, have some water in it.

ROPER: Just the water, sir.

MORE: My poor boy.

ALICE [*stopping at head of stairs, as one who will be answered*]: Why does Cromwell collect information about you?

MORE: I'm a prominent figure. Someone somewhere's collecting information about Cromwell. Now no more shirking; we must make a start. [*Shepherding Roper up the stairs*] There's a stuffed swan if you please.

[ALICE and MARGARET *exit above.*]

Will, I'd trust *you* with my life. But not your principles.

[*They mount the stairs.*]

You see, we speak of being anchored to our principles. But if the weather turns nasty you up with an anchor and let it down where there's less wind, and the fishing's better. And 'look' we say 'I'm anchored!' [*Laughing, inviting Roper to laugh with him*] 'To my principles!'

[*Exit above,* MORE *and* ROPER. *Enter* COMMON MAN *pulling basket. From it he takes an Inn Sign which he hangs on to the alcove. He inspects it.*]

COMMON MAN: 'The Loyal Subject' . . . [*to audience*] a pub [*takes from basket and puts on jacket, cap, and napkin*]. A publican. [*Places two stools at the table, and mugs and a candle which he lights.*] Oh, he's a deep one that Sir Thomas More. . . . Deep. . . It takes a lot of education to get a man as deep as that. . . . [*Straight to audience*] And a deep nature to begin with too. [*Deadpan*] The likes of me can hardly be *expected* to follow the processes of a man like that. . . . [*Sly*] Can we? [*Inspects pub.*] Right, ready. [*Goes right.*] Ready, sir!

[*Enter* CROMWELL, *carrying bottle. Goes to alcove.*]

CROMWELL: Is this a *good* place for a conspiracy, innkeeper?

PUBLICAN [*woodenly*]: You asked for a private room, sir.

CROMWELL [*looking round*]: Yes, I want one without too many little dark corners.

PUBLICAN: I don't understand you, sir. Just the four corners as you see.

CROMWELL [*sardonic*]: You don't understand me.

PUBLICAN: That's right, sir.

CROMWELL: Do you know who I am?

PUBLICAN [*promptly*]: No, sir.

CROMWELL: Don't be too tactful, innkeeper.

PUBLICAN: I don't understand, sir.

CROMWELL: When the likes of you *are* too tactful, the likes of me begin to wonder who's the fool.

PUBLICAN: I just don't understand you, sir.

[CROMWELL *puts back his head and laughs silently.*]

CROMWELL: The master statesman of us all. 'I don't understand.'
[*Looks at Publican almost with hatred.*] All right, Get out.

[*Throws coin. Exit* PUBLICAN. CROMWELL *goes to exit opposite, calling*]

Come on.

[*Enter* RICH. *He glances at bottle in Cromwell's hand and remains cautiously by the exit.*]

Yes, it may be that I am a little intoxicated. [*Leaves Rich standing.*] But not with alcohol, with success! And who has a strong head for success? None of us gets enough of it. Except Kings. And they're born drunk.

RICH: Success? What success?

CROMWELL: Guess.

RICH: Collector of Revenues for York.

CROMWELL [*amused*]: You do keep your ear to the ground don't you? No. Better than that.

RICH: High Constable.

CROMWELL: Better than that.

RICH: Better than High Constable?

CROMWELL: Much better. Sir Thomas Paget is – retiring.

RICH: Secretary to the Council!

CROMWELL: 'Tis astonishing, isn't it?

RICH [*hastily*]: Oh no – I mean – one sees, it's logical.

CROMWELL: No ceremony, no courtship. Be seated.

[RICH *sits.*]

As His Majesty would say.

[RICH *laughs nervously and involuntarily glances round.*]

Yes; see how I trust you.

RICH: Oh, I would never repeat or report a thing like that –

CROMWELL [*pouring wine*]: What kind of thing would you repeat or report?

RICH: Well, nothing said in friendship – may I say 'friendship'?

CROMWELL: If you like. D'you believe that – that you would never repeat or report anything etcetera?

RICH: Why yes!

CROMWELL: No, but seriously.

RICH: Yes!

[CROMWELL *puts down bottle.*]

CROMWELL [*not sinister, but rather as a kindly teacher with a promising pupil*]: Rich; seriously.

RICH [*pausing, then bitterly*]: . . . It would depend what I was offered.

CROMWELL: Don't say it just to please me.

RICH: It's true. It would depend what I was offered.

CROMWELL [*patting his arm*]: Everyone knows it; not many people can say it.

RICH: There are *some* things one wouldn't do for anything. Surely.

CROMWELL: Mm – that idea's like these lifelines they have on the embankment: comforting, but you don't expect to have to use them. [*Briskly*] Well, congratulations!

RICH [*suspicious*]: On what?

CROMWELL: I think you'd make a good Collector of Revenues for York Diocese.

RICH [*gripping on to himself*]: Is it in your gift?

CROMWELL: Effectively.

RICH [*with conscious cynicism*]: What do I have to do for it?

CROMWELL: Nothing. [*He lectures, pacing pedantically up and down.*] It isn't like that, Rich. There are no rules. With rewards and penalties – so much wickedness purchases so much worldly prospering – [*He breaks off and stops, suddenly struck.*] Are you sure you're not religious?

RICH: Almost sure.

CROMWELL: Get sure. [*Resumes pacing.*] No, it's not like that, it's much more a matter of convenience, administrative convenience. The normal aim of administration is to keep steady this factor of convenience – and Sir Thomas would agree. Now normally when a man wants to change his woman, you let him if it's convenient and prevent him if it's not – normally indeed it's of so little importance that you leave it to the priests. But the constant factor is this element of convenience.

RICH: Whose convenience?

[CROMWELL *stops.*]

CROMWELL: Oh ours. But everybody's too. [*Sets off again*] However, in the present instance the man who wants to change his woman is our Sovereign Lord, Harry, by the Grace of God, the Eighth of that name. Which is a quaint way of saying that if he wants to change his woman he will. So *that* becomes the constant factor. And our job as administrators is to make it as convenient as we can. I say 'our' job, on the assumption that you'll take this post at York I've offered you?

RICH: Yes . . . yes, yes. [*But he seems gloomy.*]

    [CROMWELL *sits.*]

CROMWELL [*sharply*]: It's a bad sign when people are depressed by their own good fortune.

RICH [*defensive*]: I'm not depressed!

CROMWELL: You look depressed.

RICH [*hastily buffooning*]: I'm lamenting. I've lost my innocence.

CROMWELL: You lost that some time ago. If you've only just noticed, it can't have been very important to you.

RICH [*much struck*]: That's true! Why that's true, it can't!

CROMWELL: We experience a sense of release do we, Master Rich? An unfamiliar freshness in the head, as of open air?

RICH [*takes wine*]: Collector of Revenues isn't bad!

CROMWELL: Not bad for a start. [*He watches Rich drink.*] Now our present Lord Chancellor – *there's* an innocent man.

RICH [*putting down glass, indulgently*]: The odd thing is – he *is.*

CROMWELL [*looking at him with dislike*]: Yes, I say he is. [*The light tone again*] The trouble is, his innocence is tangled in this proposition that you can't change your woman without a divorce, and can't have a divorce unless the Pope says so. And although his present Holiness is – judged even by the most liberal standards – a strikingly corrupt old person, yet he still has this word 'Pope' attached to him. And from this quite meaningless circumstance I fear some degree of . . .

RICH [*pleased, waving his cup*]: Administrative inconvenience.

CROMWELL [*nodding as to a pupil word-perfect*]: Just so. [*Deadpan*] This goblet that he gave you, how much was it worth?

    [RICH *puts down cup, looks down.*]

    [*Quite gently*] Come along, Rich, he gave you a silver goblet. How much did you get for it?

RICH: Fifty shillings.

CROMWELL: Could you take me to the shop?

RICH: Yes.

CROMWELL: Where did he get it? [*No reply.*] It was a gift from a litigant, a woman, wasn't it?

RICH: Yes.

CROMWELL: Which court? Chancery? [*Restrains Rich from filling his glass.*] No, don't get drunk. In which court was this litigant's case?

RICH: Court of Requests.

[CROMWELL *grunts, his face abstracted. Becoming aware of* RICH'S *regard he smiles.*]

CROMWELL: There, that wasn't too painful was it?

RICH [*laughing a little and a little rueful*]: No!

CROMWELL [*spreading his hands*]: That's all there is. And you'll find it easier next time.

RICH [*looking up briefly, unhappily*]: What application do they have, these titbits of information you collect?

CROMWELL: None at all, usually.

RICH [*stubbornly, not looking up*]: But sometimes.

CROMWELL: Well, there *are* these men – you know – 'upright', 'steadfast', men who want themselves to be the constant factor in the situation. Which of course they can't be. The situation rolls forward in any case.

RICH [*the same*]: So what happens?

CROMWELL [*not liking his tone, coldly*]: If they've any sense they get out of its way.

RICH: What if they haven't any sense?

CROMWELL [*the same*]: What, none at all? Well, then they're only fit for Heaven. But Sir Thomas has plenty of sense; he could be frightened.

RICH [*looking up, his face nasty*]: Don't forget he's an innocent, Master Cromwell.

CROMWELL: I think we'll finish there for tonight. [*Rising*] After all, he *is* the Lord Chancellor. [*Going.*]

RICH: You wouldn't find him easy to frighten! [*Calls after him*] You've mistaken your man this time! He doesn't know how to be frightened!

CROMWELL: [*returning*, RICH *rising at his approach*]: Doesn't know how to be frightened? Why, then he never put his hand in a candle.

... Did he? [*And seizing Rich by the wrist he holds his hand in the candle flame.*]

[RICH *screeches and darts back, hugging his hand in his armpit, regarding Cromwell with horror.*]

RICH: You enjoyed that!

[CROMWELL'S *downturned face is amazed.*]

[*Triumphantly*] You enjoyed it!

CURTAIN

ACT TWO

The scene is as for Act One.

[*When the curtain rises the stage is in darkness save for a spot, at the front of the stage, in which stands the* COMMON MAN. *He carries the book, a placed marked by his finger, and wears his spectacles.*]

COMMON MAN: The interval started early in the year 1530 and it's now the middle of May 1532. [*Explanatory*] Two years. During that time a lot of water's flowed under the bridge and among the things that have come floating along on it is . . . [*Reads*] 'The Church of England, that finest flower of our Island genius for compromise; that system, peculiar to these shores, which deflects the torrents of religious passion down the canals of moderation.' That's very well put. [*Returns to book; approvingly*] 'Typically, this great effect was achieved not by bloodshed but by simple Act of Parliament. Only an unhappy few were found to set themselves against the current of their times, and in so doing to court disaster. For we are dealing with an age less fastidious than our own. Imprisonment without trial, and even examination under torture, were common practice.'

[*Lights rise to show* MORE, *seated, and* ROPER, *standing. Exit* COMMON MAN. ROPER *is dressed in black and wears a cross. He commences to walk up and down, watched by* MORE. *A pause.*]

MORE: Must you wear those clothes, Will?

ROPER: Yes, I must.

MORE: Why?

ROPER: The time has come for decent men to declare their allegiance!

MORE: And what allegiance are those designed to express?

ROPER: My allegiance to the Church.

MORE: Well, you *look* like a Spaniard.

ROPER: All credit to Spain then!

MORE: You wouldn't last six months in Spain. You'd have been burned alive in Spain, during your heretic period.

ROPER: I suppose you have the right to remind me of it. [*Points accusingly.*] That chain of office that *you* wear is a degradation!

MORE [*glancing down at it*]: I've told you. If the bishops in Convocation submitted this morning, I'll take it off. . . . It's no degradation. Great men have worn this.

ROPER: When d'you expect to hear from Canterbury?

MORE: About now. The Archbishop promised me an immediate message.

ROPER [*recommences pacing*]: I don't see what difference Convocation can make. The Church is already a wing of the Palace is it not? The King is already its 'Supreme Head'! Is he not?

MORE: No.

ROPER [*startled*]: You are denying the Act of Supremacy!

MORE: No, I'm not; the Act states that the King –

ROPER: – is Supreme Head of the Church in England.

MORE: Supreme Head of the Church in England – [*Underlining the words*] 'so far as the law of God allows'. How far the law of God does allow it remains a matter of opinion, since the Act doesn't state it.

ROPER: A legal quibble.

MORE: Call it what you like, it's there, thank God.

ROPER: Very well: in your opinion how far does the law of God allow this?

MORE: I'll keep my opinion to myself, Will.

ROPER: Yes? I'll tell you mine – !

MORE: Don't! If your opinion's what I think it is, it's High Treason, Roper!

[*Enter* MARGARET *above, unseen.*]

Will, you remember you've a wife now! And may have children!

MARGARET: Why must he remember that?

ROPER: To keep myself 'discreet'.

MARGARET [*smiling*]: Then I'd rather you forgot it.

MORE [*unsmiling*]: You are either idiots, or children.

[*Enter* CHAPUYS, *above.*]

CHAPUYS [*very sonorous*]: Or saints, my lord!

MARGARET: Oh, Father, Signor Chapuys has come to see you.

MORE [*rising*]: Your Excellency.

CHAPUYS [*striking pose with* MARGARET *and* ROPER]: Or saints, my lord; or saints.

MORE [*grinning maliciously at Roper*]: That's it of course – saints! Roper – turn your head a bit – yes, I think I do detect, a faint radiance. [*Reproachful*] You should have told us, Will.

CHAPUYS: Come come, my lord; you too at this time are not free from some suspicion of saintliness.

MORE [*quietly*]: I don't like the sound of that, Your Excellency. What do you require of *me*? What, Your Excellency?

CHAPUYS [*awkward beneath his sudden keen regard*]: May I not come simply, to pay my respects to the English Socrates – as I see your angelic friend Erasmus calls you.

MORE [*wrinkling nose*]: Yes, I'll think of something presently to call Erasmus. [*Checks.*] Socrates! I've no taste for hemlock, Your Excellency, if that's what you require.

CHAPUYS [*with display of horror*]: Heaven forbid!

MORE [*dryly*]: Amen.

CHAPUYS [*spreads hands*]: Must I require anything? [*Sonorous*] After all, we are brothers in Christ, you and I!

MORE: A characteristic we share with the rest of humanity. You live in Cheapside, Signor? To make contact with a brother in Christ you have only to open your window and empty a chamberpot. There was no need to come to Chelsea.

[CHAPUYS *titters nervously.*]

[*Coldly*] William. The Imperial Ambassador is here on business. Would you mind?

[ROPER *and* MARGARET *begin to go.*]

CHAPUYS [*rising, unreal protestations*]: Oh no! I protest!

MORE: He is clearly here on business.

CHAPUYS [*the same*]: No; but really, I protest!

[*It is no more than token: when* ROPER *and* MARGARET *reach head of stairs he calls:*]

Dominus vobiscum filii mei!

ROPER [*pompous*]: Et cum spiritu tuo, excellencis!

[*Exit* ROPER *and* MARGARET.]

CHAPUYS [*approaching More, thrillingly*]: And how much longer shall we hear that holy language in these shores?

MORE [*alert, poker-faced*]: 'Tisn't 'holy', Your Excellency; just old.
   [CHAPUYS *sits with the air of one coming to brass tacks.*]

CHAPUYS: My Lord, I cannot believe you will allow yourself to be
   associated with the recent actions of King Henry! In respect of
   Queen Catherine.

MORE: Subjects are associated with the actions of Kings willy-nilly.

CHAPUYS: The Lord Chancellor is not an ordinary subject. He bears
   responsibility ... [*letting the word sink in while* MORE *shifts*] for what
   is done.

MORE [*agitation beginning to show through*]: Have you considered that
   what has been done badly, might have been done worse, with a
   different Chancellor.

CHAPUYS [*with mounting confidence, as* MORE'S *attention is caught*]:
   Believe me, Sir Thomas, your influence in these policies has been
   much searched for, and where it has been found it has been praised
   – *but* ... There comes a point, does there not? ...

MORE: Yes. [*Agitated*] There does come such a point.

CHAPUYS: When the sufferings of one unfortunate lady swell to an
   open attack on the religion of an entire country that point has been
   passed. Beyond that point, Sir Thomas, one is not merely 'com-
   promised', one is in truth corrupted.

MORE [*staring at him*]: What do you want?

CHAPUYS: Rumour has it that if the Church in Convocation has
   submitted to the King, you will resign.

MORE [*looking down and regaining composure*]: I see. [*Suavely*] Supposing rumour to be right. Would you approve of that?

CHAPUYS: Approve, applaud, admire.

MORE [*still looking down*]: Why?

CHAPUYS: Because it would show one man – and that man known
   to be temperate – unable to go further with this wickedness.

MORE [*the same*]: And that man known to be Chancellor of England
   too.

CHAPUYS: Believe me, my lord, such a signal would be seen –

MORE [*the same*]: 'Signal'?

CHAPUYS: Yes, my lord; it would be seen and understood.

MORE [*the same, and now positively silky*]: By whom?

CHAPUYS: By half of your fellow countrymen!

[*Now* MORE *looks up sharply.*]

Sir Thomas, I have just returned from Yorkshire and Northumberland, where I have made a tour.

MORE [*softly*]: Have you indeed?

CHAPUYS: Things are very different there, my lord. There they are ready.

MORE: For what?

CHAPUYS: Resistance!

[*Enter* ROPER, *above, excited.*]

ROPER: Sir Thomas – !

[MORE *looks up angrily.*]

Excuse me, sir – [*Indicates off.*] His Grace the Duke of Norfolk –

[MORE *and* CHAPUYS *rise.* ROPER *excitedly descends.*]

It's all over, sir, they've –

[*Enter* NORFOLK *above,* ALICE *and* MARGARET, *below.*]

NORFOLK: One moment, Roper, I'll do this! Thomas – [*Sees Chapuys.*] Oh. [*He stares at Chapuys, hostile.*]

CHAPUYS: I was on the point of leaving, Your Grace. Just a personal call. I have been trying ... er to borrow a book – but without success – you're sure you have no copy, my lord? Then I'll leave you. [*Bowing*] Gentlemen, ladies. [*Going, upstairs, but stopping unseen as Roper speaks.*]

ROPER: Sir Thomas –

NORFOLK: I'll do it, Roper! Convocation's knuckled under, Thomas. They're to pay a fine of a hundred thousand pounds. And ... we've severed the connexion with Rome.

MORE [*smiling bitterly*]: 'The connexion with Rome' is nice. [*Bitter*] 'The connexion with Rome.' Did *anyone* resist?

NORFOLK: Bishop Fisher.

MORE: Lovely man.

[NORFOLK *shrugs.*]

ROPER [*looking at More*]: Your Grace, this is quite certain is it?

NORFOLK: Yes.

[MORE *puts his hand to his chain.* CHAPUYS *exit. All turn.*]

Funny company, Thomas?

MORE: It's quite unintentional. He doesn't mean to be funny. [*Fumbles with chain.*] Help me with this.

NORFOLK: Not I.

ROPER [*taking a step forward, then, subdued*]: Shall I, sir?

MORE: No thank you, Will. Alice?

ALICE: Hell's fire – God's blood and body *no*! Sun and moon, Master More, you're taken for a wise man! Is this wisdom – to betray your ability, abandon practice, forget your station and your duty to your kin, and behave like a printed book!

MORE [*listening gravely, then*]: Margaret, will you?

MARGARET: If you want.

MORE: There's my clever girl.
[*She takes it from his neck.*]

NORFOLK: Well, Thomas, why? Make me understand – because I'll tell you now, from where I stand, this looks like cowardice!

MORE [*excited and angry*]: All right I will – this isn't 'Reformation'; this is war against the Church! . . . [*Indignant.*] Our King, Norfolk, has declared war on the Pope – because the Pope will not declare that our Queen is not his wife.

NORFOLK: And is she?

MORE [*cunning*]: I'll answer that question for one person only, the King. Aye, and that in private too.

NORFOLK [*contemptuous*]: Man, you're cautious.

MORE: Yes, cautious. I'm not one of your hawks.

NORFOLK [*walks away and turns*]: All right – we're at war with the Pope! The Pope's a Prince, isn't he?

MORE: He is.

NORFOLK: And a bad one?

MORE: Bad enough. But the theory is that he's also the Vicar of God, the descendant of St Peter, our only link with Christ.

NORFOLK [*sneer*]: A tenuous link.

MORE: Oh, tenuous indeed.

NORFOLK [*to the others*]: Does this make sense?
[*No reply; they look at More.*]
You'll forfeit all you've got – which includes the respect of your country – for a theory?

MORE [*hotly*]: The Apostolic Succession of the Pope is – [*Stops: interested.*] . . . Why, it's a theory yes; you can't see it; can't touch it; it's a theory. [*To Norfolk, very rapidly but calm*] But what matters to me is not whether it's true or not but that I believe it to be true, or rather not that I *believe* it, but that *I* believe it. . . . I trust I make myself obscure?

NORFOLK: Perfectly.

MORE: That's good. Obscurity's what I have need of now.

NORFOLK: Man, you're sick. This isn't Spain you know.

[MORE *looks at him; then takes him aside.*]

MORE [*lowered voice*]: Have I your word, that what we say here is between us and has no existence beyond these walls?

NORFOLK [*impatient*]: Very well.

MORE [*almost whispering*]: And if the King should command you to repeat what I have said?

NORFOLK: I should keep my word to you!

MORE: Then what has become of your oath of obedience to the King?

NORFOLK [*indignant*]: You lay traps for me!

MORE [*now grown calm*]: No, I show you the times.

NORFOLK: Why do you insult me with these lawyer's tricks?

MORE: Because I am afraid.

NORFOLK: And here's your answer. The King accepts your resignation very sadly; he is mindful of your goodness and past loyalty and in any matter concerning your honour and welfare he will be your good lord. So much for your fear.

MORE [*flatly*]: You will convey my humble gratitude.

NORFOLK: I will. Good day, Alice. [*Going*] I'd rather deal with you than your husband.

MORE [*with complete change of tone; briskly professional*]: Oh, Howard! [*Goes to him.*] Signor Chapuys tells me he's just made a 'tour' of the North Country. He thinks we shall have trouble there. So do I.

NORFOLK [*stolid*]: Yes? What kind of trouble?

MORE: The Church – the old Church, not the new Church – is very strong up there. I'm serious, Howard, keep an eye on the Border, this next year; and bear in mind the Old Alliance.

NORFOLK [*looks at him*]: We will. We do. . . . As for the Dago, Thomas, it'll perhaps relieve your mind to know that one of Secretary Cromwell's agents made the tour with him.

MORE: Oh. [*With a flash of jealousy*] Of course if Master Cromwell has matters in hand –

NORFOLK: – He has.

MORE: Yes, I can imagine.

NORFOLK: But thanks for the information. [*Going*] It's good to know you still have . . . some vestige of patriotism.

MORE [*anger*]: That's a remarkably stupid observation, Norfolk! [*Exit* NORFOLK.]

ALICE: So there's an end of you. What will you do now – sit by the fire and make goslings in the ash?

MORE: Not at all, Alice, I expect I'll write a bit. [*He woos them with unhappy cheerfulness.*] I'll write, I'll read, I'll think. I think I'll learn to fish! I'll play with my grandchildren – when son Roper's done his duty. [*Eager*] Alice, shall I teach you to read?

ALICE: No, by God!

MORE: . . . Son Roper, *you're* pleased with me I hope?

ROPER [*going to him: moved*]: Sir, you've made a noble gesture.

MORE [*blankly*]: A gesture? [*Eager*] It wasn't possible to continue, Will. I was not *able* to continue. I would have if I could! I make no gesture! [*Apprehensive, looks after Norfolk.*] My God, I hope it's understood I make no gesture! [*Turns back to them.*] – Alice, you don't think I would do this to you for a gesture! *That's* a gesture! [*Thumbs his nose.*] *That's* a gesture! [*Jerks up two fingers.*] I'm no street acrobat to make gestures! I'm practical!

ROPER: You belittle yourself, sir, this was not practical; [*resonant*] this was moral!

MORE: Oh now I understand you, Will. Morality's *not* practical. Morality's a gesture. A complicated gesture learned from books – that's what you say, Alice, isn't it? . . . And you, Meg?

MARGARET: It *is*, for most of us, Father.

MORE: Oh no, if you're going to plead humility – ! Oh, you're cruel. I have a cruel family.

ALICE: Yes, you can fit the cap on anyone you want, I know that well enough. If there's cruelty in this house, I know where to look for it.

MARGARET: No, Mother – !

ALICE: Oh, you'd walk on the bottom of the sea and think yourself a crab if he suggested it! [*To Roper*] And you! You'd dance him to the Tower – You'd dance him to the block! Like David with a harp! Scattering hymn-books in his path! [*To More*] Poor silly man, d'you think they'll *leave* you here to learn to fish?

MORE [*straight at her*]: If we govern our tongues they will! . . . Look, I have a word to say about that. I have made no statement. I've resigned, that's *all*. On the King's Supremacy, the King's divorce which he'll now grant himself, the marriage he'll then make – have you heard me make a statement?

ALICE: No – and if I'm to lose my rank and fall to housekeeping I want to know the reason; so make a statement now.

MORE: No –

[ALICE *exhibits indignation.*]

– Alice, it's a point of law! Accept it from me, Alice, that in silence is my safety under the law, but my silence must be absolute, it must extend to you.

ALICE: In short you don't trust us!

MORE [*impatient*]: Look – [*advancing on her*] I'm the Lord Chief Justice, I'm Cromwell, I'm the King's Head Jailer – and I take your hand [*does so*] and I clamp it on the Bible, on the Blessed Cross [*clamps her hand on his closed fist*] and I say: 'Woman, has your husband made a statement on these matters?' Now – on peril of your soul remember– what's your answer?

ALICE: No.

MORE: And so it must remain. [*He looks round at their grave faces.*] Oh, it's only a life-line, we shan't have to use it but it's comforting to have. No, no, when they find I'm silent they'll ask nothing better than to leave me silent; you'll see.

[*Enter* STEWARD.]

STEWARD: Sir, the household's in the kitchen. They want to know what's happened.

MORE: Oh. Yes. We must speak to them. Alice, they'll mostly have to go, my dear. [*To Steward*] But not before we've found them places.

ALICE: We can't find places for them all!

MORE: Yes, we can; yes, we can. Tell them so.

ALICE: God's death it comes on us quickly . . .

[*Exit* ALICE, MARGARET, *and* ROPER.]

MORE: What about you, Matthew? It'll be a smaller household now, and for you, I'm afraid, a smaller wage. Will you stay?

STEWARD: Don't see how I could then, sir.

MORE: You're a single man.

STEWARD [*awkward*]: Well, yes, sir, but I mean I've got my own –

MORE [*quickly*]: Quite right, why should you? . . . I shall miss you, Matthew.

STEWARD [*with man-to-man jocosity*]: No-o-o. You never had much time for *me*, sir. You see through *me*, sir, I know that. [*He almost winks.*]

MORE [*gently insists*]: I shall miss you, Matthew; I shall miss you.

[*Exit* MORE. STEWARD *snatches off hat and hurls it to the floor.*]

STEWARD: Now, damn me isn't that them all over! [*He broods, face downturned.*] Miss – ? . . . He – . . . Miss – ? . . . *Miss* me? . . . What's *in* me for *him* to miss. . . ? [*Suddenly he cries out like one who sees a danger at his very feet.*] WO-AH! [*Chuckling*] We-e-eyup! [*To audience*] I nearly fell for it. [*Walks away.*] 'Matthew, will you kindly take a cut in your wages?' 'No, Sir Thomas, I will not.' That's it and [*fiercely*] that's all of it! [*Falls to thought again. Resentfully*] All right, so he's down on his luck! I'm sorry. I don't mind saying that: I'm sorry! Bad luck! If I'd any good luck to spare he could have some. I wish we could *all* have good luck, *all* the time! I wish we had wings! I wish rainwater was beer! But it isn't! . . . And what with not having wings but walking – on two flat feet; and good luck and bad luck being just exactly even stevens; and rain being water – don't you complicate the job by putting things in me for me to miss! [*He takes off Steward's coat, picks up his hat: draws the curtain to alcove. Chuckling*] I did you know. I nearly fell for it.

[*Exit* COMMON MAN. NORFOLK *and* CROMWELL *enter to alcove.*]

NORFOLK: But he makes no noise, Mr Secretary; he's silent, why not leave him silent?

CROMWELL [*patiently*]: Not being a man of letters, Your Grace, you perhaps don't realize the extent of his reputation. This 'silence' of his is bellowing up and down Europe! Now may I recapitulate: he reported the Ambassador's conversation to you, informed on the

Ambassador's tour of the North-country, warned against a possible rebellion there.

NORFOLK: He did!

CROMWELL: We may say, then, that he showed himself hostile to the hopes of Spain.

NORFOLK: That's what I *say*!

CROMWELL [*patiently*]: Bear with me, Your Grace. Now if he opposes Spain, he supports us. Well, surely that follows? [*Sarcastically*] Or do you see some third alternative?

NORFOLK: No no, that's the line-up all right. And I may say Thomas More –

CROMWELL: Thomas More will line up on the right side.

NORFOLK: Yes! Crank he may be, traitor he is not.

CROMWELL [*spreading his hands*]: And with a little pressure, he can be got to say so. And that's all we need – a brief declaration of his loyalty to the present administration.

NORFOLK: I still say let sleeping dogs lie.

CROMWELL [*heavily*]: The King does not agree with you.

NORFOLK [*who glances at him; flickers, but then rallies*]: What kind of 'pressure' d'you think you can bring to bear?

CROMWELL: I have evidence that Sir Thomas, during the period of his judicature, accepted bribes.

NORFOLK [*incredulous*]: What! Goddammit he was the only judge since Cato who *didn't* accept bribes! When was there last a Chancellor whose possessions after three years in office totalled one hundred pounds and a gold chain.

CROMWELL [*rings hand-bell and calls*]: Richard! It is, as you imply, common practice, but a practice may be common and remain an offence; this offence could send a man to the Tower.

NORFOLK [*contemptuous*] I don't believe it.

[*Enter* RICH *and* A WOMAN. *He motions her to remain, and approaches the table, where* CROMWELL *indicates a seat. He has acquired self-importance.*]

CROMWELL: Ah, Richard. You know His Grace of course.

RICH [*with respectful affability*]: Indeed yes, we're *old* friends.

NORFOLK [*with a savage snub*]: Used to look after my books or something, didn't you?

CROMWELL (*clicking his fingers at the Woman*]: Come here. This woman's name is Catherine Anger; she comes from Lincoln. And she put a case in the Court of Requests in – [*Consults paper.*]

WOMAN: A property case, it was.

CROMWELL: Be quiet. A property case in the Court of Requests in April 1526.

WOMAN: And got a wicked false judgement!

CROMWELL: And got an impeccably correct judgement from our friend Sir Thomas.

WOMAN: No, sir, it was not!

CROMWELL: We're not concerned with the judgement but the gift you gave the judge. Tell this gentleman about that. The judgement for what it's worth was the right one.

WOMAN: No, sir!

[CROMWELL *looks at her: she hastily addresses Norfolk.*]

I sent him a cup, sir; an Italian Silver cup I bought in Lincoln for a hundred shillings.

NORFOLK: Did Sir Thomas accept this cup?

WOMAN: I sent it.

CROMWELL: He did accept it, we can corroborate that. You can go.

[*She opens her mouth.*]

Go!

[*Exit* WOMAN.]

NORFOLK [*scornful*]: Is that your witness?

CROMWELL: No; by an odd coincidence this cup later came into the hands of Master Rich here.

NORFOLK: How?

RICH: He gave it to me.

NORFOLK [*brutal*]: Can you corroborate that?

CROMWELL: I have a fellow outside who can; he was More's steward at that time. Shall I call him?

NORFOLK: Don't bother, I know him. When did Thomas give you this thing?

RICH: I don't exactly remember.

NORFOLK: Well, make an effort. Wait! I can tell you! I can tell you – it was that Spring– it was that night we were there together. You had a cup with you when we left; was that it?

[RICH *looks to Cromwell for guidance but gets none.*]

RICH: It may have been.

NORFOLK: Did he often give you cups?

RICH: I don't suppose so, Your Grace.

NORFOLK: That was it then. [*New realization.*] And it was April! The April of 26. The very month that cow first put her case before him! [*Triumphant*] In other words the moment he knew it was a bribe, he got rid of it.

CROMWELL [*nodding judicially*]: The facts will bear that interpretation I suppose.

NORFOLK: Oh, this is a horse that won't run, Master Secretary.

CROMWELL: Just a trial canter, Your Grace. We'll find something better.

NORFOLK [*between bullying and plea*]: Look here, Cromwell, I want no part of this.

CROMWELL: You have no choice.

NORFOLK: What's that you say?

CROMWELL: The King particularly wishes you to be active in the matter.

NORFOLK [*winded*]: He has not told me that.

CROMWELL [*politely*]: Indeed? He told me.

NORFOLK: But *why*?

CROMWELL: We feel that, since you are known to have been a friend of More's, your participation will show that there is nothing in the nature of a 'persecution', but only the strict processes of law. As indeed you've just demonstrated. I'll tell the King of your loyalty to your friend. If you like, I'll tell him that you 'want no part of it', too.

NORFOLK [*furious*]: Are you threatening me, Cromwell?

CROMWELL: My *dear* Norfolk. . . . This isn't Spain.

[NORFOLK *stares, turns abruptly, and exits.* CROMWELL *turns a look of glacial coldness upon Rich.*]

RICH: I'm sorry, secretary, I'd forgotten he was there that night.

CROMWELL [*scrutinizing him dispassionately, then*]: You must try to remember these things.

RICH: Secretary, I'm sincerely – !

[CROMWELL *dismisses the topic with a wave and turns to look after Norfolk.*]

Not such a fool as he looks, the Duke.

RICH [*with Civil Service simper*]: That would hardly be possible, Secretary.

CROMWELL: [*straightening papers, briskly*]: Sir Thomas is going to be a slippery fish, Richard; we need a net with a finer mesh.

RICH: Yes, Secretary?

CROMWELL: We'll weave one for him shall we, you and I?

RICH [*uncertain*]: I'm only anxious to do what is correct, Secretary.

CROMWELL [*smiling at him*]: Yes, Richard, I know. [*Straightfacedly*] You're absolutely right, it must be done by law. It's just a matter of finding the right law. Or making one. Bring my papers, will you?

[*Exit* CROMWELL. *Enter* STEWARD.]

STEWARD: Could we have a word now, sir?

RICH: We don't require you after all, Matthew.

STEWARD: No, sir, but about . . .

RICH: Oh yes. . . . Well, I begin to need a steward, certainly; my household is expanding. . . . [*Sharply*] But as I remember, Matthew, your attitude to me was sometimes – disrespectful! [*The last word is shrill.*]

STEWARD [*with humble dignity*]: Oh. Oh, I must contradict you there, sir; that's your imagination. In those days, sir, you still had your way to make. And a gentleman in that position often imagines these things. Then when he's risen to his proper level, sir, he stops thinking about it. [*As one offering tangible proof*] Well – I don't think you find people 'disrespectful' nowadays, do you, sir?

RICH: There may be something in that. Bring my papers. [*Going, he turns at exit and anxiously scans Steward's face for signs of impudence.*] I'll permit no breath of insolence!

STEWARD [*the very idea is shocking*]: I should hope not, sir.

[*Exit* RICH.]

Oh, I can manage this one! He's just my size!

[*Lighting changes so that the set looks drab and chilly.*]

Sir Thomas More's again gone down a bit.

[*Exit* COMMON MAN.

Enter, side, CHAPUYS *and* ATTENDANT, *cloaked. Above,* ALICE, *wearing big coarse apron over her dress.*]

ALICE: My husband is coming down, Your Excellency.

CHAPUYS: Thank you, madam.

ALICE: And I beg you to be gone before he does!

CHAPUYS [*patiently*]: Madam, I have a Royal Commission to perform.

ALICE: Aye. You said so.

  [*Exit* ALICE.]

CHAPUYS: For sheer barbarity, commend me to a good-hearted Englishwoman of a certain class. . . . [*Wraps cloak about him.*]

ATTENDANT: It's very cold, Excellency.

CHAPUYS: I remember when these rooms were warm enough.

ATTENDANT [*looking about*]: 'Thus it is to incur the enmity of a Prince.'

CHAPUYS: – A heretic Prince. [*Looking about*] Yes, Sir Thomas is a good man.

ATTENDANT: Yes, Excellency, I like Sir Thomas very much.

CHAPUYS: Carefully, carefully.

ATTENDANT: It's uncomfortable dealing with him, isn't it?

CHAPUYS: Goodness presents its own difficulties. Attend and learn now.

ATTENDANT: Excellency?

CHAPUYS: Well?

ATTENDANT: Excellency, is he really *for* us?

CHAPUYS [*testy*]: He's opposed to Cromwell. He's shown that, I think?

ATTENDANT: Yes, Excellency, but –

CHAPUYS: If he's opposed to Cromwell, he's for us. There's no third alternative.

ATTENDANT: I suppose not, Excellency.

CHAPUYS: I wish your mother had chosen some other career for you; you've no political sense whatever. Sh!

  [*Enter* MORE. *His clothes match the atmosphere of the room and he moves rather more deliberately than before.*]

MORE [*descending*]: Is this another 'personal' visit, Chapuys, or is it official?

CHAPUYS: It falls between the two, Sir Thomas.

MORE [*reaching the bottom of stairs*]: Official then.

CHAPUYS: No, I have a personal letter for you.

MORE: From whom?

CHAPUYS: From King Charles!

[MORE *puts his hands behind back.*]

You will take it?

MORE: I will not lay a finger on it.

CHAPUYS: It is in no way an affair of State. It expresses my master's admiration for the stand which you and Bishop Fisher of Rochester have taken over the so-called divorce of Queen Catherine.

MORE: I have taken no stand!

CHAPUYS: But your views, Sir Thomas, are well known –

MORE: My views are much guessed at. [*Irritably*] Oh come, sir, could you undertake to convince [*grimly*] King Harry that this letter is 'in no way an affair of State'?

CHAPUYS: My dear Sir Thomas, I have taken extreme precautions. I came here very much incognito. [*With self-indulgent chuckle*] Very nearly in disguise.

MORE: You misunderstand me. It is not a matter of your precautions but my duty; which would be to take this letter immediately to the King.

CHAPUYS [*flabbergasted*]: Sir Thomas, your views –

MORE: – Are well known you say. It seems my loyalty is less so.

[*Enter* MARGARET *bearing before her a huge bundle of bracken.*]

MARGARET: Look, Father! [*Dumps it.*] Will's getting more.

MORE: Oh, well done! [*Not with whimsy; they're cold and their interest in fuel is serious.*] Is it dry? [*Feels it expertly.*] Oh it *is*. [*Sees Chapuys staring; laughs.*] It's bracken, Your Excellency. We burn it.

[*Enter* ALICE.]

Alice, look at this [*the bracken*].

ALICE [*eyeing Chapuys*]: Aye.

MORE [*crossing to Chapuys*]: May I – ? [*Takes letter to Alice and Margaret.*] This is a letter from King Charles; I want you to see it's not been opened. I have declined it. You see the seal has not been broken? [*Returning it to Chapuys.*] I wish I could ask you to stay, Your Excellency – the bracken fire is a luxury.

CHAPUYS [*with cold smile*]: One I must forego. [*Aside to Attendant*] Come. [*Crosses to exit, pauses.*] May I say I am sure my master's admiration will not be diminished. [*Bows.*]

MORE: I am gratified. [*Bows; women curtsey.*]

CHAPUYS [*aside to Attendant*]: The man's utterly unreliable!

[*Exit* CHAPUYS *and* ATTENDANT.]

ALICE [*after a little silence, kicking the bracken*]: 'Luxury!' [*She sits wearily on the bundle.*]

MORE: Well, it's a luxury while it lasts. . . . There's not much sport in it for you, is there? . . .

[*She neither answers nor looks at him from the depths of her fatigue. After a moment's hesitation he braces himself.*]

Alice, the money from the Bishops. I wish – oh heaven how I wish I could take it! But I can't.

ALICE [*as one who has ceased to expect anything*]: I didn't think you would.

MORE [*reproachful*]: Alice, there *are* reasons.

ALICE: We couldn't come so deep into your confidence as to *know* these reasons why a man in poverty can't take four thousand pounds?

MORE [*gently but very firm*]: Alice, this isn't poverty.

ALICE: D'you know what we shall eat tonight?

MORE [*trying for a smile*]: Yes, parsnips.

ALICE: Yes, parsnips and stinking mutton! [*Straight at him*] For a knight's lady!

MORE [*pleading*]: But at the worst, we could be beggars, and still keep company, and be merry together!

ALICE [*bitterly*]: Merry!

MORE [*sternly*]: Aye, merry!

MARGARET [*her arm about her mother's waist*]: I think you should take that money.

MORE: Oh, don't you see? [*Sits by them.*] If I'm paid by the Church for my writings –

ALICE: – This had nothing to do with your writings! This was charity pure and simple! Collected from the clergy high and low!

MORE: It would *appear* as payment.

ALICE: You're not a man who deals in appearances!

MORE [*fervent*]: Oh, am I not though. . . . [*Calmly*] If the King takes this matter any further, with me or with the Church, it will be very bad, if I even appear to have been in the pay of the Church.

ALICE [*sharply*]: Bad?

MORE: If you will have it, dangerous. [*He gets up.*]

MARGARET: But you don't write against the King.

MORE: I write! And that's enough in times like these!

ALICE: You said there *was* no danger!

MORE: I don't think there is! And I don't want there to be!
    [*Enter* ROPER *carrying sickle.*]

ROPER [*steadily*]: There's a gentleman here from Hampton Court. You are to go before Secretary Cromwell. To answer certain charges.
    [ALICE *and* MARGARET, *appalled, turn to* MORE.]

MORE [*after a silence, rubbing his nose*]: Well, that's all right. We expected that. [*Not very convincing.*] When?

ROPER: Now.
    [ALICE *exhibits distress.*]

MORE: That means nothing, Alice; that's just technique. . . . Well, I suppose 'now' means now.
    [*Lighting change commences, darkness gathering on the others, leaving* MORE *isolated in the light, out of which he answers them in the shadows.*]

MARGARET: Can I come with you?

MORE: Why? No. I'll be back for dinner. I'll bring Cromwell to dinner, shall I? It'd serve him right.

MARGARET: Oh, Father, don't be witty!

MORE: Why not? Wit's what's in question.

ROPER [*quietly*]: While we are witty, the Devil may enter us unawares.

MORE: He's not the Devil, son Roper, he's a lawyer! And my case is watertight!

ALICE: They say he's a very nimble lawyer.

MORE: What, Cromwell? Pooh, he's a pragmatist – and that's the only resemblance he has to the Devil, son Roper; a pragmatist, the merest plumber.

[*Exit* ALICE, MARGARET, ROPER, *in darkness.*

Lights come up. Enter CROMWELL, *bustling, carrying file of papers.*]

CROMWELL: I'm sorry to invite you here at such short notice, Sir Thomas; good of you to come. [*Draws back curtain from alcove, revealing* RICH *seated at table, with writing materials.*] Will you take a seat? I think you know Master Rich?

MORE: Indeed yes, we're old friends. That's a nice gown you have, Richard.

CROMWELL: Master Rich will make a record of our conversation.

MORE: Good of you to tell me, Master Secretary.

CROMWELL [*laughing appreciatively, then*]: Believe me, Sir Thomas – no, that's asking too much – but let me tell you all the same, you have no more sincere admirer than myself.

[RICH *begins to scribble.*]

Not yet, Rich, not yet. | *Invites More to join him in laughing at Rich.*]

MORE: If I might hear the charges?

CROMWELL: Charges?

MORE: I understand there are certain charges.

CROMWELL: Some ambiguities of behaviour I should like to clarify – hardly 'charges'.

MORE: Make a note of that will you, Master Rich? There are no charges.

CROMWELL [*laughing and shaking head*]: Sir Thomas, Sir Thomas. . . You know it amazes me that you, who were once so effective *in* the world, and are now so *much* retired from it, should be opposing yourself to the whole movement of the times? [*He ends on a note of interrogation.*]

MORE [*nods*]: It amazes me too.

CROMWELL [*picking up and dropping paper; sadly*]: The King is not pleased with you.

MORE: I am grieved.

CROMWELL: Yet do you know that even now, if you could bring yourself to agree with the Universities, the Bishops, and the Parliament of this realm, there is no honour which the King would be likely to deny you?

MORE [*stonily*]: I am well acquainted with His Grace's generosity.

CROMWELL [*coldly*]: Very well. [*Consults paper.*] You have heard of the so-called 'Holy Maid of Kent' – who was executed for prophesying against the King?

MORE: Yes; I knew the poor woman.

CROMWELL [quick]: You sympathize with her?

MORE: She was ignorant and misguided; she was a bit mad I think. And she has paid for her folly. Naturally I sympathize with her.

CROMWELL [grunts]: You admit meeting her. You met her – and yet you did not warn His Majesty of her treason. How was that?

MORE: She spoke no treason. Our conversation was not political.

CROMWELL: My dear More, the woman was notorious! Do you expect me to believe that?

MORE: Happily there were witnesses.

CROMWELL: You wrote a letter to her?

MORE: Yes, I wrote advising her to abstain from meddling with the affairs of Princes and the State. I have a copy of this letter – also witnessed.

CROMWELL: You have been cautious.

MORE: I like to keep my affairs regular.

CROMWELL: Sir Thomas, there is a more serious charge –

MORE: Charge?

CROMWELL: For want of a better word. In the May of 1526 the King published a book, [he permits himself a little smile] a theological work. It was called A Defence of the Seven Sacraments.

MORE: Yes. [Bitterly] For which he was named 'Defender of the Faith', by His Holiness the Pope.

CROMWELL: – By the Bishop of Rome. Or do you insist on 'Pope'?

MORE: No, 'Bishop of Rome' if you like. It doesn't alter his authority.

CROMWELL: Thank you, you come to the point very readily; what is that authority? As regards the Church in other parts of Europe; [approaching] for example, the Church in England. What exactly is the Bishop of Rome's authority?

MORE: You will find it very ably set out and defended, Master Secretary, in the King's book.

CROMWELL: The book published under the King's name would be more accurate. You wrote that book.

MORE: – I wrote no part of it.

CROMWELL: – I do not mean you actually held the pen.

MORE: – I merely answered to the best of my ability certain questions on canon law which His Majesty put to me. As I was bound to do.

CROMWELL: – Do you deny that you *instigated* it?

MORE: – It was from first to last the King's own project. This is trivial, Master Cromwell.

CROMWELL: I should not think so if I were in your place.

MORE: Only two people know the truth of the matter. Myself and the King. And, whatever he may have said to you, he will not give evidence to support this accusation.

CROMWELL: Why not?

MORE: Because evidence is given on oath, and he will not perjure himself. If you don't know that, you don't yet know him.

[CROMWELL *looks at him viciously.*]

CROMWELL [*going apart, formally*]: Sir Thomas More, is there anything you wish to say to me concerning the King's marriage with Queen Anne?

MORE [*very still*]: I understood I was not to be asked that again.

CROMWELL: Evidently you understood wrongly. These charges –

MORE [*anger breaking through*]: They are terrors for children, Mr Secretary, not for me!

CROMWELL: Then know that the King commands me to charge you in his name with great ingratitude! And to tell you that there never was nor never could be so villainous a servant nor so traitorous a subject as yourself!

MORE: So I am brought here at last.

CROMWELL: Brought? You brought yourself to where you stand now.

MORE: Yes. Still, in another sense I was brought.

CROMWELL [*indifferent*]: Oh yes. [*Official*] You may go home now. For the present.

[*Exit* MORE.]

I don't like him so well as I did. There's a man who raises the gale and won't come out of harbour.

[*Scene change commences here, i.e., rear of stage becoming water-patterned.*]

RICH [*with covert jeer*]: Do you still think you can frighten him?

CROMWELL: No, he's misusing his intelligence.

RICH: What will you do now, then?

CROMWELL [*as to an importunate child*]: Oh, be quiet, Rich. . . . We'll do whatever's necessary. The King's a man of conscience and he wants either Sir Thomas More to bless his marriage or Sir Thomas More destroyed. Either will do.

RICH [*shakily*]: They seem odd alternatives, Secretary.

CROMWELL: Do they? That's because you're not a man of conscience. If the King destroys a man, that's proof to the King that it must have been a bad man, the kind of man a man of conscience *ought* to destroy – and of course a bad man's blessing's not worth having. So either will do.

RICH [*subdued*]: I see.

CROMWELL: Oh, there's no going back, Rich. I find we've made ourselves the keepers of this conscience. And it's ravenous.

[*Exit* CROMWELL *and* RICH.

Enter MORE.]

MORE [*calling*]: Boat! . . . Boat! . . . [*To himself*] Oh, come along, it's not as bad as that. . . . [*Calls*] Boat!

[*Enter* NORFOLK. *He stops.*]

[*Pleased*] Howard! . . . I can't get home. They won't bring me a boat.

NORFOLK: Do you blame them?

MORE: Is it as bad as that?

NORFOLK: It's every bit as bad as that!

MORE [*gravely*]: Then it's good of you to be seen with me.

NORFOLK [*looking back, off*]: I followed you.

MORE [*surprised*]: Were *you* followed?

NORFOLK: Probably. [*Facing him.*] So listen to what I have to say. You're behaving like a fool. You're behaving like a crank. You're not behaving like a gentleman – All right, that means nothing to you; but what about your friends?

MORE: What about them?

NORFOLK: Goddammit, you're dangerous to know!

MORE: Then don't know me.

NORFOLK: There's something further. . . . You must have realized by now there's a . . . policy, with regards to you.

[MORE *nods.*]

The King is using me in it.

MORE: That's clever. That's Cromwell. . . . You're between the upper and the nether millstones then.

NORFOLK: I am!

MORE: Howard, you must cease to know me.

NORFOLK: I do know you! I wish I didn't but I do!

MORE: I mean as a friend.

NORFOLK: You *are* my friend!

MORE: I can't relieve you of your obedience to the King, Howard. You must relieve yourself of our friendship. No one's safe now, and you have a son.

NORFOLK: You might as well advise a man to change the colour of his hair! I'm fond of you, and there it is! You're fond of me, and there it is!

MORE: What's to be done then?

NORFOLK [*with deep appeal*]: Give in.

MORE [*gently*]: I can't give in, Howard – [*smile*] you might as well advise a man to change the colour of his eyes. I can't. Our friendship's more mutable than *that*.

NORFOLK: Oh, that's immutable is it? The one fixed point in a world of changing friendships is that Thomas More will not give in!

MORE [*urgent to explain*]: To me it *has* to be, for that's myself! Affection goes as deep in me as you I think, but only God is love right through, Howard; and *that's* my *self*.

NORFOLK: And who are you? Goddammit, man, it's disproportionate! *We're* supposed to be the arrogant ones, the proud, splenetic ones – and we've all given in! Why must you stand out? [*Quiet and quick*] You'll break my heart.

MORE [*moved*]: We'll do it now, Howard: part, as friends, and meet as strangers. [*He attempts to take Norfolk's hand.*]

NORFOLK [*throwing it off*]: Daft, Thomas! Why d'you want to take your friendship from me? For friendship's sake! You say we'll meet as strangers and every word you've said confirms our friendship!

MORE [*takes a last affectionate look at him*]: Oh, that can be remedied. [*Walks away, turns: in a tone of deliberate insult*] Norfolk, you're a fool.

NORFOLK [*starts: then smiles and folds his arms*]: You can't place a quarrel; you haven't the style.

MORE: Hear me out. You and your class have 'given in' – as you rightly call it – because the religion of this country means nothing to you one way or the other.

NORFOLK: Well, that's a foolish saying for a start; the nobility of England has always been –

MORE: The nobility of England, my lord, would have snored through the Sermon on the Mount. But you'll labour like Thomas Aquinas over a rat-dog's pedigree. Now what's the name of those distorted creatures you're all breeding at the moment?

NORFOLK [*steadily, but roused towards anger by More's tone*]: An artificial quarrel's not a quarrel.

MORE: Don't deceive yourself, my lord, we've had a quarrel since the day we met, our friendship was but sloth.

NORFOLK: You can be cruel when you've a mind to be; but I've always known that.

MORE: What's the name of those dogs? Marsh mastiffs? Bog beagles?

NORFOLK: Water spaniels!

MORE: And what would you do with a water spaniel that was afraid of water? You'd hang it! Well, as a spaniel is to water, so is a man to his own self. I will not give in because I oppose it – *I* do – not my pride, not my spleen, nor any other of my appetites but I do – *I*!
[*He goes up to him and feels him up and down like an animal. MARGARET's voice is heard, well off, calling her father. MORE's attention is irresistibly caught by this; but he turns back determinedly to Norfolk.*]
Is there no single sinew in the midst of this that serves no appetite of Norfolk's but is, just, Norfolk? There is! Give *that* some exercise, my lord!

MARGARET [*off, nearer*]: Father?

NORFOLK [*breathing hard*]: Thomas...

MORE: Because as you stand, you'll go before your Maker in a very ill condition!
[*Enter MARGARET, below; she stops, amazed at them.*]

NORFOLK: Now steady, Thomas....

MORE: And he'll have to think that somewhere back along your pedigree – a bitch got over the wall!

[NORFOLK *lashes out at him; he ducks and winces. Exit* NORFOLK.]

MARGARET: Father! [*As he straightens up*] Father, what was that?

MORE: That was Norfolk. [*Looks after him wistfully.*]

[*Enter* ROPER.]

ROPER [*excited, almost gleeful*]: Do you know, sir? Have you heard?

[MORE *still looking off, unanswering; to Margaret*] Have you told him?

MARGARET [*gently*]: We've been looking for you, Father.

[MORE *the same.*]

ROPER: There's to be a new Act through Parliament, sir!

MORE [*half turning, half attending*]: Act?

ROPER: Yes, sir – about the Marriage!

MORE [*indifferent*]: Oh. [*Turning back again.*]

[ROPER *and* MARGARET *look at one another.*]

MARGARET [*putting hand on his arm*]: Father, by this Act, they're going to administer an oath.

MORE [*instantaneous attention*]: An oath! [*Looks from one to other.*] On what compulsion?

ROPER: It's expected to be treason!

MORE [*very still*]: What is the oath?

ROPER [*puzzled*]: It's about the Marriage, sir.

MORE: But what is the wording?

ROPER: We don't need to know the [*contemptuous*] wording – we know what it will mean!

MORE: It will mean what the words say! An oath is *made* of words! It may be possible to take it. Or avoid it. [*To Margaret*] Have we a copy of the Bill?

MARGARET: There's one coming out from the City.

MORE: Then let's get home and look at it. Oh, I've no boat. [*He looks off again after Norfolk.*]

MARGARET [*gently*]: What happened, Father?

MORE: I spoke, slightingly, of water spaniels. Let's get home. [*He turns and sees Roper excited and truculent.*] Now listen, Will. And, Meg, you know I know you well, you listen too. God made the *angels* to show him splendour – as he made animals for innocence and plants for their simplicity. But Man he made to serve him wittily, in the tangle of his mind! If he suffers us to fall to such a case that there is no escaping, then we may stand to our tackle as best we can, and yes, Will, then we may clamour like champions . . . if we have the spittle for it. And no doubt it delights God to see splendour where he only looked for complexity. But it's God's part, not our own, to bring ourselves to that extremity! Our natural business lies in escaping – so let's get home and study this Bill.

[*Exit* MORE, ROPER, *and* MARGARET.

Enter COMMON MAN, *dragging basket. The rear of the stage remains water-lit in moonlight. Iron grills now descend to cover all the apertures. Also, a rack, which remains suspended, and a cage which is lowered to the floor. While this takes place the* COMMON MAN *arranges three chairs behind a table. Then he turns and watches the completion of the transformation.*]

COMMON MAN [*aggrieved*]: *Now* look! . . . I don't suppose anyone enjoyed it any more than he did. Well, not much more. [*Takes from basket and dons coat and hat.*] Jailer! [*Shrugs.*] It's a job. The pay-scale being what it is they have to take a rather common type of man into the prison service. But it's a job like any other job. Bit nearer the knuckle than most perhaps.

[*Enter right,* CROMWELL, NORFOLK, CRANMER, *who sit, and* RICH, *who stands behind them. Enter left,* MORE, *who enters the cage and lies down.*]

They'd let him out if they could but for various reasons they can't. [*Twirling keys*] I'd let him out if I could but I can't. Not without taking up residence in there myself. And he's in there already, so what'd be the point? You know the old adage? 'Better a live rat than a dead lion,' and that's about it.

[*An envelope descends swiftly before him. He opens it and reads:*]

'With reference to the old adage: Thomas Cromwell was found guilty of High Treason and executed on 28 July 1540. Norfolk was found guilty of High Treason and should have been executed on 27 January 1547, but on the night of 26 January the King died of syphilis and wasn't able to sign the warrant. Thomas Cranmer.' [*Jerking thumb*] That's the other one – 'was burned alive on 21 March 1556.' [*He is about to conclude but sees a postscript.*] Oh. 'Richard Rich became a Knight and Solicitor-General, a Baron and

Lord Chancellor, and died in his bed.' So did I. And so, I hope, [*pushing off basket*] will all of you.

[*He goes to More and rouses him. Heavy bell strikes one.*]

MORE [*rousing*]: What, again?

JAILER: Sorry, sir.

MORE [*flops back*]: What time is it?

JAILER: Just struck one, sir.

MORE: Oh, this is iniquitous!

JAILER [*anxious*]: Sir.

MORE [*sitting up*]: All right. [*Putting on slippers*] Who's there?

JAILER: The Secretary, the Duke, and the Archbishop.

MORE: I'm flattered. [*Stands. Claps hand to hip.*] Ooh!

[*Preceded by JAILER limps across stage right: he has aged and is pale, but his manner, though wary, is relaxed: while that of the Commission is bored, tense, and jumpy.*]

NORFOLK [*looking at him*]: A chair for the prisoner.

[*While JAILER brings a chair and MORE sits in it, NORFOLK rattles off:*]

This is the Seventh Commission to inquire into the case of Sir Thomas More, appointed by His Majesty's Council. Have you anything to say?

MORE: No. [*To Jailer*] Thank you.

NORFOLK [*sitting back*]: Mr Secretary.

CROMWELL: Sir Thomas – [*breaks off*] – do the witnesses attend?

RICH: Mr Secretary.

JAILER: Sir.

CROMWELL [*to Jailer*]: Nearer! [*He advances a bit.*] Come where you can hear!

[*JAILER takes up stance by Rich.*]

[*To More*] Sir Thomas, you have seen this document before?

MORE: Many times.

CROMWELL: It is the Act of Succession. These are the names of those who have sworn to it.

MORE: I have, as you say, seen it before.

CROMWELL: Will you swear to it?

MORE: No.

NORFOLK: Thomas, we must know plainly –

CROMWELL [*throws down document*]: Your Grace, *please*!

NORFOLK: Master Cromwell!

[*They regard one another in hatred.*]

CROMWELL: I beg Your Grace's pardon. [*Sighing, rests head in hands.*]

NORFOLK: Thomas, we must know plainly whether you recognize the offspring of Queen Anne as heirs to His Majesty.

MORE: The King in Parliament tells me that they are. Of course I recognize them.

NORFOLK: Will you swear that you do?

MORE: Yes.

NORFOLK: Then why don't you swear to the Act?

CROMWELL [*impatient*]: Because there is more than that *in* the Act.

NORFOLK: Is that it?

MORE [*after a pause*]: Yes.

NORFOLK: Then we must find out what it is in the Act that he objects to!

CROMWELL: Brilliant.

[NORFOLK *rounds on him.*]

CRANMER [*hastily*]: Your Grace – May I try?

NORFOLK: Certainly. I've no pretension to be an expert, in Police work.

[*During next speech* CROMWELL *straightens up and folds arms resignedly.*]

CRANMER [*clears throat fussily*]: Sir Thomas, it states in the preamble that the King's former marriage, to the Lady Catherine, was unlawful, she being previously his brother's wife and the – er – 'Pope' having no authority to sanction it. [*Gently*] Is that what you deny? [*No reply.*] Is that what you dispute? [*No reply.*] Is that what you are not sure of? [*No reply.*]

NORFOLK: Thomas, you insult the King and His Council in the person of the Lord Archbishop!

MORE: I insult no one. I will not take the oath, I will not tell you why I will not.

NORFOLK: Then your reasons must be treasonable!

MORE: Not 'must be'; may be.

NORFOLK: It's a fair assumption!

MORE: The law requires more than an assumption; the law requires a fact.

[CROMWELL *looks at him and away again.*]

CRANMER: I cannot judge your legal standing in the case; but until I know the *ground* of your objections, I can only guess your spiritual standing too.

[MORE *is for a second furiously affronted; then humour overtakes him:*]

MORE: If you're willing to guess at that, Your Grace, it should be a small matter to guess my objections.

CROMWELL [*quickly*]: You do have objections to the Act?

NORFOLK [*happily*]: Well, we know *that*, Cromwell!

MORE: You don't, my lord. You may *suppose* I have objections. All you *know* is that I will not swear to it. From sheer delight to give you trouble it might be.

NORFOLK: Is it material why you won't?

MORE: It's most material. For refusing to swear my goods are forfeit and I am condemned to life imprisonment. You cannot lawfully harm me further. But if you were right in supposing I had reasons for refusing and right again in supposing my reasons to be treasonable, the law would let you cut my head off.

NORFOLK [*who has followed with some difficulty*]: Oh yes.

CROMWELL [*an admiring murmur*]: Oh, well done, Sir Thomas. I've been trying to make that clear to His Grace for some time.

NORFOLK [*hardly responding to the insult, his face gloomy and disgusted*]: Oh, confound all this. . . . [*With real dignity*] I'm not a scholar, as Master Cromwell never tires of pointing out, and frankly I don't know whether the marriage was lawful or not. But damn it, Thomas, look at those names. . . . You know those men! Can't you do what I did, and come with us, for fellowship?

MORE [*moved*]: And when we stand before God, and you are sent to Paradise for doing according to your conscience, and I am damned for not doing according to mine, will you come with me, for fellowship?

CRANMER: So those of us whose names are there are damned. Sir Thomas?

MORE: I don't know, Your Grace. I have no window to look into another man's conscience. I condemn no one.

CRANMER: Then the matter is capable of question?

MORE: Certainly.

CRANMER: But that you owe obedience to your King is not capable of question. So weigh a doubt against a certainty – and sign.

MORE: Some men think the Earth is round, others think it flat; it is a matter capable of question. But if it is flat, will the King's command make it round? And if it is round, will the King's command flatten it? No, I will not sign.

CROMWELL [leaping up, with ceremonial indignation]: Then you have more regard to your own doubt than you have to his command!

MORE: For myself, I have no doubt.

CROMWELL: No doubt of what?

MORE: No doubt of my grounds for refusing this oath. Grounds I will tell to the King alone, and which you, Mr Secretary, will not trick out of me.

NORFOLK: Thomas –

MORE: Oh, gentlemen, can't I go to bed?

CROMWELL: You don't seem to appreciate the seriousness of your position.

MORE: I defy anyone to live in that cell for a year and not appreciate the seriousness of his position.

CROMWELL: Yet the State has harsher punishments.

MORE: You threaten like a dockside bully.

CROMWELL: How should I threaten?

MORE: Like a Minister of State, with justice!

CROMWELL: Oh, justice is what you're threatened with.

MORE: Then I'm not threatened.

NORFOLK: Master Secretary, I think the prisoner may retire as he requests. Unless, you, my lord – ?

CRANMER [pettish]: No, I see no purpose in prolonging the interview.

NORFOLK: Then good night, Thomas.

MORE [hesitates]: Might I have one or two more books?

CROMWELL: You have books?

MORE: Yes.

CROMWELL: I didn't know; you shouldn't have.

[MORE turns to go: pauses.]

MORE [desperately]: May I see my family?

CROMWELL: No!

[MORE *returns to cell.*]

Jailer!

JAILER: Sir!

CROMWELL: Have you ever heard the prisoner speak of the King's divorce, or the King's Supremacy of the Church, or the King's marriage?

JAILER: No, sir, not a word.

CROMWELL: If he does, you will of course report it to the Lieutenant.

JAILER: Of course, sir.

CROMWELL: You will swear an oath to that effect.

JAILER [*cheerfully*]: Certainly, sir!

CROMWELL: Archbishop?

CRANMER [*laying cross of vestment on table*]: Place your left hand on this and raise your right hand – take your hat off – Now say after me: I swear by my immortal soul –

[JAILER *overlapping, repeats the oath with him.*]

– that I will report truly anything said by Sir Thomas More against the King the Council or the State of the Realm. So help me God. Amen.

JAILER [*overlapping*]: So help me God. Amen.

CROMWELL: And there's fifty guineas in it if you do.

JAILER [*looks at him gravely*]: Yes, sir. [*And goes.*]

CRANMER [*hastily*]: That's not to tempt you into perjury, my man!

JAILER: No, sir! [*At exit pauses; to audience*] Fifty guineas isn't tempting; fifty guineas is alarming. If he'd left it at swearing. ... But fifty – That's serious money. If it's worth that much now it's worth my neck presently. [*With decision*] I want no part of it. They can sort it out between them. I feel my deafness coming on.

[*Exit* JAILER. *The Commission rises.*]

CROMWELL: Rich!

RICH: Secretary!

CROMWELL: Tomorrow morning, remove the prisoner's books.

NORFOLK: Is that necessary?

CROMWELL [*with suppressed exasperation*]: Norfolk. With regards this case, the King is becoming impatient.

NORFOLK: Aye, with you.

CROMWELL: With all of us. [*He walks over to the rack.*] You know the King's impatience, how commodious it is!

[NORFOLK *and* CRANMER *exit.* CROMWELL *is brooding over the instrument of torture.*]

RICH: Secretary!

CROMWELL [*abstracted*]: Yes . . . ?

RICH: Sir Redvers Llewellyn has retired.

CROMWELL [*not listening*]: Mm . . . ?

[RICH *goes to other end of rack and faces him.*]

RICH [*with some indignation*]: The Attorney-General for Wales. His post is vacant. You said I might approach you.

CROMWELL [*contemptuous impatience*]: Oh, not now. . . . [*Broods.*] He must submit, the alternatives are bad. While More's alive the King's conscience breaks into fresh stinking flowers every time he gets from bed. And if I bring about More's death – I plant my own, I think. There's no other good solution! He must submit!

[*He whirls the windlass of the rack, producing a startling clatter from the ratchet. They look at each other. He turns it again slowly, shakes his head, and lets go.*]

No; the King will not permit it. [*Walks away.*] We have to find some gentler way.

[*The scene change commences as he says this and exit* RICH *and* CROMWELL. *From night it becomes morning, cold grey light from off the grey water. And enter* JAILER *and* MARGARET.]

JAILER: Wake up, Sir Thomas! Your family's here!

MORE [*starting up, with a great cry*]: Margaret! What's this? You can visit me? [*Thrusts arms through cage.*] Meg. Meg. [*She goes to him. Then, horrified*] For God's sake, Meg, they've not put *you* in here?

JAILER [*reassuring*]: No-o-o, sir. Just a visit; a short one.

MORE [*excited*]: Jailer, jailer, let me out of this.

JAILER [*stolid*]: Yes, sir. I'm allowed to let you out.

MORE: Thank you. [*Goes to door of cage, gabbling while* JAILER *unlocks it*] Thank you, thank you. [*Comes out.*]

[*He and she regard each other; then she drops into a curtsey.*]

MARGARET: Good morning, Father.

MORE [*ecstatic, wraps her to him*]: Oh, good morning – Good morning.

[*Enter* ALICE, *supported by* WILL. *She, like More, has aged and is poorly dressed.*]

Good morning, Alice. Good morning, Will.

[ROPER *is staring at the rack in horror.* ALICE *approaches* MORE *and peers at him technically.*]

ALICE [*almost accusatory*]: Husband, how do you do?

MORE [*smiling over Margaret*]: As well as need be, Alice. Very happy now. Will?

ROPER: This is an awful place!

MORE: Except it's keeping me from you, my dears, it's not so bad. Remarkably like any other place.

ALICE [*looking up critically*]: It drips!

MORE: Yes. Too near the river.

[ALICE *goes apart and sits, her face bitter.*]

MARGARET [*disengages from him, takes basket from her mother*]: We've brought you some things. [*Shows him. There is constraint between them.*] Some cheese . . .

MORE: Cheese.

MARGARET: And a custard. . .

MORE: A custard!

MARGARET: And, these other things. . . [*She doesn't look at him.*]

ROPER: And a bottle of wine. [*Offering it.*]

MORE: Oh. [*Mischievous*] Is it good, son Roper?

ROPER: I don't know, sir.

MORE [*looks at them, puzzled*]: Well.

ROPER: Sir, come out! Swear to the Act! Take the oath and come out!

MORE: Is this why they let you come?

ROPER: Yes . . . Meg's under oath to persuade you.

MORE [*coldly*]: That was silly, Meg. How did you come to do that?

MARGARET: I wanted to!

MORE: You want me to swear to the Act of Succession?

MARGARET: 'God more regards the thoughts of the heart than the words of the mouth' or so you've always told me.

MORE: Yes.

MARGARET: Then say the words of the oath and in your heart think otherwise.

MORE: What is an oath then but words we say to God?

MARGARET: That's very neat.

MORE: Do you mean it isn't true?

MARGARET: No, it's true.

MORE: Then it's a poor argument to call it 'neat', Meg. When a man takes an oath, Meg, he's holding his own self in his own hands. Like water [*cups hands*] and if he opens his fingers *then* – he needn't hope to find himself again. Some men aren't capable of this, but I'd be loathe to think your father one of them.

MARGARET: So should I. . . .

MORE: Then –

MARGARET: There's something else I've been thinking.

MORE: Oh, Meg!

MARGARET: In any state that was half good, you would be raised up high, not here, for what you've done already.

MORE: All right.

MARGARET: It's not your fault the State's three-quarters bad.

MORE: No.

MARGARET: Then if you elect to suffer for it, you elect yourself a hero.

MORE: That's very neat. But look now . . . If we lived in a State where virtue was profitable, common sense would make us good, and greed would make us saintly. And we'd live like animals or angels in the happy land that *needs* no heroes. But since in fact we see that avarice, anger, envy, pride, sloth, lust, and stupidity commonly profit far beyond humility, chastity, fortitude, justice, and thought, and have to choose, to be human at all . . . why then perhaps we *must* stand fast a little – even at the risk of being heroes.

MARGARET [*emotional*]: But in reason! Haven't you done as much as God can reasonably *want*?

MORE: Well . . . finally . . . it isn't a matter of reason; finally it's a matter of love.

ALICE [*hostile*]: You're content, then, to be shut up here with mice and rats when you might be home with us!

MORE [*flinching*]: Content? If they'd open a crack that wide [*between finger and thumb*] I'd be through it. [*To Margaret*] Well, has Eve run out of apples?

MARGARET: I've not yet told you what the house is like, without you.

MORE: Don't, Meg.

MARGARET: What we do in the evenings, now that you're not there.

MORE: Meg, have done!

MARGARET: We sit in the dark because we've no candles. And we've no talk because we're wondering what they're doing to you here.

MORE: The King's more merciful than you. He doesn't use the rack.

[*Enter* JAILER.]

JAILER: Two minutes to go, sir. I thought you'd like to know.

MORE: Two minutes!

JAILER: Till seven o'clock, sir. Sorry. Two minutes.

[*Exit* JAILER.]

MORE: Jailer – ! [*Seizes Roper by the arm.*] Will – go to him, talk to him, keep him occupied – [*Propelling him after Jailer.*]

ROPER: How, sir?

MORE: Anyhow! – Have you got any money?

ROPER [*eager*]: Yes!

MORE: No, don't try and bribe him! Let him play for it; he's got a pair of dice. And talk to him, you understand! And take this [*the wine*] – and mind you share it – do it properly, Will!

[ROPER *nods vigorously and exits.*]

Now listen, you must leave the country. All of you must leave the country.

MARGARET: And leave you here?

MORE: It makes no difference, Meg; they won't let you see me again. [*Breathlessly, a prepared speech under pressure*] You must all go on the same day, but not on the same boat; different boats from different ports –

MARGARET: After the trial, then.

MORE: There'll be no trial, they have no case. Do this for me I beseech you?

MARGARET: Yes.

MORE: Alice? [*She turns her back.*] Alice, I command it!

ALICE [*harshly*]: Right!

MORE [*looks into basket*]: Oh, this is splendid; I know who packed this.

ALICE [*harshly*]: I packed it.

MORE: Yes. [*Eats a morsel.*] You still make superlative custard, Alice.

ALICE: Do I?

MORE: That's a nice dress you have on.

ALICE: It's my cooking dress.

MORE: It's very nice anyway. Nice colour.

ALICE [*turns; quietly*]: By God, you think very little of me. [*with mounting bitterness*] I know I'm a fool. But I'm no such fool as at this time to be lamenting for my dresses! Or to relish complimenting on my custard!

[MORE *regards her with frozen attention. He nods once or twice.*]

MORE: I am well rebuked. [*Holds out his hands.*] Al – !

ALICE: No! [*She remains where she is, glaring at him.*]

MORE [*he is in great fear of her*]: I am faint when I think of the worst that they may do to me. But worse than that would be to go, with you not understanding why I go.

ALICE: I don't!

MORE [*just hanging on to his self-possession*]: Alice, if you can tell me that you understand, I think I can make a good death, if I have to.

ALICE: Your death's no 'good' to me!

MORE: Alice, you must tell me that you understand!

ALICE: I don't! [*She throws it straight at his head.*] I don't believe this had to happen.

MORE [*his face is drawn*]: If you say that, Alice, I don't see how I'm to face it.

ALICE: It's the truth!

MORE [*gasping*]: You're an honest woman.

ALICE: Much good may it do me! I'll tell you what I'm afraid of; that when you've gone, I shall hate you for it.

[MORE *turns from her: his face working.*]

MORE: Well, you mustn't, Alice, that's all.

[*Swiftly she crosses the stage to him; he turns and they clasp each other fiercely.*]

You mustn't, you –

ALICE [*covers his mouth with her hand*]: S-s-sh. . . As for understanding, I understand you're the best man that I ever met or am likely to; and if you go – well God knows why I suppose – though as God's my witness God's kept deadly quiet about it! And if anyone wants my opinion of the King and his Council they've only to ask for it!

MORE: Why, it's a lion I married! A lion! A lion! [*He breaks away from her his face shining.*] Get them to take half this to Bishop Fisher – they've got him in the upper gallery –

ALICE: It's for you, not Bishop Fisher!

MORE: Now do as I ask – [*Breaks off a piece of the custard and eats it.*] Oh, it's good, it's very, very good.

> [*He puts his face in his hands; ALICE and MARGARET comfort him; ROPER and JAILER erupt on to the stage above, wrangling fiercely.*]

JAILER: It's no good, sir! I know what you're up to! And it can't be done!

ROPER: Another minute, man!

JAILER [*to More descending*]: Sorry, sir, time's up!

ROPER [*gripping his shoulder from behind*]: For pity's sake – !

JAILER [*shaking him off*]: Now don't do that, sir! Sir Thomas, the ladies will have to go now!

MORE: You said seven o'clock!

JAILER: It's seven now. You must understand my position, sir.

MORE: But one more minute!

MARGARET: Only a little while – give us a little while!

JAILER [*reproving*]: Now, Miss, you don't want to get me into trouble.

ALICE: Do as you're told. Be off at once!

> [*The first stroke of seven is heard on a heavy, deliberate bell, which continues, reducing what follows to a babble.*]

JAILER [*taking Margaret firmly by the upper arm*]: Now come along, Miss; you'll get your father into trouble as well as me.

> [ROPER *descends and grabs him.*]

Are you obstructing me, sir?

> [MARGARET *embraces More, and dashes up the stairs and exits, followed by* ROPER. JAILER *takes Alice gingerly by the arm.*]

Now, my lady, no trouble!

ALICE [*throwing him off as she rises*]: Don't put your muddy hand on me!

JAILER: Am I to call the guard then? Then come on!

> [ALICE, *facing him, puts foot on bottom stair and so retreats before him, backwards.*]

MORE: For God's sake, man, we're saying good-bye!

JAILER: You don't know what you're asking, sir. You don't know how you're watched.

ALICE: Filthy, stinking, gutter-bred turnkey!

JAILER: Call me what you like, ma'am; you've got to go.

ALICE: I'll see you suffer for this!

JAILER: You're doing your husband no good!

MORE: Alice, good-bye, my love!

[*On this, the last stroke of the seven sounds.* ALICE *raises her hand, turns, and, with considerable dignity, exits.* JAILER *stops at head of stairs and addresses* MORE, *who, still crouching, turns from him, facing audience.*]

JAILER [*reasonably*]: You understand my position, sir, there's nothing I can do; I'm a plain simple man and just want to keep out of trouble.

MORE [*cries out passionately*]: Oh, Sweet Jesus! These plain, simple, men!

[*Immediately:*

(1) *Music, portentous and heraldic.*

(2) *Bars, rack, and cage fly swiftly upwards.*

(3) *Lighting change from cold grey to warm yellow, re-creating a warm interior.*

(4) *Several narrow panels, scarlet and bearing the monogram 'HR VIII' in gold, are lowered. Also an enormous Royal Coat-of-Arms which hangs above the table, stage right.*

(5) *The* JAILER, *doffing costume, comes down the stairs and:*

(A) *Places a chair for the Accused, helps* MORE *to it, and gives him a scroll which he studies.*

(B) *Fetches from the wings his prop basket, and produces: (i) A large hour-glass and papers which he places on table, stage right. (ii) Twelve folding stools which he arranges in two rows of six each. While he is still doing this, and just before the panels and Coat-of-Arms have finished their descent, enter* CROMWELL. *He ringingly addresses the audience (while the* COMMON MAN *is still bustling about his chores) as soon as the music ends, which it does at this point, on a fanfare.*]

CROMWELL [*indicating descending props*]:

What Englishman can behold without Awe.
The Canvas and the Rigging of the Law!
[*Brief fanfare.*]
Forbidden here the galley-master's whip –
Hearts of Oak, in the Law's Great Ship!
[*Brief fanfare.*]

[*To Common man, who is tiptoeing discreetly off stage*] Where are you going?

COMMON MAN: I've finished here, sir.

[*Above the two rows of stools the Common Man has suspended from two wires, supported by two pairs of sticks, two rows of hats for the presumed occupants. Seven are plain grey hats, four are those worn by the* STEWARD, BOATMAN, INNKEEPER, *and* JAILER. *And the last is another of the plain grey ones. The basket remains on stage, clearly visible.*]

CROMWELL: You're the Foreman of the Jury.

COMMON MAN: Oh no, sir.

CROMWELL: You are John Dauncey. A general dealer?

COMMON MAN [*gloomy*]: Yes, sir?

CROMWELL [*resuming his rhetorical stance*]: Foreman of the Jury. Does the cap fit?

[COMMON MAN *puts on the grey hat. It fits.*]

COMMON MAN: Yes, sir.

CROMWELL [*resuming rhetorical stance*]:

So, now we'll apply the good, plain sailor's art,
And fix these quicksands on the Law's plain chart!

[*Renewed, more prolonged fanfare, during which enter* CRANMER *and* NORFOLK, *who stand behind the table stage right. On their entry* MORE *and* FOREMAN *rise. As soon as the fanfare is finished,* NORFOLK *speaks.*]

NORFOLK [*taking refuge behind a rigorously official manner*]: Sir Thomas More, you are called before us here at the Hall of Westminster to answer charge of High Treason. Nevertheless, and though you have heinously offended the King's Majesty, we hope if you will even now forthink and repent of your obstinate opinions, you may still taste his gracious pardon.

MORE: My lords, I thank you. Howbeit I make my petition to

Almighty God that he will keep me in this, my honest mind, to the last hour that I shall live. . . . As for the matters you may charge me with, I fear, from my present weakness, that neither my wit nor my memory will serve to make sufficient answers. . . . I should be glad to sit down.

NORFOLK: Be seated. Master Secretary Cromwell, have you the charge?

CROMWELL: I have, my lord.

NORFOLK: Then read the charge.

CROMWELL [*approaching More, behind him, with papers; informally*]: It is the same charge, Sir Thomas, that was brought against Bishop Fisher. . . . [*as one who catches himself up punctiliously.*] The *late* Bishop Fisher I should have said.

MORE [*tonelessly*]: 'Late'?

CROMWELL: Bishop Fisher was executed this morning.

[MORE'S *face expresses violent shock, then grief; he turns his head away from Cromwell who is observing him clinically.*]

NORFOLK: Master Secretary, read the charge!

CROMWELL [*formal*]: That you did conspire traitorously and maliciously to deny and deprive our liege lord Henry of his undoubted certain title, Supreme Head of the Church in England.

MORE [*with surprise, shock, and indignation*]: But I have never denied this title!

CROMWELL: You refused the oath tendered to you at the Tower and elsewhere –

MORE [*the same*]: Silence is not denial. And for my silence I am punished, with imprisonment. Why have I been called again? [*At this point he is sensing that the trial has been in some way rigged.*]

NORFOLK: On a charge of High Treason, Sir Thomas.

CROMWELL: For which the punishment is *not* imprisonment.

MORE: Death . . . comes for us all, my lords. Yes, even for Kings he comes, to whom amidst all their Royalty and brute strength he will neither kneel nor make them any reverence nor pleasantly desire them to come forth, but roughly grasp them by the very breast and rattle them until they be stark dead! So causing their bodies to be buried in a pit and sending *them* to a judgement . . . whereof at their death their success is uncertain.

CROMWELL: Treason enough here!

NORFOLK: The death of Kings is not in question, Sir Thomas.

MORE: Nor mine, I trust, until I'm proven guilty.

NORFOLK [*leaning forward urgently*]: Your life lies in your own hand, Thomas, as it always has.

[MORE *absorbs this.*]

MORE: For our own deaths, my lord, yours and mine, dare we for shame desire to enter the Kingdom with ease, when Our Lord Himself entered with so much pain? [*and now he faces Cromwell his eyes sparkling with suspicion.*]

CROMWELL: Now, Sir Thomas, you stand upon your silence.

MORE: I do.

CROMWELL: But, Gentlemen of the Jury, there are many kinds of silence. Consider first the silence of a man when he is dead. Let us say we go into the room where he is lying; and let us say it is in the dead of night – there's nothing like darkness for sharpening the ear; and we listen. What do we hear? Silence. What does it betoken, this silence? Nothing. This is silence, pure and simple. But consider another case. Suppose I were to draw a dagger from my sleeve and make to kill the prisoner with it, and suppose their lordships there, instead of crying out for me to stop or crying out for help to stop me, maintained their silence. That *would* betoken! It would betoken a willingness that I should do it, and under the law they would be guilty with me. So silence can, according to circumstances, speak. Consider, now, the circumstances of the prisoner's silence. The oath was put to good and faithful subjects up and down the country and they had declared His Grace's Title to be just and good. And when it came to the prisoner he refused. He calls this silence. Yet is there a man in this court, is there a man in this country, who does not *know* Sir Thomas More's opinion of this title? Of course not! But how can that be? Because this silence betokened – nay this silence *was* – not silence at all, but most eloquent denial.

MORE [*with some of the academic impatience for a shoddy line of reasoning*]: Not so, Mr Secretary, the maxim is 'qui tacet consentire'. [*Turns to the Foreman.*] The maxim of the law is: [*very carefully*] 'Silence Gives Consent'. If therefore, you wish to construe what my silence 'betokened', you must construe that I consented, not that I denied.

CROMWELL: Is that what the world in fact construes from it? Do you pretend that is what you *wish* the world to construe from it?

MORE: The world must construe according to its wits. This Court must construe according to the law.

CROMWELL: I put it to the Court that the prisoner is perverting the law – making smoky what should be a clear light to discover to the Court his own wrongdoing!

[CROMWELL's *official indignation is slipping into genuine anger and* MORE *responds.*]

MORE: The law is not a 'light' for you or any man to see by; the law is not an instrument of any kind. [*To the Foreman*] The law is a causeway upon which so long as he keeps to it a citizen may walk safely. [*Earnestly addressing him*] In matters of conscience –

CROMWELL [*bitterly smiling*]: The conscience, the conscience . . .

MORE [*turning*]: The word is not familiar to you?

CROMWELL: By God, too familiar! I am very used to hear it in the mouths of criminals!

MORE: I am used to hear bad men misuse the name of God, yet God exists. [*Turning back*] In matters of conscience, the loyal subject is more bounden to be loyal *to* his conscience than to any other thing.

CROMWELL [*breathing hard: straight at More*]: – And so provide a noble motive for his frivolous self-conceit!

MORE [*earnestly*]: It is not so, Master Cromwell – very and pure necessity for respect of my own soul.

CROMWELL: – Your own self you mean!

MORE: Yes, a man's soul is his self!

[CROMWELL *thrusts his face into More's. They hate each other and each other's standpoint.*]

CROMWELL: A miserable thing, whatever you call it, that lives like a bat in a Sunday School! A shrill incessant pedagogue about its own salvation – but nothing to say of your place in the State! Under the King! In a great native country!

MORE [*not untouched*]: Can I help my King by giving him lies when he asks for truth? Will you help England by populating her with liars?

CROMWELL [*backing away, his face stiff with malevolence*]: My lords, I wish to call [*raises voice*] Sir Richard Rich!

[*Enter* RICH. *He is now splendidly official, in dress and bearing; even* NORFOLK *is a bit impressed.*]

Sir Richard [*indicating Cranmer.*]

CRANMER [*proffering Bible*]: I do solemnly swear . . .

RICH: I do solemnly swear that the evidence I shall give before the Court shall be the truth, the whole truth, and nothing but the truth.

CRANMER [*discreetly*]: So help me God, Sir Richard.

RICH: So help me God.

NORFOLK: Take your stand there, Sir Richard.

CROMWELL: Now, Rich, on 12 March, you were at the Tower?

RICH: I was.

CROMWELL: With what purpose?

RICH: I was sent to carry away the prisoner's books.

CROMWELL: Did you talk with the prisoner?

RICH: Yes.

CROMWELL: Did you talk about the King's Supremacy of the Church?

RICH: Yes.

CROMWELL: What did you say?

RICH: I said to him: 'Supposing there was an Act of Parliament to say that I, Richard Rich, were to be King, would not you, Master More, take me for King?' 'That I would,' he said, 'for then you would be King.'

CROMWELL: Yes?

RICH: Then he said –

NORFOLK [*sharply*]: The prisoner?

RICH: Yes, my lord. 'But I will put you a higher case,' he said. 'How if there were an Act of Parliament to say that God should not be God?'.

MORE: This is true; and then you said –

NORFOLK: Silence! Continue.

RICH: I said 'Ah, but I will put you a middle case. Parliament has made our King Head of the Church. Why will you not accept him?'

NORFOLK [*strung up*]: Well?

RICH: Then he said Parliament had no power to do it.

NORFOLK: Repeat the prisoner's words!

RICH: He said 'Parliament has not the competence.' Or words to that effect.

CROMWELL: He denied the title?

RICH: He did.

[*All look to More, but he looks to Rich.*]

MORE: In good faith, Rich, I am sorrier for your perjury than my peril.

NORFOLK: Do you deny this?

MORE: Yes! My lords, if I were a man who heeded not the taking of an oath, you know well I need not to be here. Now I will take an oath! If what Master Rich has said is true, then I pray I may never see God in the face! Which I would not say were it otherwise for anything on earth.

CROMWELL [*to Foreman, calmly, technical*]: That is not evidence.

MORE: Is it probable – is it probable – that after so long a silence, on this, the very point so urgently sought of me, I should open my mind to such a man as that?

CROMWELL [*to Rich*]: Do you wish to modify your testimony?

RICH: No, Secretary.

MORE: There were two other men! Southwell and Palmer!

CROMWELL: Unhappily, Sir Richard Southwell and Master Palmer are both in Ireland on the King's business.

[MORE *gestures helplessly.*]

It has no bearing. I have their deposition here in which the Court will see they state that being busy with the prisoner's books they did not hear what was said. [*Hands deposition to Foreman, who examines it with much seriousness.*]

MORE: If I had really said this is it not obvious he would instantly have called these men to witness?

CROMWELL: Sir Richard, have you anything to add?

RICH: Nothing, Mr Secretary.

NORFOLK: Sir Thomas?

MORE [*looking at Foreman*]: To what purpose? I am a dead man. [*To Cromwell*] You have your desire of me. What you have hunted me for is not my actions, but the thoughts of my heart. It is a long road you have opened. For first men will disclaim their hearts and presently they will have no hearts. God help the people whose Statesmen walk your road.

NORFOLK: Then the witness may withdraw.

[RICH *crosses stage, watched by* MORE.]

MORE: I *have* one question to ask the witness.

[RICH *stops.*]

That's a chain of office you are wearing.

[*Reluctantly* RICH *faces him.*]

May I see it?

[NORFOLK *motions him to approach.* MORE *examines the medallion.*]

The red dragon. [*To Cromwell*] What's this?

CROMWELL: Sir Richard is appointed Attorney-General for Wales.

MORE [*looking into Rich's face: with pain and amusement*]: For Wales? Why, Richard, it profits a man nothing to give his soul for the whole world. . . . But for Wales – !

[*Exit* RICH, *stiff-faced, but infrangibly dignified.*]

CROMWELL: Now I must ask the Court's indulgence! I have a message for the prisoner from the King: [*urgently*] Sir Thomas, I am empowered to tell you that even now –

MORE: No, no. It cannot be.

CROMWELL: The case rests!

[NORFOLK *is staring at More.*]

My lord!

NORFOLK: The Jury will retire and consider the evidence.

CROMWELL: Considering the evidence it shouldn't be necessary for them to retire. [*Standing over Foreman*] Is it necessary?

[FOREMAN *shakes his head.*]

NORFOLK: Then is the prisoner guilty or not guilty?

FOREMAN: Guilty, my lord!

NORFOLK [*leaping to his feet, all rising save More.*]: Prisoner at the bar, you have been found guilty of High Treason. The sentence of the Court –

MORE: My lord!

[NORFOLK *breaks off.* MORE *has a sly smile. From this point to end of* play his manner is of one who has fulfilled all his obligations and will now consult no interests but his own.]

My lord, when I was practising the law, the manner was to ask the prisoner, *before* pronouncing sentence, if he had anything to say.

NORFOLK [*flummoxed*]: Have you anything to say?

MORE: Yes. [*He rises: all others sit.*] To avoid this I have taken every path my winding wits would find. Now that the court has determined to condemn me, God knoweth how, I will discharge my mind ... concerning my indictment and the King's title. The indictment is grounded in an Act of Parliament which is directly repugnant to the Law of God. The King in Parliament cannot bestow the Supremacy of the Church because it is a Spiritual Supremacy! And more to this the immunity of the Church is promised both in Magna Carta and the King's own Coronation Oath!

CROMWELL: Now we plainly see that you *are* malicious!

MORE: Not so, Mr Secretary! [*He pauses, and launches, very quietly, ruminatively, into his final stock-taking.*] I am the King's true subject, and pray for him and all the realm. . . . I do none harm, I say none harm, I think none harm. And if this be not enough to keep a man alive, in good faith I long not to live. . . . I have, since I came into prison, been several times in such a case that I thought to die within the hour, and I thank Our Lord I was never sorry for it, but rather sorry when it passed. And therefore, my poor body is at the King's pleasure. Would God my death might do him some good. . . . [*With a great flash of scorn and anger*] Nevertheless, it is not for the Supremacy that you have sought my blood – but because I would not bend to the marriage!

[*Immediately scene change commences, while* NORFOLK *reads the sentence.*]

NORFOLK: Prisoner at the bar, you have been found guilty on the charge of High Treason. The sentence of the Court is that you shall be taken from this Court to the Tower, thence to the place of execution, and there your head shall be stricken from your body, and may God have mercy on your soul!

[*The scene change is as follows:*

(1) *The trappings of justice are flown upwards.*

(2) The lights are dimmed save for three areas: spots, left and right front, and the arch at the head of the stairs, which begins to show blue sky.

(3) Through this arch – where the axe and the block are silhouetted against a light of steadily increasing brilliance – comes the murmuration of a large crowd, formalized almost into a chant and mounting, so that NORFOLK *has to shout the end of his speech.*

In addition to the noise of the crowd and the flying machinery there is stage activity: FOREMAN *doffs cap, and, as* COMMON MAN, *removes the prisoner's chair and then goes to the spot, left.*

CRANMER *also goes to spot, left.*

MORE *goes to spot, right.*

WOMAN *enters, up right, and goes to spot, left.*

NORFOLK *remains where he is.*

When these movements are complete – they are made naturally, technically – CROMWELL *goes and stands in the light streaming down the stairs. He beckons the Common Man who leaves spot, left, and joins him.* CROMWELL *points to the head of the stairs.* COMMON MAN *shakes his head and indicates in mime that he has no costume. He drags basket into the light and again indicates that there is no costume in it.* CROMWELL *takes a small black mask from his sleeve and offers it to him. The* COMMON MAN *puts it on, thus, in his black tights, becoming the traditional headsman. He ascends the stairs, straddles his legs, and picks up the axe, silhouetted against the bright sky. At once the crowd falls silent.*

Exit CROMWELL, *dragging basket.*

NORFOLK *joins More in spot, right.*]

NORFOLK: I can come no further, Thomas. [*Proffering goblet*] Here, drink this.

MORE: My master had easel and gall, not wine, given him to drink. Let me be going.

MARGARET: Father! [*She runs to him in the spot from right and flings herself upon him.*] Father! Father, Father, Father, Father!

MORE: Have patience, Margaret, and trouble not thyself. Death comes for us all; even at our birth [*he holds her head and looks down at it for a moment in recollection*] – even at our birth, death does but stand aside a little. It is the law of nature, and the will of God.

[*He disengages from her. Dispassionately*] You have long known the secrets of my heart.

WOMAN: Sir Thomas! [*He stops.*] Remember me, Sir Thomas? When you were Chancellor, you gave a false judgement against me. Remember that now.

MORE: Woman, you see how I am occupied. [*With sudden decision goes to her in spot, left. Crisply*] I remember your matter well, and if I had to give sentence now I assure you I should not alter it. You have no injury; so go your ways; and content yourself; and trouble me not!

[*He walks swiftly to the stairs. Then stops, realizing that* CRANMER, *carrying his Bible, has followed him.*]

[*Quite kindly*] I beseech Your Grace, go back.

[*Offended*, CRANMER *does so. The lighting is now complete, i.e., darkness save for three areas of light, the one at head of stairs now dazzlingly brilliant. When* MORE *gets to head of stairs by the Heads-man, there is a single shout from the crowd. He turns to Headsman.*]

Friend, be not afraid of your office. You send me to God.

CRANMER [*envious rather than waspish*]: You're very sure of that, Sir Thomas.

[MORE *takes off his hat, revealing the grey disordered hair.*]

MORE: He will not refuse one who is so blithe to go to him. [*Kneel-ing.*]

[*Immediately, harsh roar of kettledrums and total blackout at head of stairs. While the drums roar,* WOMAN *backs into* CRANMER *and exit together.* NORFOLK *assists* MARGARET *from the stage, which is now 'occupied' only by the two spots left and right front. The drums cease.*]

HEADSMAN [*from the darkness*]: Behold – the head – of a traitor!

[*Enter into spots left and right,* CROMWELL *and* CHAPUYS. *They stop on seeing one another, arrested in postures of frozen hostility while the light spreads plainly over the stage, which is empty save for them-selves.*

Then simultaneously they stalk forward, crossing mid-stage with heads high and averted. But as they approach their exits they pause, hesitate, and slowly turn. Thoughtfully they stroll back towards one another. CROMWELL *raises his head and essays a smile.* CHAPUYS *responds.*]

They link arms and approach the stairs. As they go we hear that they are chuckling. There is nothing sinister or malignant in the sound; rather it is the self-mocking, self-indulgent, rather rueful laughter of men who know what the world is and how to be comfortable in it. As they go, THE CURTAIN FALLS.]

ALTERNATIVE ENDING

In the London production of this play at the Globe Theatre the play ended as follows.

Instead of the Cromwell and Chapuys entrance after the Headsman's line 'Behold – the head – of a traitor!', the Common Man came to the centre stage, having taken off his mask as the executioner, and said:

'I'm breathing. ... Are you breathing too? ... It's nice isn't it? It isn't difficult to keep alive friends ... just don't make trouble – or if you must make trouble, make the sort of trouble that's expected. Well, I don't need to tell you that. Good night. If we should bump into one another, recognize me.' [Exits.]

CURTAIN

JOHN WHITING

The Devils

A PLAY BASED ON A BOOK
BY ALDOUS HUXLEY

First presented in London at the Aldwych Theatre on 20 February 1961 by the Royal Shakespeare Company, with the following cast:

MANNOURY	Ian Holm
ADAM	James Bree
LOUIS TRINCANT	P. G. Stephens
PHILLIPE TRINCANT	Diana Rigg
JEAN D'ARMAGNAC	Patrick Allen
DE CERISAY	Peter Jeffrey
A SEWERMAN	Clive Swift
URBAIN GRANDIER	Richard Johnson
NINON	Yvonne Bonnamy
DE LA ROCHEPOZAY	Derek Godfrey
FATHER RANGIER	David Sumner
FATHER BARRÉ	Max Adrian
SISTER JEANNE OF THE ANGELS	Dorothy Tutin
SISTER CLAIRE	Stephanie Bidmead
SISTER LOUISE	Mavis Edwards
DE LAUBARDEMONT	Patrick Wymark
FATHER MIGNON	Donald Layne-Smith
SISTER GABRIELLE	Patsy Byrne
PRINCE HENRI DE CONDÉ	Derek Godfrey
RICHELIEU	John Cater
LOUIS XIII	Philip Voss
BONTEMPS	Stephen Thorne
FATHER AMBROSE	Roy Dotrice
A CLERK	John Cater

Townspeople, People from the Country, Capuchins, Carmelites, Jesuits, and Soldiers played by:

Tracey Lloyd, Maroussia Frank, Wendy Gifford, Meg Richie, Christopher Cruise, Edward Argent, William Austin, Alan Downer, Stuart Hoyle, James Keen, Peter Russell, Robert Langley, Larry Viner

Directed by Peter Wood	Setting by Sean Kenny
Costumes by Desmond Heeley	Lighting by John Wyckham

CHARACTERS

MANNOURY, *a surgeon*

ADAM, *a chemist*

LOUIS TRINCANT, *the Public Prosecutor*

PHILLIPE TRINCANT

JEAN D'ARMAGNAC, *the Governor of Loudun*

A SEWERMAN

URBAIN GRANDIER, *the Vicar of St Peter's Church*

NINON, *a widow*

DE LA ROCHEPOZAY, *the Bishop of Poitiers*

FATHER RANGIER

FATHER BARRÉ

SISTER JEANNE OF THE ANGELS, *the prioress of St Ursula's Convent*

SISTER CLAIRE

SISTER LOUISE

DE LAUBARDEMONT, *the King's Special Commissioner to Loudun*

FATHER MIGNON

SISTER GABRIELLE

PRINCE HENRI DE CONDÉ

RICHELIEU

LOUIS XIII, *King of France*

BONTEMPS, *a gaoler*

FATHER AMBROSE

A CLERK

Townspeople, People from the Country, Capuchins, Carmelites, Jesuits, and Soldiers

The action of the play takes place in and near the town of Loudun, and briefly at Paris, between the years 1623 and 1634.

ACT ONE

The streets of Loudun. Day.
A corpse hangs from the municipal gallows. Near by, a sewerman works in
a shallow drain.

>   [*People are coming from Saint Peter's Church.* ADAM, *a chemist, and*
>   MANNOURY, *a surgeon, among others.*]

MANNOURY: Shall we go together?

ADAM: By all means.

MANNOURY: Don't catch my sleeve. He spoke as if he were God.

ADAM: Grandier?

MANNOURY: Grandier.

ADAM: Very rousing to the spirit.

MANNOURY: You think so? Hm.

ADAM: So small a town is lucky to have such a caretaker of souls.
   Did I say that as if I meant it?

MANNOURY: No. There are things, my dear Adam.

ADAM: Things, Mannoury?

MANNOURY: Don't gape. Things said and things done.

ADAM: By the priest? Yes, I've heard.

MANNOURY: Then see.

>   [NINON, *a young widow, has come from the church. She goes away*
>   *along the street.*]

ADAM: With my own eyes.

MANNOURY: I've attended her. Medically.

ADAM: Have you?

MANNOURY: It's not widowhood gives that contentment. That walk.

ADAM: It takes a visit.

MANNOURY: It does.

>   [*They have come beneath the gallows.*]

ADAM: Hoo, he dangles.

MANNOURY: What idiot is this?

ADAM: They put him up last night.

MANNOURY: Compelling sight. What resides, Adam?

123

ADAM: I don't understand you.

MANNOURY: What's left, man? After that.

ADAM: Ah, you've something in your head.

MANNOURY: Has he? That's the point. Come to dinner.

[ADAM *and* MANNOURY *go.*

LOUIS TRINCANT *and his daughter,* PHILLIPE, *have come from the church.*]

TRINCANT: Fold your hands, child. You walk like a peasant.

PHILLIPE: Who's to see?

TRINCANT: The world. Let it set eyes on a lady.

[*They have come near the gallows.*]

PHILLIPE: Was he young or old?

TRINCANT: Don't look.

PHILLIPE: You want me to be filled with nice and useful experience, Father, so tell me something: does death unmask the face in heaven?

TRINCANT: A question for a priest.

PHILLIPE: I'm sorry. Let's talk of how my legs move in the dance. And of marriage. And love. Not death. For death smells bad. And there is scent upon a pillow.

TRINCANT: Chatter. Come along. Mind the step.

[TRINCANT *and* PHILLIPE *go.*

JEAN D'ARMAGNAC, *Governor of the town,* and GUILLAUME DE CERISAY, *the Chief Magistrate, have come from the church into the street.*]

D'ARMAGNAC: Grandier seems to have got it into his head that the forces of good are a kind of political party, needing a leader.

DE CERISAY: His mind's been running on such things.

D'ARMAGNAC: Politics? All the same, the terms seem strange coming from a pulpit.

DE CERISAY: So does wit.

D'ARMAGNAC: Yes. I disgraced myself this morning. I laughed aloud. Is that more becoming to the Governor of the town than yawning his way through the sermon, as I used to do before Grandier came here?

DE CERISAY: Have you sent the carriage on?

D'ARMAGNAC: Yes, I thought we'd walk. Tell me –

DE CERISAY: Yes?

D'ARMAGNAC: This is a small town. Can it contain a Father Grandier? That proud man. Shall we go this way?

[D'ARMAGNAC *and* DE CERISAY *go.*
The crowd has gone. The church doorway is empty.

FATHER URBAIN GRANDIER, *Vicar of Saint Peter's Church, appears. He comes into the street. A bucket of filth dredged up by the sewerman splashes his gown.*]

SEWERMAN: Sorry.

GRANDIER: It doesn't matter.

SEWERMAN: It's wrong, though. Shit on the holy purple.

GRANDIER: My son –

SEWERMAN: Father?

GRANDIER: Your words suit your condition.

SEWERMAN: How would you have it?

GRANDIER: Otherwise.

SEWERMAN: But I'm a man, sir. A dirty, sinful man. And my job is in the drains of the city. Why expect clean words from me? Let me oblige you, all the same. I regret, sir, splashing your gown with the excrement of the poor. Better?

GRANDIER [*he laughs*]: It'll do.

SEWERMAN: Lovely day. Hot.

GRANDIER: Yes. How can you bear to work down there?

SEWERMAN: Well, I used to keep my mind on higher things.

GRANDIER: I'm very pleased to hear it. What were they?

SEWERMAN: My wife and my dinner.

GRANDIER: I see. But now –

SEWERMAN: There's not the need. I've grown used to the stink. Nobody can live forty-three years and not have it happen. If you were a man, sir, and not a priest, perhaps I could make you understand.

GRANDIER: Try, even so.

SEWERMAN: Well, every man is his own drain. He carries his main sewer with him. Gutters run about him to carry off the dirt –

GRANDIER: They also carry the blood of life.

SEWERMAN: Mere plumbing. Elementary sanitation. Don't interrupt. And what makes a man happy? To eat, and set the drains awash. To sit in the sun and ferment the rubbish. To go home, and find comfort in his wife's conduit. Then why should I feel ashamed or out of place down here?

GRANDIER: Put in that way I can see no reason at all. It must be almost a pleasure.

SEWERMAN: It's clear, sir, that your precious juices will never flow here. As this misguided creature has dripped through his toes all night.

GRANDIER: Don't mock the thing!

SEWERMAN: Sorry.

GRANDIER: He was a man. A young man. Eighteen years old. They brought him to kneel at the church door on his way here. He told me his sins.

SEWERMAN: What were they?

GRANDIER: Being alive.

SEWERMAN: Comprehensive.

GRANDIER: Heinous, it seemed. Manhood led him into the power of the senses. With them he worshipped in total adoration a young girl. But he learnt too quickly. He learnt that only gold can decorate the naked body. And so he stole.

SEWERMAN: And so he hanged.

GRANDIER: He confessed something to me alone. It was not for God to hear. It was a man speaking to a man. He said that when he adorned the girl the metal looked colourless, valueless, against her golden skin. That was repentance. When will they take him down?

SEWERMAN: Tomorrow. When it's dark.

GRANDIER: See that it's done with some kind of decency.

[GRANDIER *goes.*]

[DE CERISAY: D'ARMAGNAC: TRINCANT.]

D'ARMAGNAC: Provincial life, my dear Trincant.

TRINCANT: You feel it has a bad effect on the art of poetry?

D'ARMAGNAC: Ask De Cerisay.

DE CERISAY: Well, you and I, Trincant, as Public Prosecutor and Magistrate, are brought close to the ground by our work. I've always understood poetry to be an elevated art.

TRINCANT: I assure you that during composition I think the right thoughts. My mind, if I may put it this way, is filled with nobility.

DE CERISAY: Why don't you show this latest bunch of Latin epigrams to Grandier?

TRINCANT: The priest?

DE CERISAY: As a priest his secular senses are well developed. Make a selection. Submit them. The man is a scholar.

TRINCANT: Very well. I don't seek praise, but I'll do as you say. Yes.

[TRINCANT *goes*.]

D'ARMAGNAC: Poor Trincant. He loves the Muses but, alas, they don't seem to love him. I hope your suggestion about Grandier was not malicious.

DE CERISAY: Not at all, sir. As with any author, the greater Trincant's audience the less burden of doubt on his closer friends.

D'ARMAGNAC: Grandier came to see me this morning. I was having breakfast in the garden. He didn't know that I could observe him as he walked towards me. Vulnerable: smiling. He visibly breathed the air. He stopped to watch the peacocks. He fondled a rose as if it were the secret part of a woman. He laughed with the gardener's child. Then he composed himself, and it was another man who sat down beside me and talked for an hour. Where will this other man climb on his ladder of doubt and laughter?

DE CERISAY: Probably to the highest offices of the church.

D'ARMAGNAC: And the man I saw in the garden?

[*Silence*.]

[GRANDIER *with* NINON. *A disordered bed: biretta on the bedpost*.]

NINON: Tell me.

GRANDIER: Now what do you need to be told? Words are playthings in our situation. Expect music from them, but not sense.

NINON: Don't laugh at me. I never understand. I'm not a clever woman.

GRANDIER: You're too humble, Ninon. It's a female vice. It will never do. Ask your question.

NINON: Why do you come to me?

GRANDIER: That would be a wise question if we were in your drawing room. As it is –

NINON: There are pretty young girls in the town.

GRANDIER: They didn't need consolation for the untimely death of their husband, the rich wine merchant. That was the reason for my first visit, remember. How many Tuesdays ago was it? I asked you to believe that God loved you, and had you in His eternal care. That the bursting of your husband's heart at the dinner table, when his blood ran with his wholesale wine, was an act of love. That all things, however incomprehensible, are an act of love. But you couldn't bring yourself to believe any of this. Your soul is as tiny as your mind, Ninon, and you had to fall back on a most human gesture: you wept. Tears must be wiped away. How can that be done without a caress?

NINON: I saw you that day just as a man. What's the matter?

GRANDIER: I wish words like that could still hurt me. [*He is putting scent on his handkerchief.*]

NINON: I've never seen you as anything but a man. Do you want to be more?

GRANDIER: Of course. Or less.

NINON: But how can you be a man of God without being a man?

GRANDIER: My dear child, you ask questions out of your time, and far beyond your experience. Your mouth . . .

[*A bell is sounding.*]

NINON: You possess me.

GRANDIER: Go to sleep now. You've been a good little animal today. Let the thought of it comfort you. Be happy.

[GRANDIER *goes.*]

[ADAM *and* MANNOURY: *a table between them.*]

MANNOURY: This human head fills me with anticipation, my dear Adam.

ADAM: It's a common enough object.

MANNOURY: Every man wears one on his shoulders, certainly. But when a head comes into my hands disassociated from the grosser parts of the body I always feel an elevation of spirit. Think, this is the residence of reason.

ADAM: Indeed! Ah, yes. Very true.

MANNOURY: Isn't it possible that one day in the most commonplace dissection I might find –

ADAM: What Mannoury? Don't hesitate to tell me.

MANNOURY: I might stumble upon the very meaning of reason. Isn't it possible that the divinity of man, enclosed in an infinitesimal bag, might rest upon the point of my knife? I have dreamed of the moment. I have seen myself. I lift the particle, taken from the cerebellum and, Adam, I know!

ADAM: What do you know, Mannoury?

MANNOURY: Come, my dear friend, I am speaking in the most comprehensive sense. I know – everything. All – is revealed.

ADAM: God bless my soul!

MANNOURY: Let's take this thing to your house. We'll spend the evening on it.

[*They begin to go down into the street.*]

MANNOURY: Everyone is speaking of your treatment of the Duke's love disease.

ADAM: Yes, I think we're getting on top of it. Too soon to be certain.

MANNOURY: Your metallic compound. Does it affect the potency?

ADAM: Disastrously. But as I jokingly told the Duke, Science must concern itself with primary causes. It cannot turn its head to observe destructive side issues.

MANNOURY: And never will, we must hope.

ADAM: Is Madam Who Shall Be Nameless delivered?

MANNOURY: Prematurely. The foetus was interesting. It had a tiny cap drawn over its head.

ADAM: Hardly surprising with all this talk about the coachman.

[*They are now in the street.* GRANDIER *is approaching them.*]

MANNOURY: Look who's coming.

ADAM: Studied indifference, if you please.

GRANDIER: Good evening, Mister Surgeon. And Mister Chemist.

MANNOURY: Good evening, sir.

ADAM: Sir.

GRANDIER: It's been a fine day.

MANNOURY: Yes.

ADAM: It has.

GRANDIER: But now – rain, do you think?

ADAM: The sky is clear.

MANNOURY: It is.

GRANDIER: But it may cloud before night.

ADAM: Indeed.

MANNOURY: Indeed, it may.

GRANDIER: Darken, you know. What have you got in that bucket?

MANNOURY: A man's head.

GRANDIER: A friend?

MANNOURY: A criminal.

ADAM: The body was taken down from the gallows last night.

GRANDIER [*after silence*]: I hope they didn't overcharge you, in the interest of Science.

MANNOURY: Ninepence.

GRANDIER: Reasonable. A bargain. Let me see. Poor pickle.

ADAM: Yes. Mannoury and I have been discussing the human predicament with this relic as centrepiece.

GRANDIER: I'm sure you said some very interesting things.

ADAM: Well, Mannoury did observe that the seat of reason is situated here.

GRANDIER: How true! But you'll have said that, Adam.

ADAM: I did.

GRANDIER: And we mustn't forget looking down on this pudding that man's fiddledeevinity is what you may say only to the greater purpose of his hohumha.

ADAM: I beg your pardon.

GRANDIER: I quite agree. But I mustn't stay exchanging profundities with you, however much you may tempt me. So good-bye, Mister Surgeon and Mister Chemist.

[GRANDIER *goes. The bell is sounding.*]

MANNOURY: You fell into his trap, Adam. Never engage Mister Clever.

ADAM: He smelled of the widow woman. Filth.

MANNOURY: Of course. He's just come from her.

ADAM: After tickling himself in the confessional with the sins of young girls this morning –

MANNOURY: He consummates himself in the widow's bed this afternoon –

ADAM: And then comes and yawns in our faces.

MANNOURY: Tonight –

ADAM: Tonight he'll spend in some great house. D'Armagnac's, De Cerisay's. Fed, comforted, and flattered by the laughter of women.

MANNOURY: What a – I'm so sorry. What were you going to say?

ADAM: I was going to say, What a life!

MANNOURY: So was I.

ADAM: We're never asked to such places.

MANNOURY: I've thought of it often.

ADAM: How do you console yourself?

MANNOURY: By remembering that I'm an honest man doing an honest job.

ADAM: Is that enough?

MANNOURY: What do you mean?

ADAM: Pick up the head and come with me.

[*They go along the street and into a house.*]

[GRANDIER *enters the church. He kneels at the altar: prays.*]

GRANDIER: O my dear Father, it is the wish of Your humble child to come to Your Grace. I speak in the weariness of thirty-five years. Years heavy with pride and ambition, love of women and love of self. Years scandalously marred by adornment and luxury, time taken up with being that nothing, a man.

I prostrate myself before You now in ravaged humility of spirit. I ask You to look upon me with love. I beg that You will answer my prayer. Show me a way. Or let a way be made.

[*Silence.*]

O God, O my God, my God! Release me. Free me. These needs! Have mercy. Free me. Four o'clock of a Tuesday afternoon. Free me.

[*He rises: cries out*]

Rex tremendae majestatis, qui salvandos salvas gratis, salva me, salva me, fons pietatis!

[DE LA ROCHEPOZAY, *Bishop of Poitiers: Capuchins and Carmelites.*]

DE LA ROCHEPOZAY: I have been alone for many days now. You will want to know if I have found some kind of grace. Perhaps, for I am filled with weariness and disgust at the folly and wickedness of mankind. Is this the beneficence of God, you ask? It may well be. Let me tell you the circumstances of the revelation.

Shut in my room for seven days, fasting and at prayer, I came to see myself as the humble instrument of God's will. It was a state of such happiness, such bliss, and such abasement that I wished never to return to you. I longed for this husk to wither away, leaving only the purity of spirit. But my sense of duty as your bishop forced me to leave this paradise. I came back to the world.

A priest of Loudun, called Grandier, wished to see me. He is my child, as you all are, my darling, and I would wish to love him. But his handkerchief was scented.

If this man had struck me in the face it would have humiliated me less. The assault on my senses was so obscene that I was in a state of terror. Scent, for a man to whom the taste of water was like fire, and the sound of the birds in the garden like the screams of the damned.

I am very tired. Take these rings from my fingers.

Perhaps on your way here from your parish a child smiled at you, or you were attracted by a flower, or the smell of new grass by the road. Did you think of these things with anything but pleasure? One of you may have lost your way and been directed by a stranger. Did you think of it as anything but kindness?

Let me say this to you. There is no innocence, none! Suspect goodness in men, and reject kindness.

For all vanities are an assertion of self, and the assertion of self in Man is the ascendancy of the Devil.

When that handkerchief was flourished in my face this morning I saw it as if in a vision. It became a mighty banner flung across the world, stinking, enveloping, overwhelming our beloved Church in shamelessness and lust. We are in peril!

Take me away. Take me away.

[DE LA ROCHEPOZAY *is led away.* FATHER BARRÉ *and* FATHER RANGIER *are left alone.*]

RANGIER: How are things in your part of the world?

BARRÉ: I'm kept very busy.

RANGIER: Is he among you?

BARRÉ: Incessantly.

RANGIER: Can we name him?

BARRÉ: If you want to. Satan.

RANGIER: How is the struggle?

BARRÉ: I shan't give up.

RANGIER: You look tired.

BARRÉ: It goes on day and night.

RANGIER: Your spirit is shining.

BARRÉ: Unbroken, at any rate. But there's never a moment's peace at Chinon now. Only the other day I was conducting a marriage. Everything was going very well. I had before me a young couple, ignorant, I thought, but pure. It never entered my head that they were anything else. I'd reached the blessing, and was about to send them out to the world as man and wife, when there was a disturbance at the west door. A cow had come into the church, and was trying to force its way through the congregation. I knew at once, of course.

RANGIER: That it was he?

BARRÉ: Say it, Rangier, say it. [*He shouts*] It was Satan!

RANGIER: You're never taken in.

BARRÉ: Before I could act he had passed from the cow to the bride's mother, who fell to the ground in a kind of convulsion. There was the most dreadful confusion, of course, but I began exorcism at once. There's a couple that won't forget their wedding day in a hurry.

RANGIER: How did it end?

BARRÉ: The spirit screamed from the church like a great wind. A kind of black slime was found smeared on the girl's forehead. She said she'd fallen, but of course I know better. That's not all. Two days later the husband came to me and said he'd found himself quite unable to perform his necessary duty. The usual kind of spell, you know. I've now started investigations into the whole family.

RANGIER: This sort of thing must bring a lot of people to Chinon.

BARRÉ: Thousands.

RANGIER: There's great popular interest in evil nowadays.

BARRÉ: It's certainly helped to offset the sadly declining attendance at my shrine. The image of Notre-Dame de Recouvrance.

RANGIER: Well, you know how that's come about.

BARRÉ: Certainly. They all flock to Loudun now. This Grandier person, who's upset the bishop, is responsible for that. He touts for his place disgracefully.

RANGIER: There are fashions in miracle-working images, just as there are in women's hats.

BARRÉ: That's true. But there's a satisfying constancy in evil. I must go.

RANGIER: Anything interesting?

BARRÉ: I have to call at a farm. They say that something is speaking through the umbilicus of a child. The child herself is now in conversation with it, and I'm told the two voices have evolved a quite astonishing creed of profanation.

[BARRÉ *and* RANGIER *go separate ways.*]

[GRANDIER *alone. He has a sheaf of poems in his hand.* TRINCANT *comes to him.*]

TRINCANT: So good of you to call, Father Grandier.

GRANDIER: Not at all. I've brought back your poetry.

TRINCANT: So I see. D'Armagnac holds that any insufficiency must be put down to life in the provinces.

GRANDIER: You write them when you get back from the office.

TRINCANT: Every day.

GRANDIER: Amid the cooking smells.

TRINCANT: They drift up.

GRANDIER: And the clatter of family life.

TRINCANT: It intrudes.

GRANDIER: And so naturally you achieve – these.

TRINCANT: Put me out of my misery. I want an honest opinion.

GRANDIER: You're an important man in this town, Trincant. Men in public positions can't expect honesty.

TRINCANT: Speak to me as a poet, not as Public Prosecutor.

GRANDIER: Very well. Your poetry –

[PHILLIPE TRINCANT *has come in.*]

TRINCANT: What is it?

PHILLIPE: I want my sewing, Father.

TRINCANT: Please take it. [*To Grandier*] This is my elder daughter, Phillipe. What were you saying?

GRANDIER: I was about to say that your creations – these – have great merit. They seem to be moral observations of a most uncommon kind.

TRINCANT: Really?

GRANDIER [*to Phillipe*]: Don't you think so? I'm speaking of your father's poetry.

TRINCANT: She's very ignorant about such things. Young girls, you know, dear me. Dancing, music, and laughter. Finer things can go hang.

GRANDIER: She should be instructed.

TRINCANT: It's so difficult to find anyone suitable in this town. Unless –

GRANDIER [*to Phillipe*]: Do you speak any Latin?

PHILLIPE: A little.

GRANDIER: That's not enough.

TRINCANT: Unless –

GRANDIER: It's an exact language. Makes it possible to say just what you mean. That's rare nowadays. Don't you agree?

PHILLIPE: Yes, it is.

TRINCANT: Unless you, Father Grandier, would undertake the instruction.

GRANDIER: Of your daughter?

TRINCANT: Yes.

GRANDIER: I'm a busy man.

TRINCANT: Just one day a week. A few hours in the appreciation of finer things. It could be done by conversation. Perhaps the reading of suitable Latin verse.

GRANDIER: Very well.

TRINCANT: Shall we say Tuesday?

GRANDIER: No. Not Tuesday. The next day.

[ADAM *and* MANNOURY: *they sit in the pharmacy, beneath a stuffed crocodile and hanging bladders. Light is reflected through bottles which hold malformed creatures.*]

ADAM [*he is reading from a small book*]: At half past five on Tuesday he left the widow's house.

MANNOURY: The man is a machine. Interesting, though. Can sexual response be conditioned by the clock?

ADAM: At half past seven he was observed in public conversation with D'Armagnac. The subject is in doubt, although Grandier was seen to snigger twice. He dined alone, later than usual, at nine o'clock. A light burned in his room until after midnight.

MANNOURY: I suppose it's possible. I say to a woman: at four-thirty on Tuesday I shall arrive to pleasure you. I do so on the dot for some weeks. It no longer becomes necessary to say that I shall do so. Anticipation speaks for me. Tuesday: half past four. Usual physiological manifestations. Subject for treatise. Must think.

ADAM [*he turns a page*]: Discovered at dawn prostrate before altar. Great languor through the morning. A meal at a quarter past two. Sweetbreads in cream, followed by a rank cheese. Wine. Three o'clock: entered Trincant's house for instruction of Trincant's daughter, Phillipe.

MANNOURY: Adam, you're a wit.

ADAM: Am I, now?

MANNOURY: Your inflexion on the word 'instruction' was masterly.

ADAM: Thank you.

MANNOURY: But forgive me, my dear friend, if I ask you something. How do we go on? Your observations of Grandier's movements are a marvel. But these are the habits of any man. We shall never catch him on such evidence.

ADAM: You must give me time, Mannoury. We shall never expose him on his habits, certainly. But lust is leading him by the nose. And lust must have a partner. The widow, Ninon? Phillipe Trincant? Another? Who knows? But there will be a time. Patience.

[SISTER JEANNE-DES-ANGES *alone: kneeling.*]

JEANNE: I dedicate myself humbly to Your service. You have made me, both in stature and in spirit, a little woman. And I have a small imagination, too. That is why, in Your infinite wisdom, You have given me this visible burden on my back to remind me day by day of what I must carry. O my dear Lord, I find it difficult to turn in my bed, and so in the small and desperate hours I am reminded of Your burden, the Cross, on the long road.

You have brought meaning to my life by my appointment to this Ursuline house. I will try to guide the Sisters of this place. I will do my duty as I see it. [*Silence.*] Lord . . . Lord, I have had great difficulty with prayer ever since I was a little girl. I have longed for another and greater voice within me to praise you. By Your grace I have come young to this office. Have mercy on Your child. Let her aspire. Meanwhile, the floors shall be swept, the beds neatly made, and the pots kept clean.

[*Silence.*] Mercy. [*Silence.*] I will find a way. Yes, I will find a way to You. I shall come. You will enfold me in Your sacred arms. The blood will flow between us, uniting us. My innocence is Yours.

[*Silence: precisely*] Please God, take away my hump so that I can lie on my back without lolling my head. [*Silence.*] There is a way to be found. May the light of Your eternal love . . . [*whispers*]. Amen

[SISTER JEANNE *rises: goes.*]

[GRANDIER *and* PHILLIPE: *she is reading.*]

PHILLIPE: Foeda est in coitu et brevis voluptas, et taedet
          Veneris statis peractae.

GRANDIER: Translate as you go. Line by line.

PHILLIPE: Pleasure in love is . . .

GRANDIER: Lust.

PHILLIPE: Pleasure in lust is nasty and short, And sickness . . .

GRANDIER: Weariness.

PHILLIPE: And weariness follows on desire.

GRANDIER: Go on.

PHILLIPE: non ergo ut pecudes libidinosae caeci protinus irruamus
          illuc (nam languescit amor peritque flamma); [*pause*]

    We're not like animals to rush at it,
    Love dies there, and the flame goes out.

GRANDIER: Prosaic, but fair. Give me the book. [*He translates*]

        But in everlasting leisure,
        Like this, like this, lie still
        And kiss time away.
        No weariness and no shame,
        Now, then and shall be all pleasure.
        No end to it,
        But an eternal beginning.

My child, why are you crying?

PHILLIPE: I haven't been well.

GRANDIER: Do you find our little lessons too much for you?

PHILLIPE: No, no, I love – I enjoy them very much.

GRANDIER: Well, we've only had six. I thought they might go on say to the end of the year.

PHILLIPE: Of course. As long as you like.

GRANDIER: As long as *you* like, Phillipe. They're for your benefit.

PHILLIPE: I want very much to understand. All things.

GRANDIER: All things?

PHILLIPE: There are forces inside me as a woman which must be understood if they are to be resisted.

GRANDIER: What forces, Phillipe?

PHILLIPE: Inclinations –

GRANDIER: Go on.

PHILLIPE: Inclinations towards sin.

    [*Silence.*]

[D'ARMAGNAC *stands at a high point on the fortifications of the town. A Council of State. Distant figures:* LOUIS XIII, *King of France, and* RICHELIEU.]

RICHELIEU: It is a simple matter to understand sir. You have that paper upside down. The self-government of the small provincial towns of France must be brought to an end. The first step is to pull down all kinds of fortification.

    [GRANDIER *has approached D'Armagnac from below.*]

D'ARMAGNAC: So it's the turn of this city.

GRANDIER: Is everything to come down?

D'ARMAGNAC: That's what they want. It's a trick, of course. Richelieu sits with the King in Paris. He whispers in his ear.

RICHELIEU: France must be free within herself if she is to determine her own destiny.

D'ARMAGNAC: Ignorant and crafty provincials like us cannot see beyond the city walls. So we have this order from the Cardinal to tear them down. Will it broaden our view?

RICHELIEU: Such men as your friend D'Armagnac, sir, see with little vision. Their loyalty is to their town, not to France.

GRANDIER: Have they given any reason for this order?

D'ARMAGNAC: When a man's intent on power, as Richelieu is, he can justify his actions with absurdities.

RICHELIEU: Such fortifications provide opportunities for an uprising by the Protestants.

D'ARMAGNAC: Look. An old city. Those walls keep out more than the draught. Those towers are more than ornament. And from that fortress I have tried to administer my small sovereignty with reasonable wisdom. For I love the place.

GRANDIER: You must refuse to destroy it. Will other provincial governors stand against the order?

D'ARMAGNAC: It's very doubtful.

GRANDIER: Shall we?

D'ARMAGNAC: We?

GRANDIER: Let me help you in this matter, sir.

D'ARMAGNAC: Do you mean it? There is a churchman beside the King in Paris. As another, beside me here, do you also want to use this matter for your own ends?

GRANDIER: Conflict attracts me, sir. Resistance compels me.

D'ARMAGNAC: They can destroy you.

GRANDIER: I am weak, it's true. But equal power cannot be conflict. It is negation. Peace. So let me help you with all the passion of my failure.

D'ARMAGNAC: Don't smile. They can destroy you.

[DE LAUBARDEMONT, *the King's Commissioner, has come to stand below Richelieu and the King.* RICHELIEU *speaks to him.*]

RICHELIEU: D'Armagnac, the Governor of Loudun, has refused to obey the order. Go to the town. You've served me before. Wait. There is a man. His name is Grandier. He is a priest. Yes, there is a man called Grandier. Remember that.

[DE LAUBARDEMONT *goes*.]

An unseen woman's voice:

> Lux aeterna luceat eis, Domine, cum sanctis
> tuis in aeternum, quia pius est.
> Requiem aeternam dona eis, Domine, et lux
> perpetua luceat eis.

[SISTER JEANNE DES ANGES: SISTER CLAIRE OF ST JOHN: SISTER LOUISE OF JESUS: SISTER GABRIELLE OF THE IN-CARNATION: *they enter*.]

JEANNE: We have suffered a great loss, Sisters. Canon Moussaut was a good old man.

CLAIRE: It is God's will.

LOUISE: God's will.

JEANNE: So we have been taught. All the same, his death leaves us with a problem. We lack a director. The old man served this place well for many years, it's true, but the life of sinful children must go on. Penitents, we must have a confessor.

LOUISE: Have you chosen, Mother?

JEANNE: God will choose.

CLAIRE: We will pray.

JEANNE: Do so. There is a – [*fit of coughing*]. Don't touch my back! [*Stillness: exhaustion*.] There is a man. His name is Grandier. He is young. I have never seen him, but God has often put him in my thoughts lately. I mean to . . . [*silence*].

CLAIRE: What's the matter?

JEANNE: Claire?

CLAIRE: Why stare at me like that? Have I done something wrong?

JEANNE [*seeing the girl*]: No, no. I mean to write to this good man and invite him to be our new director. Grandier. Grandier. It is guidance, you understand. He has been put in my thoughts. Grandier.

CLAIRE: It is God's will.

LOUISE: God's will.

JEANNE [*sudden harsh laughter*]: I am tired to death. [*Silence: calmly*] It is a very excellent and practical solution. He can advise us on the method of education for the children put in our care. He will oversee our spiritual needs. [*Laughter again.*] He can sort out these damned problems of theological progression which muddle me day after day. Yes, it will be a good appointment. Leave me alone.

[*The Sisters go:* JEANNE *calls back* CLAIRE.]

JEANNE: Claire!

CLAIRE: Yes?

JEANNE: They say I have beautiful eyes. Is it true?

CLAIRE: Yes, Mother.

JEANNE: Too beautiful to close even in sleep, it seems. Go with the others.

[JEANNE *alone.*]

JEANNE: A summer morning. Children playing. Boy and girl. Paper boats sail the pond. Sun shone so hot upon the head that day. Children crouched, staring at each other across the sheet of water. Was it love? Flick. A toad upon a slab. Croak. Boy, head to one side, smiling, gentle voice whispering over the water: Look. Speak to your brother, Jeanne. There. Green brother, Hophop. Speak to him, Jeanne. [*Laughter: silence.*] God, forgive my laughter. But you haven't given me much defence, have You?

[JEANNE *goes to a window and opens it. She stares down through the grille upon:*]

[*A street. There is a market stall. People of the town are coming and going, buying and selling. Children. A cart passes. A song is heard.* GRANDIER *comes through the crowd. He is in full canonicals, magnificent, golden, in the dying light of day. His tread is quick, confident, and gay.*

JEANNE *cries out.*

The sound is not heard by the crowd, but GRANDIER *stops. He looks around him, into the faces of the crowd, wondering which man or woman could have been moved to such a cry of agony in the middle of*

such careless activity. GRANDIER *goes on by way of ascending steps.*
JEANNE *is writing. Rapid, angular hand, ornamented.*]

[*The street.* ADAM *and* MANNOURY *are among the crowd. They
come forward.*]

MANNOURY: The first thing to do is to draw up some kind of document.

ADAM: An accusation against Grandier.

MANNOURY: Exactly. We know about his debauchery.

ADAM: Profanity.

MANNOURY: And impiety.

ADAM: Is it enough?

MANNOURY: It'll have to do.

ADAM: For the time being.

MANNOURY: We'll present the paper to the Bishop.

ADAM: It must be properly done.

MANNOURY: Of course. Framed in correct language, decent to
handle –

ADAM: Something's just occurred to me.

MANNOURY: Oh?

ADAM: What a lot of criticism we middle classes come in for just
because we like things nice. I'm sorry. Go on. What will the
document say?

MANNOURY: Say? [*Pause.*] We shall have to decide.

ADAM: It's not important.

MANNOURY: No. Just the means.

ADAM: We must keep the end in sight.

MANNOURY: Always.

[*They go.*]

[*A confessional:* GRANDIER *and* PHILLIPE. *They speak in whispers
throughout.*]

GRANDIER: When was your last confession, child?

PHILLIPE: A week ago, Father.

GRANDIER: What have you to tell me?

PHILLIPE: Father, I have sinned. I have suffered from pride.

GRANDIER: We must always be on guard.

PHILLIPE: I finished some needlework yesterday, and I was pleased with myself.

GRANDIER: God allows us satisfaction in the work we do.

PHILLIPE: I have been in error through anger.

GRANDIER: Tell me.

PHILLIPE: My sister teased me. I wished her – elsewhere.

GRANDIER: You're absolved. Anything else? [*Silence.*] Come now, others are waiting.

PHILLIPE: I've had unclean thoughts.

GRANDIER: Of what nature?

PHILLIPE: About a man.

GRANDIER: My child –

PHILLIPE: In the early hours of the morning ... my bedroom is suffocatingly hot ... I've asked them to take away the velvet curtains ... my thoughts fester ... and yet they are so tender ... my body ... Father ... my body ... I wished to be touched.

GRANDIER: Have you tried to suppress these thoughts?

PHILLIPE: Yes.

GRANDIER: Are they an indulgence?

PHILLIPE: No. I have prayed.

GRANDIER: Do you wish to be saved from this? [*Silence.*] Answer, child.

PHILLIPE: No! I want him to take – no, possess – no, destroy me. I love you. Him. I love him!

[GRANDIER *comes out from the box: compassion. After a moment he draws aside the curtain and* PHILLIPE *is seen. They stand facing each other.*]

[DE LA ROCHEPOZAY. ADAM *and* MANNOURY *humbly before him.*]

DE LA ROCHEPOZAY: I have considered this document you have presented against the priest, Grandier. He is known to us as an impious and dangerous man. A few months ago we ourselves suffered insult and humiliation by his presence. But this is neither here nor there. What is your complaint?

MANNOURY: We feel, my lord bishop, that Grandier should be forbidden to exercise the sacerdotal function.

DE LA ROCHEPOZAY: What is your profession?

MANNOURY: I'm a surgeon.

DE LA ROCHEPOZAY: Would it amuse you if I came and instructed you in your business?

MANNOURY: I'm always prepared to take advice.

DE LA ROCHEPOZAY: Don't talk like a fool. This grubby and ill-composed document tells us nothing we did not know about the man. Vague and yet somewhat hysterical accusations concerning lonely widows and amorous virgins are all that I can find here. I'm not prepared to conduct the affairs of this diocese on the level of a police court.

ADAM: He has powerful friends.

DE LA ROCHEPOZAY: Stop whispering. What did you say?

ADAM: Grandier is protected by his friends.

DE LA ROCHEPOZAY: What are their names?

MANNOURY [to Adam: a nudge]: Go on.

ADAM: D'Armagnac. De Cerisay. Others.

DE LA ROCHEPOZAY: I'll accept your reasonable intentions in coming here. Although, God knows, if there's anyone I distrust it's the good citizen going about his civic duty. His motive is usually hate or money. But I will not accept your opinions, your advice, nor, for a moment longer, your presence.

[ADAM and MANNOURY go.]

DE LA ROCHEPOZAY [to his attendant]: It is vital that the Church should be protected from the democratic principle that every man must have his say. Those two probably spoke the truth, but they must not be allowed to think that they influence our judgements in any way.

[JEANNE alone: a book of devotions. Night. CLAIRE comes to her.]

CLAIRE: This was just delivered at the gate.

[JEANNE takes a letter from Claire, breaks it open, and reads.]

JEANNE: He has refused.

CLAIRE: Father Grandier?

JEANNE [*she reads aloud*]: My dear Sister: It is with great regret that I must refuse your invitation to become Director of your House. The pressing duties I have in the town would not allow me the time to devote my energies to the advantage of your Sisterhood. I very much appreciate all you say of my qualities and . . .

[JEANNE *tears the letter across and presses it to her body.*]

JEANNE: Thank you, Sister.

[CLAIRE *goes.*

JEANNE *alone.*]

JEANNE: What is this divine mystery? Let me see. Let me see. [*Laughter.*] I was about to address myself to God in this matter. Habit. Habit. It would never do. No. It must be to Man.

[*She whispers the name:* 'Grandier.']

You wake up. Dawn has broken over others before you. Look at the little grey window. Then turn. She lies beside you. The attitude is of prayer or the womb. Her mouth tastes of wine and the sea. Her skin is smooth and silky, rank with sweat. The native odours of her body have exhausted in the night the scents of day.

[PHILLIPE, *naked, is seen making love with* GRANDIER. *They will continue to be seen in the touching formal attitudes of passion throughout* JEANNE'S *words.*]

JEANNE: Look down at her. What do you feel? Sadness? It must be sadness. You are a man. Ah, now she stretches her arms above her head. Are you not moved? This is not the sophistry of a whore, whatever you may pretend. She shifts her legs, entwines them, lays a finger on your lips and her mouth upon her finger. She whispers. Those words were taught. She only repeats the lesson. Such filth is love to her, and the speaking of it is an act of faith. [*Sudden laughter.*] What was that you did? Stretching out to clutch the falling bedclothes. Was it to cover your nakedness? Is there modesty here?

[*Silence: in wonder*] How strange. Can you laugh, too? That's something I didn't know. Pain, oblivion, unreason, mania. These I thought would be in your bed. But laughter . . .

How young you both look. Quiet again.

The girl is heavy in your arms. She yawned, and you have taken up the shudder of her body. You tremble, in spite of yourself. Look, the sun is breaking up the mists in the fields. You're going to be engulfed by day. Take what you can. Let both take what they can. Now.

Now.

[*She weeps.*] This frenzy, this ripping apart, this meat on a butcher's slab. Where are you? Love? Love? What are you? Now. Now. Now.

> [JEANNE *falls on her knees, convulsed. Grandier and Phillipe can no longer be seen.*]

JEANNE [*suffocated, young voice*]: O my God, is that it? Is that it?
> [*Darkness.*]

[D'ARMAGNAC: DE CERISAY: DE LAUBARDEMONT.]

LAUBARDEMONT: It's not a question of compromise. I'm here as His Majesty's Special Commissioner, but I have no power to negotiate. I'm sorry, D'Armagnac.

D'ARMAGNAC: You know, Laubardemont, grown men in this country are getting a little tired of the father figures which keep arising, so we are told, for our own good. France may very well be looked on as a woman, and submissive, but she's not a baby.

LAUBARDEMONT: I'm inclined to agree with you. But I'm not here for argument. I simply brought a message.

D'ARMAGNAC: An order. Pull down the fortifications.

LAUBARDEMONT: That was the message. What answer may I take back?

D'ARMAGNAC: That I refuse.

LAUBARDEMONT: I have a curious feeling.

D'ARMAGNAC: Fear?

LAUBARDEMONT: No, no. Just that you've been influenced in this decision. And that there is pressure behind your obduracy.

D'ARMAGNAC: The decision is entirely mine. As governor of the town.

[GRANDIER *approaches*.]

D'ARMAGNAC: Do you know Father Grandier?

LAUBARDEMONT: I've heard of him.

D'ARMAGNAC: Well, this is he.

LAUBARDEMONT [*turning*]: Ah, Father. Can't you bring your influence to bear on the Governor in this matter of the demolition. As a man of peace I'm sure you want it brought about.

GRANDIER: As a man of peace, I do. As a man of principle, I'd prefer the city walls to remain standing.

LAUBARDEMONT: I see. Well, I seem to be alone in this. If you change your mind, and I earnestly hope you will, I shall be in Loudun for a few days.

[LAUBARDEMONT *goes*.]

D'ARMAGNAC: Look at him, Grandier.

GRANDIER: A funny little man.

D'ARMAGNAC: My dear fellow, we are all romantic. We see our lives being changed by a winged messenger on a black horse. But more often than not it turns out to be a shabby little man, who stumbles across our path.

[*A cloister*. JEANNE *and* FATHER MIGNON, *a foolish old man, walking together*.]

JEANNE: We are all of us so happy, Father Mignon, that you've been able to accept. We shall look forward to having you as our director for many years to come.

MIGNON: You're very kind, my child. You have a direct simplicity which an old man like myself finds very touching.

JEANNE: There are many problems in a place like this. I shall need your advice and guidance.

MIGNON: Always at your disposal.

JEANNE: For example, nearly all the Sisters here are young women. I think you'll agree that youth is more exposed to temptation than age.

MIGNON: That's so. I remember when I was a young man –

JEANNE: I have myself –

MIGNON: What's that?

JEANNE: I was about to say that I have myself recently suffered from visions of a diabolical nature.

MIGNON: In living close to God one becomes a natural prey to the Devil. I shouldn't worry about them too much.

JEANNE: I can speak about this in the daytime. But at night –

MIGNON: It is a well-known fact, my dear, that the spirit is at its weakest in the small hours.

JEANNE: Yes. I managed to resist the vision. Several hours of prayer and I was myself again. But the visitation –

MIGNON: Visitation?

JEANNE: The dead Canon Moussaut, your predecessor, came to me in the night. He stood at the foot of my bed.

MIGNON: But this was a visit of love, my child. Moussaut was a good man. You were fond of him. Did he speak to you?

JEANNE: Yes.

MIGNON: What did he say?

JEANNE: Filth.

MIGNON: What's that?

JEANNE: He spoke filth. Dirt. Jeering, contemptuous, hurtful obscenity.

MIGNON: My beloved Sister –

JEANNE: He was not in his own person.

MIGNON: What do you mean?

JEANNE: He came to me as another. A different man.

MIGNON: Did you recognize this man?

JEANNE: Yes.

MIGNON: Who was it?

JEANNE: Grandier. Father Grandier.

[Silence.]

MIGNON: My dear, do you understand the seriousness of what you're saying?

JEANNE [calmly]: Yes. Help me, Father.

[GRANDIER: in the pulpit.]

GRANDIER: ... For some lewd fellows go about the town and

148

speak against me. I know them. And you will know them when I say that Surgery and Chemistry go hand in hand, vermination against the wall. They have borne false witness. They spy. They sneak. They snigger. And the first sinful man was called Adam, and he begot murder. Why do they pursue me? I am not sick!

If they be here, in this holy place, let them stand before me and declare their hatred, and give the reason for it. I am not afraid to speak openly of what they attempt to discover secretly. If they be in this church let them stand before me. [*Silence.*] No, they are in some hole in the ground, scratching, so that more venom may come to the surface, and infect us all; distilling bile in retorts; revealing lust, envy, and blight with the turn of a scalpel.

[*During this* DE LAUBARDEMONT, *with two attendants, has approached, listened, and moved on.*]

O my dear children, I should not speak to you so from this place. And I should not speak to you in bitterness as your pastor.

Do they provoke me to anger? saith the Lord: do they not provoke themselves to the confusion of their own faces?

[*The pharmacy:* ADAM *and* MANNOURY.]

ADAM: It's after ten o'clock. Would you believe it?

MANNOURY: Well, we have had a nice talk.

ADAM: Have we got anywhere?

MANNOURY: Somebody at the door.

ADAM: Can't be.

MANNOURY: Is.

[ADAM *opens the door.* LAUBARDEMONT *stands there.*]

ADAM: No business. Shut.

LAUBARDEMONT: My name is Jean de Martin, Baron de Laubardemont. I am His Majesty's Special Commissioner to Loudun.

ADAM: Can I help you?

LAUBARDEMONT: I hope so.

[LAUBARDEMONT *comes into the shop.*]

LAUBARDEMONT: I am visiting the town for a kind of investigation.

MANNOURY [*carefully*]: We are both honest men.

LAUBARDEMONT: I know. That's why I'm here. I've always found in cases like this that there are perhaps two incorruptible men in the town. Usually close friends, professional men, middle class, backbone of the nation. Deep civic interest. Patriotic. Lost sons in a war. Happily married. Managing to make ends meet in spite of taxation. Austere lives, but what they have they like to be nice. Gentlemen, am I right?

ADAM: Quite correct.

LAUBARDEMONT: Good. I want you to tell me all you know about a man called Grandier. Father Grandier, of Saint Peter's Church.

ADAM: My dear Mannoury, at last!

[GRANDIER *and* PHILLIPE: *a secluded place.*]

PHILLIPE: I must go home now.

GRANDIER: Yes.

PHILLIPE: I don't like walking through the streets at night. Dogs bark. Listen, they're at it now.

GRANDIER: I wish I could come with you. I would like – oh, words, words!

PHILLIPE: What is it?

GRANDIER: Come here. Gently. I want to tell you –

PHILLIPE: Yes?

GRANDIER: You know the love-making –

PHILLIPE: Yes.

GRANDIER: I want to tell you, Phillipe. Among the clothes dropped on the floor, the soiled linen, the instruction, the apparatus, the surgery – among all this there is a kind of passion of the heart.

PHILLIPE: I know. It is love. Human love.

[*Silence.*]

GRANDIER: You understand it that way?

PHILLIPE: I think so.

GRANDIER: Do I love you?

PHILLIPE: I believe so.

GRANDIER: Then what comfort can I give you?

[*Silence.*]

PHILLIPE: I am a simple person. I see the world and myself as I have been taught. I am deeply sinful, but my love of God has not deserted me. It is said by Man that those in our state should stand before God. I believe this to be right. And I would not be afraid to declare myself to Him with you beside me, even in our transgression, for I believe Him to be good, wise, and always merciful.

[*Silence.*]

GRANDIER: You shame me.

[*The pharmacy.* DE LAUBARDEMONT: MANNOURY: ADAM. *They have been joined by* FATHER MIGNON.]

MIGNON: I couldn't get any more out of the prioress. I can prove nothing. She may be just a hysterical woman.

ADAM: Does it matter?

MIGNON: I'd very much like you, as a surgeon, Mannoury, and you Adam, as a chemist, to be there.

LAUBARDEMONT: May I attend as a disinterested party?

MIGNON: Certainly. If this is a genuine case, the more the – [*He stops.*]

LAUBARDEMONT: Were you going to say merrier?

MIGNON: I've sent a message to Father Barré, at Chinon. He's our great local expert in these matters.

MANNOURY: I shall be only too happy to give you any medical advice, Father.

ADAM: And I'll comment on any chemical or biological manifestations.

MIGNON: She already complains of a spasmodic but acute swelling of the belly.

ADAM: Fascinating!

MANNOURY: Not unusual. Sense of false pregnancy. Known it before. Nothing to do with the Devil. Wind?

LAUBARDEMONT: Conjecture is useless. It'll soon be morning.

[*Dawn.* JEANNE *at prayer beside her simple bed.*]

JEANNE: Please God, make me a good girl. Take care of my dear father and mother and look after my dog, Captain, who loved me and didn't understand why I had to leave him behind all that time ago. Lord ... Lord, I would like to make formal prayers to

You, but I can only do that out of a book in the chapel. [*Silence.*]
Love me. [*Silence.*] Love me. Amen.

[JEANNE *gets up and goes from the room to a great open space where
stand:*

DE LAUBARDEMONT: MANNOURY: ADAM: MIGNON:
RANGIER: BARRÉ. JEANNE *approaches them.*]

BARRÉ: Let me deal with this. Good morning, Sister. Are you well?

JEANNE: I'm very well, thank you, Father.

BARRÉ: Excellent. Will you kneel down?

[JEANNE *does so.* BARRÉ *goes to her.*]

BARRÉ [*sudden shout*]: Are you there! Are you there! [*Silence: to the
others*] They never answer at once. Afraid of committing themselves. [*To Jeanne*] Come now, declare yourself! In the name of
Our Lord Jesus Christ –

[*Suddenly* JEANNE *throws back her crooked head and peals of masculine laughter pour from her open, distorted mouth.*]

BARRÉ [*with satisfaction: to the others*]: Always does the trick.

JEANNE [*deep man's voice*]: Here we are, and here we stay.

BARRÉ: One question.

JEANNE: Pooh!

BARRÉ: Don't be impudent. One question. How did you gain entry
to this poor woman?

JEANNE [*deep voice*]: Good offices of a friend.

BARRÉ: His name?

JEANNE: Asmodeus.

BARRÉ: That's your name. What is the name of your friend?

[JEANNE *is swaying on her knees. She gives inarticulate cries which
gradually form themselves into the word:*]

JEANNE: Grandier! Grandier! Grandier!

[*Deep, sullen laughter.*]

CURTAIN

ACT TWO

Saint Peter's Church. Night.
> [GRANDIER *is at the altar.* PHILLIPE *kneels below him.*
> GRANDIER *holds up a salver. Speaks:*]

GRANDIER: Benedic, ✠ Domine, hunc annulum, quem nos in tuo nomine benedicimus, ✠ ut quae eum gestaverit, fidelitatem integram suo sponso tenens, in pace et voluntate tua permaneat, atque in mutua caritate semper vivat. Per Christum Dominum nostrum.

PHILLIPE: Amen.

> [GRANDIER *sprinkles the ring with holy water, and then, taking the ring from the salver, comes down to kneel beside Phillipe.*]

GRANDIER: With this ring I thee wed: this gold and silver I thee give; with my body I thee worship; and with all my worldly goods I thee endow.

> [GRANDIER *places the ring on the thumb of Phillipe's hand, saying:*]

GRANDIER: In the name of the Father: [*then on the second finger, saying*] And of the Son: [*then on the third finger, saying*] And of the Holy Ghost: [*lastly on the fourth finger, saying*] Amen.

> [*And there he leaves the ring.*
> GRANDIER *mounts the altar steps.*]

GRANDIER: Confirma hoc, Deus, quod operatus es in nobis.

PHILLIPE: A templo sancto tuo, quod est in Jerusalem.

GRANDIER: Kyrie eleison.

PHILLIPE: Christe eleison.

GRANDIER: Kyrie eleison.

> [*They speak together:*]

Pater noster –

> [– *and their voices whisper into silence.*]

A street.
> [THE SEWERMAN *is sitting at ease. He holds a cage with a bird in it.*
> GRANDIER *and* PHILLIPE *come from the church.*]

PHILLIPE: We should step out into the sunlight. Bells should tell the world about us. It shouldn't be night. And as quiet as this. Dear God, my husband, kiss me.

[*They kiss.* THE SEWERMAN *speaks.*]

SEWERMAN: So it's done. I saw you go into the church.

GRANDIER: It's done. And well done. Does the bird sing?

SEWERMAN: Not its purpose. Tongueless.

GRANDIER: Do you carry it for love?

SEWERMAN: An idea which would only occur to a good man. Or one careless with hope. No, I carry the thing so that it may die, and I live. He's my saviour. Who's yours?

GRANDIER: You –

SEWERMAN: Blaspheme?

GRANDIER: Yes.

SEWERMAN: Sorry. You know the pits at the edge of the town? Where even your beloved here sends in my buckets. Well, there are days when the place gives off poison. So I always approach it with this creature on a pole before me. His many predecessors have died in the miasma. When this happens I know it's no place for me. So I let the drains run foul for a day or two, and I spend my time catching another victim to shut up here. You'll understand what I mean.

[*Silence.*]

GRANDIER: I have put my trust in this child. She is not a victim.

SEWERMAN: Just as you say.

GRANDIER: Come now, even at this hopeless hour you must admit more passes between human beings than the actions which provide you and the laundry with a job.

SEWERMAN: I'm not arguing.

GRANDIER: There is a way of salvation through each other.

SEWERMAN: Are you trying to convince me?

GRANDIER: I'd like to.

SEWERMAN: What about yourself? Has the little ceremony in there done the trick?

GRANDIER: It has given me hope.

SEWERMAN: Hope of what?

GRANDIER: Hope of coming to God by way of a fellow being. Hope that the path, which taken alone, in awful solitude, is a way of despair, can be enlightened by the love of a woman. I have come to believe that by this simple act of commital, which I have done with my heart, it may be possible to reach God by way of happiness.

SEWERMAN: What was that last word?

GRANDIER: Happiness.

SEWERMAN: I don't know what it means. You must have made it up for the occasion. It's getting light.

PHILLIPE: I must go.

SEWERMAN: Yes. They mustn't find the bed empty. On the other hand, they mustn't find it too full.

PHILLIPE [to Grandier]: Speak to me.

SEWERMAN: Say it.

GRANDIER: I love you, Phillipe.

[PHILLIPE goes.]

SEWERMAN: Speaking of love, some very odd things are going on up at the convent.

GRANDIER: So I'm told.

SEWERMAN: It seems your name is being bandied about by the crazy ladies.

GRANDIER: We must pity them.

SEWERMAN: Will they pity you, that's the point?

GRANDIER: What do you mean? They're deluded.

SEWERMAN: What were you, a few minutes ago, with that girl?

GRANDIER: I was in my right mind, and I knew what I was doing. You may mock me, my son, if you wish. What seems to you a meaningless act, the marriage of an unmarriageable priest, has meaning for me. The lonely and the proud sometimes need to avail themselves of simple means. I, too, have made fun of the innocent before now. Your debasement has given you an unholy elevation. From your superior position be kind, be wise. Pity me. Pity me.

SEWERMAN: All right. Let's hope the good women of Saint Ursula's will do the same.

Daylight.

> [JEANNE, *on her knees. Facing her,* BARRÉ, RANGIER, *and* MIG-NON.]

BARRÉ: Exorcise te, immundissime spiritus, omnis incursio adversarii, omne phantasma, omnis legio, in nomine Domini nostri Jesus Christi, eradicare et effugare ab hoc plasmate Dei.

> [RANGIER *and* MIGNON *come forward.* RANGIER *splashes holy water:* MIGNON *lays on the stole.* ASMODEUS, *in a deep voice, speaks through* JEANNE.]

ASMODEUS: You gentlemen are wasting your time. You're soaking the lady, but you're not touching me.

BARRÉ [*to Mignon*]: Give me the relic.

> [MIGNON *hands Barré a small box. It is applied to Jeanne's back.*]

Adjure te, serpens antique, per judicem vivorum et mortuorum....

ASMODEUS: Excuse me.

BARRÉ: ... per factorum tuum, per factorum mundi. ...

ASMODEUS: I'm sorry to interrupt you.

BARRÉ: Well, what is it?

ASMODEUS: I don't understand a word you're saying. I'm a heathen devil. Latin – I suppose it is Latin – is a foreign language to me.

BARRÉ: It is customary to carry out exorcism in Latin.

ASMODEUS: Hidebound, that's what you are. Can't we continue our earlier conversation, which interested me so much, about the sexual activities of priests?

BARRÉ: Certainly not!

ASMODEUS: Is it true that men of your parish ... [*insane giggles*] ... is it true that they ... Bend low. Let me whisper.

JEANNE: O dear God, release this thing from me.

ASMODEUS: Be quiet, woman. You're interrupting a theological discussion.

JEANNE: Father, help me.

BARRÉ: My dear child, I'm doing all I can.

> [BARRÉ *takes* RANGIER *and* MIGNON *aside: speaks to Rangier.*]

BARRÉ: The wretch thinks I'm defeated.

ASMODEUS: You are.

BARRÉ: He seems at the moment to be lodged in the lower bowel. Are Adam and Mannoury here?

RANGIER: They're waiting. In there.

BARRÉ: Ask them to get ready, will you. Consecrate the water, while you're about it.

[RANGIER *goes out through the small, low door.* BARRÉ *turns to Jeanne.*]

BARRÉ: My beloved Sister, it must be extreme measures.

JEANNE: What do you mean, Father?

BARRÉ: The fiend must be forced from you.

JEANNE: Is there any way, but exorcism?

BARRÉ: Haha! They say the devil takes residence only in the innocent. It's true in this case, it seems. Yes, child, there is another way. [*He shouts*] Do you hear me, Asmodeus?

ASMODEUS [*is it Jeanne's voice?*]: Mercy. Mercy.

BARRÉ [*a scream*]: Nonsense!

[*Silence.*

RANGIER *comes out from the inner room.*]

BARRÉ: My dear boy, you look quite pale. The use of such methods in our job distresses you. Wait till you've been at it as long as I have. Anyway, the Church must keep up with the times. [*To Jeanne*] Come, my dear Sister. Through that little door. There lies your salvation. She looks like a child, doesn't she? Touching. Um. Go along, now. Pretty, pretty. A few steps.

[JEANNE *moves forward towards the small door.*]

Let the power of good propel you. Not much further. There!

[JEANNE *is standing in the doorway staring into the small, dark room – and then at once she is struggling in Barré's arms, a howling animal.*]

BARRÉ [*powerful: confident*]: Help me, Rangier!

[RANGIER *comes to Barré, and together they hold the woman.*]

JEANNE: No, no! I didn't mean it!

BARRÉ: Too late, Asmodeus. Do you expect mercy now, after your blasphemy and filth against Our Lord?

JEANNE: Father! Father Barré, it is I speaking to you now, Sister Jane of the Angels –

BARRÉ: Ah, Asmodeus, you spoke with many voices.

JEANNE: But it's I, Father. Beloved Mother of this dear convent, protector of little children –

BARRÉ: Silence, beast! Let's get her in there, Rangier. Are you ready, Adam?

ADAM[*from within*]: Quite ready.

[BARRÉ *and* RANGIER *carry the struggling woman into the room. The door slams shut.* MIGNON, *left alone, gets down on his knees and begins to pray.*

There is a scream from JEANNE *inside the room: it dissolves into sobs and laughter.* MIGNON *prays louder. His empty, excited little voice ascends to nothingness.*]

[D'ARMAGNAC, DE CERISAY, *and* GRANDIER *move into the foreground.*]

DE CERISAY: The devil, it seems, departed from the woman at two o'clock precisely.

D'ARMAGNAC: What about the others?

DE CERISAY: The Fathers are working on them now.

D'ARMAGNAC: Same method?

DE CERISAY: No. It seems that after the Prioress more normal methods of exorcism are proving successful. A little holy water – applied externally – a few prayers, and the devils go.

D'ARMAGNAC: Then we can hope for some peace.

DE CERISAY: I don't know.

D'ARMAGNAC: Can't you do something if it starts again? As Magistrate, I'd say such goings-on constitute a civil disorder.

DE CERISAY: I saw Barré and Rangier the other day and questioned the legality of their methods. Next time the convent door was shut in my face. I put myself in a difficult position if I use force against priests. They've asked me to be present at an interrogation of Sister Jane. I'm on my way there now.

D'ARMAGNAC [*to Grandier*]: You know your name is constantly being mentioned in this affair.

GRANDIER: Yes, sir.

D'ARMAGNAC: Wouldn't it be a good thing to take steps to clear yourself?

DE CERISAY: Have you offended this woman in some way?

GRANDIER: I don't know how that's possible. I've never seen her.

DE CERISAY: Then why has she chosen you as the devilish perpetrator?

GRANDIER: You look frightened, De Cerisay. Forgive me.

D'ARMAGNAC: You're the one who should be frightened, Father. There was a case some years ago – I forget the man's name –

GRANDIER: I don't, poor devil. There have been many cases, sir.

D'ARMAGNAC: You're in danger.

GRANDIER: Of death? But surely not by a farce such as the convent's putting on. Come, sir, death must be more magnificent, more significant for a man of my kind.

D'ARMAGNAC: How did these other men end?

GRANDIER: At the stake. But they were ridiculous and obscure. Proper matter for sacrifice, that's all.

DE CERISAY: D'Armagnac and I will give you any help we can, Father.

GRANDIER: Can't I talk either of you out of this? When I came here this morning I heard the stories on the streets. I laughed. I thought you'd be doing the same. Is the possession genuine?

DE CERISAY: Not from the evidence I have. As I say, I shall see the woman today. I'll let you know what happens. But you haven't answered my question. Why should it be you?

GRANDIER: Secluded women. They give themselves to God, but something remains which cries out to be given to Man. With the truly pure in heart it can be given in the form of charity, but for the weaker members it is not so easy. It's sad. Very sad, indeed, when you think about it. Imagine being awakened in the night by a quite innocent dream. A dream of your childhood, or of a friend not seen for many years, or even the vision of a good meal. Now, this is a sin. And so you must take up your little whip and scourge your body. We call that discipline. But pain is sensuality, and in its vortex spin images of horror and lust. My beloved Sister in Jesus seems to have fixed her mind on me. There is no reason, De Cerisay. A dropped handkerchief, a scribbled note, a piece of gossip. Any of these things found in the desert of mind and body caused by continual prayer can bring hope. And with hope comes love. And, as we all know, with love comes hate. So I possess this woman. God help her in her terror and unhappiness. God help her.

[*To D'Armagnac*] Now, sir, the business I called on. I've the new plans for your garden summer-house. Will you come and see them? I've revised and modified the frivolity of the design. As you wished.

[GRANDIER *and* D'ARMAGNAC *go.* DE CERISAY *stares after them for a moment, and then moves on to enter –*]

[*A high-ceilinged room, furnished with two small beds. One is occupied by* JEANNE. BARRÉ, RANGIER, *and* MIGNON *are present. Also* ADAM *and* MANNOURY. *A* CLERK *sits writing.*]

BARRÉ: Dear Sister in Christ, I must question you further.

JEANNE: Yes, Father.

BARRÉ: Do you remember the first time your thoughts were turned to these evil things?

JEANNE: Very well.

BARRÉ: Tell us.

JEANNE: I was walking in the garden. I stopped. Lying at my feet was a stick of hawthorn. I was sinfully possessed by anger, for that very morning I'd had cause to admonish two of the Sisters for neglecting their duties in the garden. I picked up the unsightly thing in rage. It must have been thorned, for blood ran from my body. Seeing the blood, I was filled with tenderness.

RANGIER: But this revelation may have come from a very different source.

BARRÉ: All the same – [*To the clerk*] Are you getting this down?

JEANNE: There was another time.

BARRÉ: Tell us.

JEANNE: A day or two later. It was a beautiful morning. I'd had a night of dreamless sleep. On the threshold of my room lay a bunch of roses. I picked them up and tucked them into my belt. Suddenly, I was seized by a violent trembling in my right arm. And a great knowledge of love. This persisted throughout my orisons. I was unable to put my mind to anything. It was entirely filled with the representation of a man which had been deeply and inwardly impressed upon me.

BARRÉ: Do you know who sent those flowers?

JEANNE [*long silence: quietly*]: Grandier. Grandier.

BARRÉ: What is his rank?

JEANNE: Priest.

BARRÉ: Of what church?

JEANNE: Saint Peter's.

[BARRÉ *turns to stare in silence at De Cerisay.*]

DE CERISAY [*quietly*]: This is nothing.

[BARRÉ *turns back to Jeanne.*]

BARRÉ: We are unconvinced, my dear Sister. And if our conviction remains untouched I do not have to remind you that you face eternal damnation.

[JEANNE *suddenly throws herself across the bed: she utters grunts like a small pig: she grinds her teeth: she disorders the bed. The men draw back from her.* JEANNE *sits upright, staring at them.*]

BARRÉ [*with great urgency*]: Speak! Speak!

JEANNE: It ... was ... night. Day's done!

BARRÉ: Yes?

JEANNE: I had tied back my hair, and scrubbed my face. Back to childhood, eh? Poor Jane. Grown woman. Made for – for....

BARRÉ: Go on.

JEANNE: He came to me.

BARRÉ: Name him!

JEANNE [*at once*]: Grandier! Grandier! The beautiful, golden lion entered my room, smiling.

BARRÉ: Was he alone?

JEANNE: No. Six of his creatures were with him.

BARRÉ: Then?

JEANNE: He took me gently in his arms and carried me to the chapel. His creatures each took one of my beloved sisters.

BARRÉ: What took place?

JEANNE [*smiling*]: Oh, my dear Father, think of our little chapel, so simple, so unadorned. That night it was a place of luxury and scented heat. Let me tell you. It was full of laughter and music. There were velvets, silks, metals, and the wood wasn't scrubbed, no, not at all. Yes, and there was food. High animal flesh, and wine, heavy, like the fruit from the East. I'd read about it all. How we stuffed ourselves.

DE CERISAY: This is an innocent vision of hell.

BARRÉ: Ssh! Go on.

JEANNE: I forgot. We were beautifully dressed. I wore my clothes as if they were part of my body. Later, when I was naked, I fell among the thorns. Yes, there were thorns strewn on the floor. I fell among them. Come here.

[*She beckons to* BARRÉ, *who leans towards her. She whispers and then laughs.*]

BARRÉ [*bleakly*]: She says that she and her sisters were compelled to form themselves into an obscene altar, and were worshipped.

JEANNE: Again.

[*Again she whispers: laughs.*]

BARRÉ: She says demons tended Grandier, and her beloved sisters incited her. You'll understand what I mean, gentlemen.

[JEANNE *again draws Barré to her. She whispers frantically, and gradually her words become audible.*]

JEANNE: ... and so we vanquished God from his house. He fled in horror at the senses fixed in men by another hand. Free of Him, we celebrated His departure again and again. [*She lies back.*] To one who has known what I have known, God is dead. I have found peace.

[*Silence.* MIGNON *has fallen on his knees and is praying.* BARRÉ *takes De Cerisay by the arm. As they speak they will move far from Jeanne and the others.*]

BARRÉ: This was an innocent woman.

DE CERISAY: That was no devil. She spoke with her own voice. The voice of an unhappy woman, that's all.

BARRÉ: But the degraded imagination and filthy language she used in other depositions. These cannot spring unaided from a cloistered woman. She is a pupil.

DE CERISAY: Of Grandier?

BARRÉ: Yes.

DE CERISAY: But the man swears he's never been in the place.

BARRÉ: Not in his own person.

DE CERISAY: There must be some way of proving what she says. Will you let my people into the house? They will conduct an investigation on a police level.

BARRÉ: Proof? Three of the Sisters have made statements saying that they have undergone copulation with demons and been deflowered. Mannoury has examined them, and it's true that none of them is intact.

DE CERISAY: My dear Father, I don't want to offend your susceptibilities, but we all know about the sentimental attachments which go on between the young women in these places.

BARRÉ: You don't wish to be convinced.

DE CERISAY: I do. Very much. One way or another.

[DE CERISAY goes. BARRÉ turns. MANNOURY and ADAM are approaching.]

ADAM: Well, there, now.

MANNOURY: Fascinating.

ADAM: Unusual.

MANNOURY: Must say. Hell can't be as dull as some people make out. Haha! What?

ADAM: Such things.

MANNOURY: You know, I think a privately printed testament of this case might have quite a sale. Shall we write it up?

ADAM: Let's.

[They have approached Barré.]

BARRÉ: Have you examined her?

MANNOURY: Yes. I'll let you have my report later.

BARRÉ: Can you give me anything to go on, meantime?

MANNOURY: As a professional man –

ADAM: He speaks for me.

MANNOURY: I don't like to commit myself.

BARRÉ: Even so –

MANNOURY: Well, let's put it this way. There's been hanky-panky.

BARRÉ: Don't mince words. There's been fornication!

MANNOURY: Rather!

BARRÉ: Lust! She's been had!

ADAM: I'll say.

BARRÉ: Thank you, gentlemen. That's all I need. Look.

[They are silent. GRANDIER is walking in the distance. BARRÉ, MANNOURY, and ADAM go.

GRANDIER approaches. PHILLIPE comes quickly to him.]

PHILLIPE: They said you were at the Governor's house.

GRANDIER: I've just come from there. What's the matter?

PHILLIPE: I want to know. Was I restless last night? I had to leave you before it was light. I went as quietly as I could. Did I disturb you? It's important that I should know.

GRANDIER: I can't remember. Why is it important?

PHILLIPE: You can't remember.

[*She gives a sudden, startling, harsh laugh.*]

GRANDIER: Walk to the church with me.

PHILLIPE: No.

GRANDIER: Very well.

PHILLIPE: There's no need to go into the confessional to say what I have to tell you. I'm pregnant.

[*Silence.*]

GRANDIER: So it ends.

PHILLIPE: I'm frightened.

GRANDIER: Of course. How can I own the child?

PHILLIPE: I'm very frightened.

GRANDIER: And there was such bravery in love, wasn't there, Phillipe? All through the summer nights. How unafraid we were each time we huddled down together. We laughed as we roused the animal. Remember? Now it has devoured us.

PHILLIPE: Help me.

GRANDIER: And we were to have been each other's salvation. Did I really believe it was possible?

PHILLIPE: I love you.

GRANDIER: Yes, I did believe it. I remember leaving you one day – you had been unusually adroit –

PHILLIPE: O God!

GRANDIER: I was filled with that indecent confidence which comes after perfect coupling. And as I went I thought – yes, solemnly I thought – the body can transcend its purpose. It can become a thing of such purity that it can be worshipped to the limits of imagination. Anything is allowed. All is right. And such perfection makes for an understanding of the hideous state of existence.

PHILLIPE: Touch me.

GRANDIER: But what is it now? An egg. A thing of weariness, loathing, and sickness. So it ends.

PHILLIPE: Where is love?

GRANDIER: Where, indeed? Go to your father. Tell him the truth. Let him find some good man. They exist.

PHILLIPE: Help me.

GRANDIER: How can I help you? Take my hand. There. Like touching the dead, isn't it? Good-bye. Phillipe.

[GRANDIER *goes*.]

[*The pharmacy.* ADAM, MANNOURY, *and* FATHER MIGNON. *There is a harsh cry from* FATHER BARRÉ *as he appears at the top of the stairway. He moves like a drunken man. The others scatter in alarm.*]

BARRÉ: I was denied entrance to the convent tonight. By armed guards.

MIGNON: My God, my God, what's wrong?

BARRÉ: The Archbishop has issued an ordinance against further exorcism or investigation.

MIGNON: Never!

BARRÉ: It was done at the request of De Cerisay and D'Armagnac. What's more, the Archbishop's personal physician – that rationalist fool! – got hold of the women without my knowledge. He examined them, and gave it as his opinion that there was no genuine possession.

MIGNON: What shall we do? Oh, what shall we do?

[BARRÉ *comes down into the room.*]

BARRÉ: De Cerisay sees it as an act of justice. He doesn't understand that such things play straight into the hands of the devil. Allow reasonable doubt for a man's sin, and the devil snaps it up. [*He shouts wearily*] There can be no reasonable doubt in sin. All or nothing!

MIGNON: Of course. Of course. Justice has nothing to do with salvation. Sit down. Sit down.

BARRÉ: My life's work is threatened by a corrupt archbishop, a liberal doctor, and an ignorant lawyer. Ah, gentlemen, there'll be happiness in hell tonight.

[*Silence.*]

MANNOURY: Are we done for, then?

ADAM: Seems so.

MANNOURY: All up.

ADAM: Dear me.

MANNOURY: Pity.

MIGNON: Let us pray.

ADAM: I beg your pardon?

MIGNON: Let us pray.

ADAM: What for?

MIGNON: Well, let me think –

ADAM: Right you are.

MIGNON: I know!

ADAM: Yes?

MIGNON: Let us pray that the Archbishop has a diabolic vision. . . .

BARRÉ [to Mannoury]: I shall go back to my parish.

MIGNON [to Adam]: . . . of a particularly horrible nature. . . .

BARRÉ [to Mannoury]: There's work for me there.

MIGNON [to Adam]: He's an old man, too. Perhaps we can frighten him to death.

BARRÉ: Be quiet, Mignon. You rave.

MIGNON: Don't leave us.

BARRÉ: I must.

MIGNON: You're naturally a little depressed by this setback. But we'll find a way.

BARRÉ: No. The Archbishop's ordinance has made evil impossible in this place. For the moment. But the ordinance doesn't apply in my parish, and you can be sure that Satan is trumpeting there. I must answer the call.

MIGNON: We shall miss you very much.

BARRÉ: My dear friend, a whisper from hell and I shall be back.

[D'ARMAGNAC *and* DE CERISAY *at a table.* GRANDIER *formally approaches them.*]

GRANDIER: I believe I must thank you, De Cerisay, for having this persecution stopped. Very well. I do so now.

DE CERISAY: I acted for you, Father, but not entirely on your behalf.

The circus up at the convent was beginning to attract a lot of unwelcome attention to the town. It's my job to keep some sort of order in the place.

D'ARMAGNAC: You don't make it easy for your friends, Grandier. Trincant has told me about his daughter. You have your whores. Why did you have to do this?

GRANDIER: It seemed a way.

D'ARMAGNAC: A way to what?

GRANDIER: All worldly things have a single purpose for a man of my kind. Politics, power, the senses, riches, pride, and authority. I choose them with the same care that you, sir, select a weapon. But my intention is different. I need to turn them against myself.

D'ARMAGNAC: To bring about your end?

GRANDIER: Yes. I have a great need to be united with God. Living has drained the need for life from me. My exercise of the senses has flagged to total exhaustion. I am a dead man, compelled to live.

D'ARMAGNAC: You disgust me. This is a sickness.

GRANDIER: No, sir. It is the meaning and purpose.

D'ARMAGNAC: I'm not one for sophisticated argument, but tell me something. I can see that the obvious short cut, self-destruction, is not possible. But isn't creating the circumstances for your death, which is what you seem to be doing, equally sinful?

GRANDIER: Leave me some hope.

D'ARMAGNAC: The hope that God will smile upon your efforts to create an enemy so malignant as to bring you down, and so send you – up?

GRANDIER: Yes.

D'ARMAGNAC: I've a letter here from Paris. It should make you happy. By supporting me in this matter of the fortifications you have made an excellent enemy. Richelieu. So far the King is standing with me against the Cardinal. But should the King fail or falter this city will come down, and you will probably have your wish, for you are deeply implicated. All the same, I shall continue to protect you from what I think to be a most dreadful course, and a most blasphemous philosophy.

GRANDIER: It is what I seek, sir. Don't hold it from me. Think what it must be like. I reach the end of a long day. I am warm, fed and satisfied. I go home. On the way I stare at a stranger across the street, perhaps a child. I greet a friend. I lie looking down on the face of a sleeping woman. I see these with wonder and hope, and ask myself: Is this, perhaps, the means to my end? And I am denied.

[GRANDIER *suddenly hides his face in his hands.*]

O my God, my God! All things fail me.

D'ARMAGNAC: Afraid, Grandier?

GRANDIER: Yes. Yes. Yes. Forsaken.

[*The convent garden.* JEANNE *and* CLAIRE *are sitting on a bench.* LOUISE *and* GABRIELLE *are on the ground at their feet. Two lay sisters stand near-by. Great stillness.*]

LOUISE: What shall we do, Mother?

JEANNE: Do?

LOUISE: People are taking their children away from us.

JEANNE: Who can blame them?

CLAIRE: There's no one to help. We have to do all the housework ourselves. It's very tiring.

JEANNE [*sudden laughter*]: Why don't you ask the devils to lend a hand?

CLAIRE: Mother!

GABRIELLE: I've taken in a little washing and sewing. I hope you don't mind, Mother.

JEANNE: Sensible girl. When hell fails to provide one can fall back on hard work, eh?

GABRIELLE: I know you've never liked us to do menial tasks.

JEANNE: I said it diminished women in our vocation. [*She laughs*] Did I say that?

GABRIELLE: Yes.

[*Silence.*]

LOUISE: Mother –

JEANNE: Yes, child?

LOUISE: Why has the Archbishop forbidden Father Barré to come and see us any more?

JEANNE: Because the Archbishop has been told that we are foolish and deluded women.

LOUISE: Mother –

JEANNE: Yes?

LOUISE: Have we sinned?

JEANNE: By what we've done?

LOUISE: Yes. Have we mocked God?

JEANNE: It was not the intention.

But to make a mockery of Man. That's a different matter! For what a splendid creature he makes to be fooled. He might have been created for no other purpose. With his head in the air, besotted with his own achievement, he asks to be tripped. Deep in the invention of mumbo-jumbo to justify his existence, he is deaf to laughter. With no eyes for anything but himself, he's blind to the gesture of ridicule made in front of his face.

So, drunk, deaf, and blind, he goes on. The perfect subject for the practical joke. And that, my sisters, is where the children of misfortune – like me – play a part. We do not mock our beloved Father in Heaven. Our laughter is kept for His wretched and sinful children who get above their station, and come to believe they have some other purpose in this world than to die.

After the delusions of power come the delusions of love. When men cannot destroy they start to believe they can be saved by creeping into a fellow human being. And so perpetuating themselves. Love me, they say over and over again, love me. Cherish me. Defend me. Save me. They say it to their wives, their whores, their children, and some to the whole human race. Never to God. These are probably the most ridiculous of all, and most worthy of derision. For they do not understand the glory of mortality, the purpose of man: loneliness and death.

Let us go in.

On the fortifications. Night.

[D'ARMAGNAC *and* DE CERISAY *enter from different ways. They are wrapped against the rain, and they shout above the wind.*]

DE CERISAY: D'Armagnac, are you there?

D'ARMAGNAC: The horseman fell at the gate. They found these papers, scattered.

DE CERISAY: What are they?

D'ARMAGNAC: The king has gone back on his word. Richelieu has won. The town fortifications are to come down. It is to be a little place. I shall have no more power than a tradesman.

[GRANDIER *has appeared far below them.*]

D'ARMAGNAC: Is that the priest?

DE CERISAY: Yes. [*He shouts*] Grandier!

D'ARMAGNAC: He will suffer. [*He shouts*] Grandier!

GRANDIER: What's the matter?

D'ARMAGNAC: The Cardinal has moved against us.

DE CERISAY: The King has lost his nerve.

D'ARMAGNAC: All this is to come down.

DE CERISAY: You are mentioned –

D'ARMAGNAC: We shan't stand here much longer.

DE CERISAY: – named for your resistance.

D'ARMAGNAC: You are in danger.

GRANDIER: Thank God.

D'ARMAGNAC: What do you say? I can't hear you. Are you mad? Is he mad? Let's go down.

[D'ARMAGNAC *and* DE CERISAY *go.* GRANDIER *kneels. The wind and rain sweep about him.*]

GRANDIER: Heavenly Father, You have restored strength to my enemies, and hope to Your sinful child. I give myself into the hands of the world secure in the faith of Your mysterious ways. You have made the way possible. I understand, and I accept. But You work beyond a curtain of majesty. I am afraid to raise my eyes, and see. Reveal Yourself. Reveal Yourself.

[*His voice is lost.*]

Stillness.

[DE LAUBARDEMONT *and* MIGNON.]

LAUBARDEMONT: We shall have to act quickly.

MIGNON: Yes. Yes.

LAUBARDEMONT: I must start for Paris tonight.

MIGNON: So soon?

LAUBARDEMONT: Can it be done in the time?

MIGNON: We must try.

LAUBARDEMONT: Sort out your thoughts on the subject.

MIGNON: I've been reading it up. There was the appalling Gauffridy case. In Marseilles, twenty years ago. The priest bewitched and debauched several Ursulines –

LAUBARDEMONT: We don't need precedents. We need results. Here and now. Call them in.

[MIGNON *leads* JEANNE *forward. They are followed by* CLAIRE, LOUISE, GABRIELLE, *and the two lay sisters.* DE LAUBARDEMONT *stands apart.*]

MIGNON: My beloved sisters in Christ, I am only a foolish old man who hasn't much time left on this earth to do God's will –

LAUBARDEMONT: Well then, get on with it.

MIGNON: My children, do you trust me?

JEANNE: Of course, Father.

MIGNON: As your spiritual instructor, do you trust me?

JEANNE: Always.

MIGNON: Very well. I am deeply disturbed by this sudden cessation of diabolical manifestations in you. Dreadful stories are being put about in the town and farther afield. They say you were not truly possessed by demons, but that you were playing parts, making a mockery both of your sublime state, and your superiors in the Church.

JEANNE: That is what we were told by the Archbishop's doctor. He talked about hysteria. The cry from the womb.

MIGNON: But as a good woman it was up to you to prove him wrong. Oh, assure me that it was true. You were possessed.

JEANNE: It was true. We were possessed by hell.

MIGNON: And the instigator, the foul magician –

JEANNE: Grandier! Grandier!

THE SISTERS: Grandier! Grandier!

MIGNON: But now I fear for you in another way. The evidence is all against you. The silence of the devils condemns you.

[*Silence.*]

MIGNON: You see, they do not speak. There is no proof of your virtue. Ah, my sisters, this stillness presages your eternal damnation. I fear for you. I dread. Forsaken by God and forsaken by the Devil you stand in the most desolate limbo for ever. I beg you, consider your position.

JEANNE: Father, we are afraid.

MIGNON: And well you may be, my child.

JEANNE: Don't leave us!

MIGNON: What else can I do? I will pray for you.

[MIGNON *turns away towards De Laubardemont.*]

LEVIATHAN [*speaking through Jeanne*]: May I put in a word?

MIGNON: God be praised! What is your name?

LEVIATHAN: Leviathan.

MIGNON: Where are you lodged, unholy thing?

LEVIATHAN: In the lady's forehead.

BEHERIT [*speaking through Jeanne*]: I am in the woman's stomach. My name is Beherit.

ISACAARON [*speaking through Jeanne*]: Isacaaron speaking. From under the last rib on the left.

ELYMI [*speaking through Claire*]: I am here. [*Another voice*] And I.

EAZAZ [*speaking through Louise*]: And I. [*Another voice*] And I am here.

[*Clamour of diabolical voices. Derisive laughter: grunts, squeals, howls.*]

[DE LAUBARDEMONT *moves to Mignon.*]

LAUBARDEMONT: Well done. Barré must be got back from Chinon. He must begin exorcism at once. In public. A representative of the Court will attend. See to it.

[DE LAUBARDEMONT *goes.* MIGNON *runs forward, shouting:*]

MIGNON: Open the gates! Open the gates!

[*A crowd floods into the palace. Men and women of the town. The Sewerman. Adam and Mannoury. Trincant. A dwarf. A creature. A trumpeter. Laughing women. Dogs. Children climb to points of vantage and look down.*

Below: the Sisters laboriously perform their antics. JEANNE *is on her hands and knees, snuffling the ground.* CLAIRE *has the skirts of her habit over her head, exposing herself in a dull promenade.* LOUISE *and* GABRIELLE *are locked in an embrace, making a beast. And from all of them come the hoarse, masculine cries of diabolical voices: inarticulate, whining, commanding, a dissonance of obscenity.*

The townspeople are very amused. They point out especially delectable gestures to each other. Some urge the Sisters to greater excesses. A lay sister, agile as a tumbler, is applauded. A party has settled down to eat and drink and watch.

Thunder of bells from Saint Peter's spire.

BARRÉ *enters in glory. He carries a gold, jewelled crucifix, which twists and glitters in his nervous hands.* RANGIER *comes from another way.* THREE CARMELITES *from another.* MIGNON *approaches them. All meet.*]

BARRÉ: I have been sent for.

MIGNON: Yes. Yes.

BARRÉ: The triumph of good!

MIGNON: It is. Yes.

BARRÉ: De Cerisay –

MIGNON: Bah!

BARRÉ: D'Armagnac –

MIGNON: Filth!

BARRÉ: Are they here?

MIGNON: No.

RANGIER: Dare not show their faces.

BARRÉ: The triumph of good! I am in love with the words. I must say them again. It is the triumph of good!

[*A* LAY SISTER *is scrabbling at Barré's feet.*]

BARRÉ: Peace, Sister.

[BARRÉ *lays on the crucifix. It has no effect, so he savagely kicks the woman aside.*]

RANGIER: The King's man is here.

BARRÉ: Who have they sent?

RANGIER: Prince Henri de Condé.

BARRÉ: One of the blood!

RANGIER: No less.

BARRÉ: Excellent. [*He shouts*] Constables!

[ARCHERS *enter, and press back the crowd. Near silence. The archers range themselves against the crowd, isolating the Sisters.*]

LEVIATHAN [*speaking through Jeanne in a loud voice*]: Where is the enemy?

BARRÉ [*in great exaltation*]: I am here.

LEVIATHAN: Who are you?

BARRÉ: I am only a humble man. But I speak for the Lord Jesus Christ.

[*A terrible scream from* LEVIATHAN. *Babel of voices from the other devils. Delight of the crowd.*]

BARRÉ: Mignon: water, a missal, the stoles, the ciborium, the saint's fingernail, the piece of the true cross. Let me have them all.

MIGNON: God's armoury! It's here.

[THE CARMELITES *have brought forward and are arranging the relics.*]

BARRÉ: I must prepare myself.

[BARRÉ *falls on his knees: prays. The crowd is silent.*

HENRI DE CONDÉ *enters. This exquisite and handsome sodomite is supported by painted boys. He regards Barré for a moment: speaks.*]

DE CONDÉ: I don't wish, my dear Father, to disturb your devotions, and I would never suggest that a member of the royal family took precedence over God . . . all the same. . . .

BARRÉ [*he has got to his feet*]: I'm at your service, sir.

DE CONDÉ: Thank you. These are the raving women, I take it.

BARRÉ: All of them are possessed by one or more devils.

DE CONDÉ: And the instigator is a man of your own people?

BARRÉ: A priest, yes.

DE CONDÉ: You don't seem amused.

BARRÉ: Amused?

DE CONDÉ: Never mind.

BARRÉ: If you'll take your place, sir, I'll proceed.

DE CONDÉ: Very well.

[DE CONDÉ *goes to a prepared part near by, and sits overlooking the scene. The boys play around him like butterflies.*

The Sisters are now in an untidy heap, exhausted, mere rubbish on the ground. BARRÉ *is robing and preparing himself with the help of* MIGNON *and* RANGIER.

DE CONDÉ *draws one of the boys to him.*]

DE CONDÉ: These are women, darling. Look well. Vomit, if you wish. Man is born of them. Gross things. Nasty. Breeding ground. Eggs hatch out in hot dung. Don't wrinkle your little nose, pet.

Take this scent. Some men love them. The priest, Grandier, for example. He's picked the gobbets from the stew. He's –

[DE CONDÉ *whispers in the boy's ear. The child's eyes widen.* DE CONDÉ *laughs.*

BARRÉ *has come forward.*]

BARRÉ With your permission, sir, I'll begin.

DE CONDÉ: Please do so.

BARRÉ: But first I have a declaration to make. This, sir – [*he holds up the ciborium*] – contains the holy eucharist.

[BARRÉ *places the ciborium on his head and kneels.*]

BARRÉ: Heavenly Father, I pray that I may be confounded and that the maledictions of Dathan and Abiram may fall upon me, if I have sinned or been at fault in any way in this affair.

DE CONDÉ: A very commendable gesture. Bravo!

[BARRÉ *rises, and goes towards Jeanne.*]

BARRÉ: Leviathan! Leviathan!

LEVIATHAN [*speaking through Jeanne: sleepy*]: Go away.

BARRÉ: Rouse yourself.

LEVIATHAN [*speaking through Jeanne*]: You bore me.

BARRÉ: In the name of Our Lord Jesus Christ –

LEVIATHAN [*speaking through Jeanne*]: Don't keep bringing that impostor's name into the conversation.

BARRÉ: It disturbs you, eh?

LEVIATHAN [*speaking through Jeanne*]: I don't tolerate fools gladly. All that talk about love. It has a softening effect on the character. And what's more, the fellow wasn't a gentleman.

DE CONDÉ: Reverend Father –

BARRÉ: Yes, sir?

DE CONDÉ: I notice that you don't speak to these creatures in Latin, as is usual. Why is that?

BARRÉ: They're not conversant with the language. You'll understand, sir, that there are uneducated as well as educated devils.

DE CONDÉ: Quite.

LEVIATHAN [*speaking through Jeanne*]: I haven't travelled much.

[*Deep laughter, taken up by the other devils.*]

BARRÉ: Listen, Filth –

LEVIATHAN [*speaking through Jeanne*]: You're always so personal.

BARRÉ: I'm going to speak a name to you. Grandier!

LEVIATHAN [*speaking through Jeanne*]: Oh, that's a sweet noise. Do it again.

BARRÉ: Grandier!

LEVIATHAN [*speaking through Jeanne*]: Yes, I like that.

BARRÉ: You know him?

LEVIATHAN [*speaking through Jeanne*]: We serve him. Don't we?

ZABULON [*speaking through Claire*]: Yes.

ISACAARON [*speaking through Jeanne*]: We do. We do.

BEHERIT [*speaking through Jeanne*]: Grandier! Grandier!

EAZAZ [*speaking through Louise*]: Oh, my love, my darling, hold me, take – take – aah! –

ZABULON [*speaking through Claire*]: Grandier! Grandier!

BEHERIT [*speaking through Jeanne*]: Grandier! Grandier!

EAZAZ [*speaking through Louise*]: Grandier! Grandier!

LEVIATHAN [*speaking through Jeanne*]: Grandier! Grandier!

[*Pandemonium.*]

BARRÉ: Let one speak for all!

[RANGIER *and* MIGNON *move in among the Sisters scattering holy water. The screams and shouts gradually die away.*]

DE CONDÉ: Father, may I question these things?

BARRÉ: By all means, sir.

[RANGIER, MIGNON, *and the* CARMELITES *hustle the wretched Sisters forward until they are ranged in front of* DE CONDÉ, *who stares down at them.*]

DE CONDÉ [*addressing the Sisters*]: Gentlemen. You have given us your views on the character and worth of our blessed Saviour. [*Hissing from the devils.*] Which of you will answer me on a matter of merely national importance?

BEHERIT [*speaking through Jeanne*]: I'll try.

DE CONDÉ: You will? Good. What's your name?

BEHERIT [*speaking through Jeanne*]: Beherit.

DE CONDÉ: Well, Beherit, tell me this. What's your opinion of His Majesty, the King of France, and his adviser, the great Cardinal? [*Silence.*]

DE CONDÉ: Come now, as a political devil you must have some

views. Or do you find yourself in the quandary of most Oppositions? Having to speak with more than one voice.

BEHERIT [*speaking through Jeanne: muttering*]: Don't understand.

DE CONDÉ: You understand very well. If you, Beherit, praise the King and his minister you condone, and imply that their policy is hellish. If you, Sister Jane, dispraise them, you run the risk of treason against powerful men. I sympathize with your difficulty. Father Barré –

[BARRÉ *comes forward, as* DE CONDÉ *takes a small box from one of the boys.*]

DE CONDÉ: I have here a relic of the most holy worth. It has been lent to me by a great cathedral of the north. I feel the bits and pieces which you've assembled from local sources may not be powerful enough to dispel these impudent demons. So why not try this?

BARRÉ: What is in the box, sir?

DE CONDÉ: A phial of the blood of our Lord Jesus Christ.

[BARRÉ *reverently takes the box in his hands: kisses it.*]

DE CONDÉ: Tell me, Father, what effect would the close proximity of this relic have on devils such as these?

BARRÉ: It would put them to flight.

DE CONDÉ: At once?

BARRÉ: Immediately. I couldn't guarantee, of course, that when the relic was removed they wouldn't return.

DE CONDÉ: Of course not. That would be asking too much. Would you like to try?

[BARRÉ *goes towards Jeanne.*]

BARRÉ: In the name of our Heavenly Father, I conjure thee, most frightful beings, by this most sacred substance, to depart!

[BARRÉ *applies the box to Jeanne's forehead. At once, in a number of horrible screams, the devils leave her body by way of her distorted mouth. Silence. Then* JEANNE *rises to her full height. She speaks calmly, with the voice of a young girl, in her own person.*]

JEANNE: I am free. I am free.

[*She goes to* DE CONDÉ, *kneels, and kisses his hands.*]

DE CONDÉ: I'm very pleased to have been of some service, madam.

BARRÉ [*triumphantly*]: You see!

[DE CONDÉ *takes the box from* BARRÉ, *opens it, and holds it upside down: it is empty.*]

DE CONDÉ: You see, Father?

BARRÉ [*after a moment*]: Ah, sir, what sort of trick have you played on us?

DE CONDÉ: Reverend Sir, what sort of trick are you playing on *us*?

[*Silence between the two men,* DE CONDÉ *smiling: hushed crowd: terrified women.*

The moment is broken by MIGNON. *He starts to run in tiny circles, holding his little head in his hands.*]

LEVIATHAN [*speaking through Mignon*]: Fooled again!

BEHERIT [*speaking through Mignon*]: Make way!

[MIGNON *cries out, as Beherit forces an entry.*

RANGIER *suddenly begins to neigh like a horse, and high-stepping in fine style, proceeds to exhibit. The* SISTERS *begin to grunt and groan in sympathy, one of them offering herself obscenely to* RANGIER, *who mounts. Only* JEANNE *stands alone and still. A* BOY *by De Condé begins to laugh in a ringing, hysterical way. There is a disturbance in the crowd. Two women have become possessed.*

BARRÉ *stares about him in horror. Then, wielding the crucifix like a club, he plunges among the devils, laying about him.*]

BARRÉ: We are besieged! Clear the place at once!

[*The* CARMELITES *hurry away the Sisters, and the dancing Mignon and Rangier. The guards disperse the crowd.* BARRÉ *is passing among the people, laying the cross on possessed and unpossessed alike, and shouting:*]

BARRÉ: ... per factorem mundi, per eum qui habet potestatem mittendi te in gehennam, ut ab hoc famulo Dei, qui ad sinum Ecclesiae recurrit, cum metu et exercitu furoris tui festinus discedas.

[RANGIER, MIGNON, *and the* SISTERS *go into the distance, followed by* BARRÉ. *The crowd go yawning home.*

The BOY *standing beside* DE CONDÉ *still laughs himself to tears.*]

DE CONDÉ [*smiling*]: Be quiet, child.

[DE CONDÉ *stares across at* JEANNE, *who stands alone, some way off.*]

DE CONDÉ: Mother, I am often accused of libertinage. Very well. Being born so high I have to stoop lower than other men. Soiled, dabbling myself, I know what I am doing and what I must give. I'd say you'll have your wish about this man Grandier, seeing the way the world goes. But do you know what you must give? [*Casually*] Your immortal soul to damnation in an infinite desert of eternal bestiality.

[DE CONDÉ *and the* BOYS *go.*

CLAIRE *and* LOUISE *enter apart from* JEANNE. *Gay voices.*]

CLAIRE: I was never any good at prayer.

LOUISE: Neither was I.

CLAIRE: We could have spent our lives on our knees.

LOUISE: And no one would have heard of us.

CLAIRE: They're selling my picture in the town.

LOUISE: We're famous all over France.

CLAIRE: Are you still worried about being damned?

LOUISE: Not any more.

CLAIRE: Not since your beautiful legs have been so admired.

LOUISE: Sweetheart, what do you think of in chapel now?

CLAIRE: This and that. New ways.

LOUISE: To amuse?

CLAIRE: Yes. [*A bell.*] Come on.

[*Laughing, they go.* JEANNE *stands silent for a moment. Then:*]

LEVIATHAN [*speaking through Jeanne*]: Clear your mind of cant, you absurd little monster.

JEANNE: I'm afraid.

LEVIATHAN [*speaking through Jeanne*]: Nonsense. We'll support you in anything you do.

JEANNE: I wish to be pure.

LEVIATHAN [*speaking through Jeanne*]: There is no such thing.

JEANNE: O God: God, yes, there is.

[*Women's voices are raised from the near-by chapel.*]

LEVIATHAN [*speaking through Jeanne*]: No, there isn't. Now think, my dear. Remember the night-time visions. He and – [*obscene giggles*] – oh, that thing – and you, agape – no, no, my darling, not purity, not even dignity. What are you thinking of? Not only all impure, but all absurd. Remember?

[JEANNE *starts to laugh:* LEVIATHAN *joins her.*
Darkness.]

A Council of State. Night.

> [LOUIS XIII, RICHELIEU, FATHER JOSEPH, *and* LA VRILLIERE, *Secretary of State.*
>
> DE CONDÉ *is apart.*
>
> DE LAUBARDEMONT *comes forward and speaks to the Council. A clerk stands beside him, handing over relevant papers from time to time.*]

LAUBARDEMONT: Your Majesty. Your Eminence. You have asked me to report on the case of possession at Loudun. The man's name is Urbain Grandier.

DE CONDÉ: He is innocent.

> [*Both men speak to the Council.*]

LAUBARDEMONT: I have been advised by priests of the district and by reputable medical men that the possession is genuine.

DE CONDÉ: I have also been there. The man is innocent.

LAUBARDEMONT: Grandier's house has been searched. Various manuscripts have been found. There was a pamphlet written some years ago and directed against Your Eminence. Other papers confirmed Grandier's support of D'Armagnac in his defiant attitude about the fortifications of the town, which has distressed you so much, Your Majesty. There were letters and notebooks of a more personal kind. A treatise on Sacerdotal Celibacy was found. The man seems to have been in love when this was written. It is reported that a mock marriage took place with a daughter of the Public Prosecutor. There were letters from other women, one of which appears to suggest that he has committed the veneric act in church.

DE CONDÉ: For the love of Jesus Christ, if you wish to destroy the man, then destroy him. I'm not here to plead for his life. But your methods are shameful. He deserves better. Any man does. Kill him with power, but don't pilfer his house, and hold evidence of this sort against him. What man could face arraignment on the idiocy of youth, old love letters, and the pathetic objects stuffed in drawers or at the bottom of cupboards, kept for the fear that one day he would need to be reminded that he was once loved? No. Destroy a man for his opposition, his strength, or his majesty. But not for this!

[*Silence.*]

LAUBARDEMONT [*to the Council*]: I should now give you any evidence in the man's favour. . . . [*He is interrupted by a sign from Richelieu.*]

RICHELIEU: The Devil must never be believed, even when he tells the truth.

LAUBARDEMONT: I shall act on your instructions at once.

[DE LAUBARDEMONT *comes forward.* GUARDS *gather about him. They move off.*]

A brilliant morning.

[GRANDIER *comes to the Sewerman, carrying flowers.*]

SEWERMAN: Why, whatever's this?

GRANDIER: I must have picked them somewhere. I can't remember. You have them.

SEWERMAN: Thank you. They smell sweet. Very suitable.

GRANDIER: Can I sit with you?

SEWERMAN: Of course. I've no sins this morning, though. Sorry.

GRANDIER: Let me look at you.

SEWERMAN: Do you like what you see?

GRANDIER: Very much.

SEWERMAN: What's happened? You're drunk with mystery.

GRANDIER: I've been out of the town. An old man was dying. I sat with him for two nights and a day. I was seeing death for the hundredth time. It was an obscene struggle. It always is. Once again a senile, foolish, and sinful old man had left it rather late to come to terms. He held my hand so tightly that I could not move. His grimy face stared up at me in blank surprise at what was happening to him. So I sat there in the rancid smell of the kitchen, while in the darkness the family argued in whispers, between weeping, about how much money there would be under the bed.

He was dirty and old and not very bright. And I loved him so much. I envied him so much, for he was standing on the threshold of everlasting life. I wanted him to turn his face to God, and not peer back through the smoky light, and stare longingly at this mere preliminary. I said to him: Be glad, be glad. But he did not understand.

His spirit weakened at dawn. It could not mount another day. There were cries of alarm from the family. I took out the necessary properties which I travel in this bag. The vulgar little sins were confessed, absolved, and the man could die. He did so. Brutally, holding on to the last. I spoke my usual words to the family, with my priest's face. My duty was done.

But I could not forget my love for the man.

I came out of the house. I thought I'd walk back, air myself after the death cell. I was very tired. I could hear Saint Peter's bell.

The road was dusty. I remembered the day I came here. I was wearing new shoes. They were white with dust. Do you know, I flicked them over with my stole before being received by the bishop. I was vain and foolish, then. Ambitious, too.

I walked on. They were working in the fields and called to me. I remembered how I loved to work with my hands when I was a boy. But my father said it was unsuitable for one of my birth.

I could see my church in the distance. I was very proud, in a humble way. I thought of my love for the beauty of this not very beautiful place. And I remembered night in the building, with the gold, lit by candlelight, against the darkness.

I thought of you. I remembered you as a friend.

I rested. The country was stretched out. Do you know where the rivers join? I once made love there.

Children came past me. Yes, of course, that's where I got the flowers. I didn't pick them. They were given to me.

I watched the children go. Yes, I was very tired. I could see far beyond the point my eyes could see. Castles, cities, mountains, oceans, plains, forests – and –

And then – oh, my son, my son – and then – I want to tell you –

SEWERMAN: Do so. Be calm.

GRANDIER: My son, I – Am I mad?

SEWERMAN: No. Quite sane. Tell me. What did you do?

GRANDIER: I created God!

[Silence.]

GRANDIER: I created Him from the light and the air, from the dust of the road, from the sweat of my hands, from gold, from filth, from the memory of women's faces, from great rivers, from children, from the works of man, from the past, the present, the future, and the unknown. I caused Him to be from fear and despair. I gathered in everything from this mighty act, all I have known, seen, and experienced. My sin, my presumption, my vanity, my love, my hate, my lust. And last I gave myself and so made God. And He was magnificent. For He is all these things.

I was utterly in His presence. I knelt by the road. I took out the bread and the wine. Panem vinum in salutis consecramus hostiam. And in this understanding He gave Himself humbly and faithfully to me, as I had given myself to Him.

[*Silence.*]

SEWERMAN: You've found peace.

GRANDIER: More. I've found meaning.

SEWERMAN: That makes me happy.

GRANDIER: And, my son, I have found reason.

SEWERMAN: And that is sanity.

GRANDIER: I must go now. I must go to worship Him in His house, adore Him in His shrine. I must go to church.

[GRANDIER *moves forward and enters the church.*

SOLDIERS *lounge against the altar.* DE LAUBARDEMONT *comes forward.*]

LAUBARDEMONT: You are forbidden this place.

GRANDIER: Forbidden?

LAUBARDEMONT: You are an impious and libertine priest. You must not enter.

GRANDIER: It is my church! My beloved church!

LAUBARDEMONT: No longer. You're under arrest. Charges will be read. Come with me. Bring him.

[GRANDIER, *between soldiers, is brought from the church into the sunlight,* DE LAUBARDEMONT *leading the way. They pass through the street.*

ADAM, MANNOURY, *and* TRINCANT *lean from an upper window, jeering.*

PHILLIPE TRINCANT, *with a silent old man beside her, watches.*]

RANGIER *and* MIGNON *move in the church with a censer, intoning, exorcizing.*

BARRÉ *is on his knees in the street as* GRANDIER *passes.*

THE SEWERMAN *watches. A crowd of townspeople gather round him, noisy and inquiring.*

And as GRANDIER *moves on, the street and the church are filled with the clamour and laughter of devils, issuing from every mouth. Laughter. Laughter.*]

CURTAIN

ACT THREE

Night.
A cell. Another room above.
> [GRANDIER *alone.*
> *Distant shouts and laughter from an unseen crowd.*
> BONTEMPS, *a gaoler, comes to Grandier.*]

BONTEMPS: Have you slept?

GRANDIER: No. No, the noise. The crowd. Have they slept?

BONTEMPS: Thirty thousand people have come into the town. Where do you expect them to find beds?

GRANDIER: Why should they want to sleep, anyway? Did I, as a child, the night before the treat?

BONTEMPS: They're certainly looking forward to it.

GRANDIER: What? Say it.

BONTEMPS: The execution.

GRANDIER: I haven't been tried yet.

BONTEMPS: All right. Have it your own way. The trial, then.

GRANDIER: Are you a merciful man?

BONTEMPS: Look, this is your system. Just be thankful that you can get men to do the job. Don't ask that they should be humane as well. I came to tell you that you're to be called early. So try and get some sleep.

GRANDIER: Thank you.

BONTEMPS: Is there anything you want? There's not much I can offer.

GRANDIER: Nothing. Nothing.

> [JEANNE *and* FATHER MIGNON.]

JEANNE: Don't go!

MIGNON: It's three o'clock in the morning. I'm an old man. Need sleep.

JEANNE: I don't want to be left alone with him.

MIGNON: With your persecutor? Grandier?

JEANNE: Yes.

MIGNON: He's under close guard.

JEANNE: No. He's here. Within me. Like a child. He never revealed to me what sort of man he was. I knew him to be beautiful. Many said he was clever, and many said he was wicked. But for all his violence to my soul and body he never came to me in anything but love. No, let me speak. He's within me, I say. I'm possessed. But he is still, lying beneath my heart, living through my breath and my blood. And he makes me afraid. Afraid that I may have fallen into the gravest error in this matter.

MIGNON: What do you mean?

JEANNE: Have I been mistaken? Did Satan take on the person of my love, my darling, so as to delude me?

MIGNON: Never. The man is his agent.

JEANNE: I have such a little body. It is a small battleground in which to decide this terrible struggle between good and evil, between love and hate. Was I wrong to allow it?

MIGNON: No, no. Don't you understand? These very thoughts are put in your mind by the forces of dread. It's wrong to believe that Hell always fights with the clamour of arms. It is now, in the small hours, that Satan sends his secret agents, whispering, with their messages of doubt.

JEANNE: I don't know. I don't know. You all speak with so many voices. And I am very tired. [*She cries out*] Father! Father!

[GRANDIER *alone in his cell.*]

GRANDIER: There will be pain. It will kill God. My fear is driving Him out already.

Yes. Yes. We are flies upon the wall. Buzzing in the heat. That's so. That's so. No, no. We're monsters made up in a day. Clay in a baby's hands. Horrible, we should be bottled and hung in the pharmacy. Curiosities, for amusement only.

So. Nothing.

Shall I withstand the pain? Mother, mother, remember my fear! Oh, nothing. This morning on the road. What was that? It was a little delusion of meaning. A trick of the sun, some fatigue of the body, and a man starts to believe that he's immortal. Look at me now. Wringing my hands, trying to convince myself that this flesh and bone is meaningful.

Sad, sad, though, very sad. To make a man see in the morning what the glory might be, and by night to snatch it from him.

Most Heavenly Father, though I struggle in Your arms like a fretful child –

This need to create a meaning. What arrogance it is! Expendable, that's what we are. Nothing proceeding to nothing.

Let me look into this void. Let me look into myself. Is there one thing, past or present, which makes for a purpose? [*Silence.*] Nothing. Nothing.

Who's there?

[FATHER AMBROSE, *an old man, has come in.*]

AMBROSE: My name is Ambrose.

GRANDIER: I know you, Father.

AMBROSE: I was told of your trouble, my son. The night can be very long.

GRANDIER: Yes. Stay with me.

AMBROSE: I thought I might read to you. Or, if you'd like it better, we can pray together.

GRANDIER: No. Help me.

AMBROSE: Let me try.

GRANDIER: They are destroying my faith. By fear and loneliness now. Later, by pain.

AMBROSE: Go to God, my son.

GRANDIER: Nothing going to nothing.

AMBROSE: God is here, and Christ is now.

GRANDIER: Yes. That is my faith. But how can I defend it?

AMBROSE: By remembering the will of God.

GRANDIER: Yes. Yes.

AMBROSE: By remembering that nothing must be asked of him, and nothing refused.

GRANDIER: Yes. But this is all in the books. I've read them, and understood them. And it is not enough. Not enough. Not now.

AMBROSE: God is here, and Christ is here.

GRANDIER: You're an old man. Have you gathered no more than this fustian in all your years? I'm sorry. You came in pure charity. The only one who has done so. I'm sorry.

[AMBROSE *opens a book.*]

AMBROSE: Suffering must be willed, affliction must be willed, humiliation must be willed, and in the act of willing –

GRANDIER: They'll be understood. I know. I know.

AMBROSE: Then you know everything.

GRANDIER: I know nothing. Speak to me as a man, Father. Talk about simple things.

AMBROSE: I came to help you, my son.

GRANDIER: You can help me. By speaking as a man. So shut your books. Forget other men's words. Speak to me.

AMBROSE: Ah, you believe there is some secret in simplicity. I am a simple man, it's true. I've never had any great doubt. Plain and shy, I have been less tempted than others, of course. The devil likes more magnificence than I've ever been able to offer. A peasant boy who clung to the love of God because he was too awkward to ask for the love of man. I'm not a good example, my son. That's why I brought the books.

GRANDIER: You think too little of yourself. What must we give God?

AMBROSE: Ourselves.

GRANDIER: But I am unworthy.

AMBROSE: Have you greatly sinned?

GRANDIER: Greatly.

AMBROSE: Even young girls come to me nowadays and confess things I don't know about. So it's hardly likely that I'll understand the sins of a young man of the world such as you. But let me try.

GRANDIER: There have been women and lust: power and ambition: worldliness and mockery.

AMBROSE: Remember. God is here. You speak before Him. Christ is now. You suffer with Him.

GRANDIER: I dread the pain to come. The humiliation.

AMBROSE: Did you dread the ecstasy of love?

GRANDIER: No.

AMBROSE: Or its humiliation?

GRANDIER: I gloried in it. I have lived by the senses.

AMBROSE: Then die by them.

GRANDIER: What did you say?

AMBROSE: Offer God pain, convulsion, and disgust.

GRANDIER: Yes. Give Him myself.

AMBROSE: Let Him reveal Himself in the only way you can understand.

GRANDIER: Yes! Yes!

AMBROSE: It is all any of us can do. We live a little while, and in that little while we sin. We go to Him as we can. All is forgiven.

GRANDIER: Yes. I am His child. It is true. Let Him take me as I am. So there is meaning. There is meaning, after all. I am a sinful man and I can be accepted. It is not nothing going to nothing. It is sin going to forgiveness. It is a human creature going to love.

[BONTEMPS *has come in.*]

BONTEMPS: He's got to leave. If you want a priest they say you can ask for Father Barré or Father Rangier.

GRANDIER: They say?

BONTEMPS: Out there.

GRANDIER: De Laubardemont?

BONTEMPS: That's right.

AMBROSE: Must I go? Does he say I must go?

GRANDIER: Yes, Father. You are dangerous in your innocence. But they are too late.

AMBROSE: I don't understand.

GRANDIER: It is better that way. Let me kiss you.

[BONTEMPS *and* FATHER AMBROSE *go.*
GRANDIER *alone.*]

GRANDIER: What? Tears? When was the last time this happened? What are they for? They must be for what is lost, not for what has been found.

For God is here.

Sudden daylight. Laughter.

[CLAIRE, GABRIELLE, *and* LOUISE *come into the open air.*]

GABRIELLE: The town's like a fairground.

CLAIRE: They were singing not far from my window all night.

GABRIELLE: There are acrobats. I wish we could see them. I loved acrobats.

CLAIRE: Haven't we entertained each other enough in that way?
  [*They laugh.*]

LOUISE: We don't seem to amuse other people any more. None of the Fathers or the great Parisians have been near us for days.
  [JEANNE *has come up to them, unobserved.*]

JEANNE: You must understand, Louise, that the darlings of the public have their day, which ends, like any other.

LOUISE: Is it all over, Mother?

JEANNE: Soon. He's appearing before his judges this morning to make his last statement.

LOUISE: I didn't mean Father Grandier. I meant us. What shall we –

JEANNE: Then they'll speak the sentence. And at last there will be the Question.

LOUISE: But what will become of us, Mother?

JEANNE: We shall live. You've a lifetime before you, pretty Louise. Think of that.

  [*A cell:* MANNOURY *alone.*
  ADAM *is let in.*]

ADAM: Hullo.

MANNOURY: Hullo.

ADAM: Were you sent for?

MANNOURY: Yes?

ADAM: So was I. By De Laubardemont?

MANNOURY: That's it.

ADAM: I've brought my things. Have you?

MANNOURY: Yes.

ADAM: What I thought would be necessary.

MANNOURY: Difficult to say, isn't it?

ADAM: Have you done this before?

MANNOURY: No.

ADAM: Neither have I. Hm. Cold in here.

MANNOURY: Yes.

ADAM: Cold out.

MANNOURY: 'Tis.

ADAM: For a summer day.

MANNOURY: August. Yes.

[DE LAUBARDEMONT *comes in.*]

LAUBARDEMONT: Good morning, gentlemen. Glad to find you here. He's being brought back from the court. Should be on his way now.

MANNOURY: What exactly do you want us to do?

LAUBARDEMONT: Prepare the man. A decision has been reached. Unanimously. He is condemned.

ADAM: Well, well.

MANNOURY: Not surprising.

ADAM: There it is.

LAUBARDEMONT: I want you to be as quick as you can. There was an extraordinary amount of sympathy for the creature when he made his statement. There were even some unhealthy tears. So I want him ready and back there to hear the sentence as soon as possible.

MANNOURY: We'll do our best.

LAUBARDEMONT: Adam, would you be good enough to go and see the gaoler? He's getting all the necessary stuff together. Bring it in when he's done.

ADAM: All right.

[ADAM *goes.*]

LAUBARDEMONT: The man made something of an impression. Father Barré explained that it was the devil's doing. He said the calm was the brazen insolence of hell, and the dignity nothing but unrepentant pride. Still, the man made quite an impression.

[GRANDIER *is brought in by a Captain of the Guard. Grandier is dressed in full canonicals, looking his finest.*]

GRANDIER: Good morning, Mister Surgeon.

MANNOURY: And good morning to you.

GRANDIER: De Laubardemont I've already seen.

LAUBARDEMONT: You must return to the court at once.

GRANDIER: Very well.

LAUBARDEMONT: For the sentence.

GRANDIER: I understand.

LAUBARDEMONT: So now I must ask you to undress.

GRANDIER: Undress?

LAUBARDEMONT: You can't go like that.

GRANDIER: I suppose not.

[GRANDIER *takes off his biretta, and then begins to remove his cape.* ADAM *comes in with* BONTEMPS, ADAM *carries a tray, on which there is a bowl of water, some oil, and a razor.*]

GRANDIER: Good morning, Mister Chemist. What have you got there?

ADAM [*stammering*]: It's a razor.

GRANDIER [*after a moment: to De Laubardemont*]: Must it be this way?

LAUBARDEMONT: Yes. Order of the court.

[MANNOURY *has taken the razor: tests it on his thumb.*]

GRANDIER: Well, Mister Surgeon, all your study and training have brought you only to this. Those late nights spent discussing the existence of existence have brought you only here. To be a barber.

LAUBARDEMONT: Get on with it.

GRANDIER: Just a moment.

[GRANDIER *touches his black curls, and then fingers his moustaches.*]

GRANDIER: Have you a glass?

LAUBARDEMONT: No, no. Of course not.

BONTEMPS: There's this.

[BONTEMPS *takes an empty metal cup from the tray. He polishes the base of the cup on his sleeve and gives it to* GRANDIER.

GRANDIER *stands looking long and deeply at his reflection.*]

A public place.

[*A large crowd. Town and country people. Yawning, at ease, calling to each other. Apart: an enclosure holding some well-dressed women of the bourgeoisie. Chatter from them. There is a* CLERK *within a mountain of books.*

Sudden silence. All heads turn towards us.

The CLERK *rises. He reads:*]

CLERK: Urbain Grandier, you have been found guilty of commerce with the devil. And that you used this unholy alliance to possess, seduce, and debauch certain Sisters of the holy order of Saint Ursula (they are fully named in this document). You have also been found guilty of obscenity, blasphemy, and sacrilege.

It is ordered that you proceed and kneel at the doors of Saint Peter's and Saint Ursula's and there, with a rope round your neck and a two pound taper in your hand, ask pardon of God, the King, and Justice. Next, it is ordered that you be taken to the Place Sainte-Croix, tied to a stake, and burned alive: after which your ashes will be scattered to the four winds.

It has been decided that a commemorative plaque shall be set up in the Ursulines' chapel. The cost of this, yet to be ascertained, will be chargeable to your confiscated estate.

Lastly, before sentence is carried out, you will be subjected to the Question, both ordinary and extraordinary.

Pronounced at Loudun, 18 August 1634, and executed the same day.

[GRANDIER *slowly comes into sight. His hands are tied behind his back. He is dressed in a nightgown and slippers, but with a skull cap and biretta on his head.* DE LAUBARDEMONT, MANNOURY, *and* ADAM *accompany him. Also* BARRÉ, RANGIER, *and* MIGNON, *who are scattering holy water with consecrated whisks and intoning formulas of exorcism.*

DE LAUBARDEMONT *steps forward. He snatches the hat and cap from Grandier's head, and flings them to the ground.* GRANDIER *is revealed. He is completely shaven. Gone are the magnificent curls, the moustaches, even the eyebrows. He stands, a bald fool.*

There is a sudden, hysterical giggle from the women in the enclosure. Silence.

GRANDIER *speaks to us.*]

GRANDIER: My lords, I call God the Father, God the Son, and God the Holy Ghost, together with the Virgin, to witness that I have never been a sorcerer. The only magic I have practised is that of the Holy Scripture. I am innocent.

[*Silence. Then murmurs from the women: a silly laugh.*]

I am innocent, and I am afraid. I fear for my salvation. I am prepared to go and meet God, but the horrible torment you have ordered for me on the way may drive my wretched soul to despair. Despair, my lords. It is the gravest of sins. It is the short way to eternal damnation. Surely in your wisdom you do not mean to kill a soul. So may I ask you, in your mercy, to mitigate, if only a little, my punishment.

[GRANDIER *looks from face to face: silence.*]

Very well. When I was a child I was told about the martyrs. I loved the men and women who died for the honour of Jesus Christ. In a time of loneliness I have often wished to be of their company. Now, foolish and obscure priest that I am, I cannot presume to place myself among these great and holy men. But may I say that I have the hope in my heart that as this day ends Almighty God, my beloved Father in Heaven, will glance aside and let my suffering atone for my vain and disordered life. Amen.

[*Silence. Then somewhere in the crowd a man's voice clearly echoes Grandier's amen. Then another. Silence again. Only the sound of a woman bitterly weeping.*

DE LAUBARDEMONT *to the Captain of the Guard:*]

LAUBARDEMONT: Get them all out of here!

[*At once the guards begin to clear the place. The public go away along corridors and down steps, complaining, some protesting.*

GRANDIER *is left with* DE LAUBARDEMONT, *the* CLERK, BARRÉ, RANGIER, *and* MIGNON. *He has not moved, as he stands facing his judges.*

DE CERISAY *and* D'ARMAGNAC *can be seen. They are apart, overlooking the scene.*

DE LAUBARDEMONT *faces Grandier: speaks to him.*]

LAUBARDEMONT: Confess your guilt. Tell us the names of your accomplices. Then perhaps my lords, the judges, will consider your appeal.

GRANDIER: I cannot name accomplices I've never had, nor confess to crimes I've not done.

LAUBARDEMONT: This attitude will do you no good. You will suffer for it.

GRANDIER: I know that. And I am proud.

LAUBARDEMONT: Proud, sir? That word does not become your situation. Now look here, my dear fellow – untie his hands – this document is a simple confession. Here is a pen. Just put your name to this paper and we can forget the next stage of the proceedings.

GRANDIER: You must excuse me. No.

LAUBARDEMONT: I just want your signature. Here. That's all.

GRANDIER: My conscience forbids me to put my name to something which is untrue.

LAUBARDEMONT: You'll save us all a lot of trouble if you'll sign. The document being true, of course. [*He shouts*] True! You've been found guilty.

GRANDIER: I'm sorry.

LAUBARDEMONT: I fear for you, Grandier. I fear for you very much. I have seen men before you take this brave standing in the shadow of the Question. It was unwise, Grandier. Think again.

GRANDIER: No.

LAUBARDEMONT: You will go into the darkness before your death. Let me talk to you for a moment about pain. It is very difficult for us standing here, both healthy men, to imagine the shattering effect of agony. The sun's warm on your face at the moment, isn't it? And you can curl your toes if you want in your slippers. You are alive, and you know it. But when you are stretched out in that little room, with the pain screaming through you like a voice, let me tell you what you will think. First: how can man do this to man? Then: how can God allow it? Then: there can be no God. Then: there is no God. The voice of pain will grow stronger, and your resolution weaker. Despair, Grandier. You used the word yourself. You called it the gravest sin. Don't reject God at this moment. Reconcile yourself. For you have bitterly offended Him. Confess.

GRANDIER: No.

D'ARMAGNAC: Are those tears on De Laubardemont's face?

DE CERISAY: I'm afraid so.

D'ARMAGNAC: Does he believe what he's saying?

DE CERISAY: Yes. Touching, isn't it?

LAUBARDEMONT [*to Grandier*]: Very well. I ask you once more. Once more! Will you sign?

   [GRANDIER *shakes his head.*]

LAUBARDEMONT: Take him away.

   [*The guard surrounds Grandier.*]

GRANDIER: I would like to ask something.

LAUBARDEMONT: What?

GRANDIER: May I have Father Ambrose with me?

LAUBARDEMONT: No.

GRANDIER: He's a harmless old man. He won't impede you.

LAUBARDEMONT: He's no longer in the town. He's been sent away. If you want spiritual consolation address yourself to one of these gentlemen.

[GRANDIER *stares at Barré, Rangier, and Mignon for a moment before turning away between the guards and going.* DE LAUBARDEMONT *and the* CLERK *follow.*]

MIGNON: I found the Commissioner's last appeal very moving.

RANGIER: Very.

BARRÉ: I suppose you understand that Grandier's refusal to sign was the final proof of guilt.

MIGNON: Yes. Yes, I suppose so.

BARRÉ: Lucifer has sealed his mouth: hardened his heart against repentance.

MIGNON: Of course. That's the reason.

BARRÉ: Shall we go?

[BARRÉ, RANGIER, *and* MIGNON *go.*]

D'ARMAGNAC: Come to my house with me, De Cerisay.

DE CERISAY: All right, sir.

D'ARMAGNAC: I don't want you to talk to me.

DE CERISAY: Very well.

D'ARMAGNAC: We'll just sit together. And think over the day. Two – I hope – reasonable men. We'll sit and – we'll drink. Yes, that's it, we'll get drunk. Drunk enough to see visions. Come on.

[D'ARMAGNAC *and* DE CERISAY *go.*]

[*A garden.* JEANNE *enters. She is bare-headed, and dressed only in a simple white under-garment. Her little, deformed person looks child-like. She has a rope round her neck, and carries a candle in her hand. She stands quite still.*

CLAIRE, GABRIELLE, *and* LOUISE *gather some little way from* JEANNE, *frightened, watching her. Then* CLAIRE *comes forward to her.*]

CLAIRE: Come in, dear Mother.

JEANNE: No, child.

CLAIRE: But the sun is very hot after the rain. It will do you no good.

JEANNE: Find me a place – it needn't be so high – where I can tie this rope. I have been looking.

CLAIRE: No, Mother. It is the most terrible sin.

JEANNE: Sin?

CLAIRE: Yes.

[CLAIRE *unknots the rope and takes it away.* LOUISE *comes forward with a cloak, which she puts about Jeanne.*]

LOUISE: Don't frighten us, Mother.

JEANNE: I have been woken night after night by the sound of weeping. I've gone about trying to find out who it is. I have a heart like anyone else. It can be broken by such a sound.

LOUISE: It's no one here.

JEANNE: I'd never have thought it was possible for anyone to suffer such despair, such desolation.

LOUISE: But it's no one.

JEANNE: No one?

CLAIRE: It is the devil. He can snivel to order. Yes, Mother, think. Father Grandier would have you go to hell with him. So he gets the devil to cry at night and break your heart, makes you put a rope round your neck, and hang yourself. Don't be deceived.

JEANNE: Is there no way? And is that Claire speaking? Claire, who used to talk to me of the innocence of Christ? What's the time?

LOUISE: Just past noon.

JEANNE: Let me sit here. I promise not to harm myself. Leave me.

[CLAIRE, LOUISE, *and* GABRIELLE *go, leaving* JEANNE *alone. The silence is broken by a hideous sound of hammering. A scream.*]

[*The upper room.* GRANDIER *is stretched on the floor, bound. His legs, from the knees to the feet, are enclosed in a kind of box. Movable boards within the box, driven inward by huge wedges, crush his legs.*

BONTEMPS *is hammering the wedges home.*

MANNOURY, ADAM, *and* MIGNON *are crouched in the lower room.*

BARRÉ, *who is sitting by Grandier's head, leans forward.*]

BARRÉ: Will you confess?

[*Slowly,* GRANDIER *shakes his head.* BARRÉ *glances at* DE LAU-BARDEMONT, *who stands against the wall.*]

LAUBARDEMONT [*to Bontemps*]: Another.

[BONTEMPS *picks up another wedge, but it is at once snatched out of his hand by* RANGIER.]

RANGIER: Just a moment! [*He sprinkles the wedge with holy water, and makes signs over it.*] Very necessary. The devil has the power, you see, to make the pain less than it should be.

BONTEMPS: Finished?

RANGIER: Yes.

[*He gives the wedge to* BONTEMPS, *who inserts it.*]

BARRÉ: Hit! Hit!

[BONTEMPS *strikes with the mallet. A scream.*

In the lower room.]

MANNOURY: What's the cubic capacity of a man's breath?

ADAM: Don't know.

MANNOURY: Just wondered.

ADAM: It doesn't occur to you when you start something, that – Hm.

MANNOURY: What did you say?

ADAM: Nothing. Just thinking aloud.

[*A blow with the mallet.* BARRÉ *leans forward.*]

BARRÉ: Confess.

GRANDIER: I'm only too ready to confess my real sins. I have been a man, I have loved women. I have been proud. I have longed for power.

BARRÉ: That's not what we want. You've been a magician. You've had commerce with devils.

GRANDIER: No. No.

BARRÉ: Another. Oh, give it to me!

[BARRÉ *snatches the wedge and the mallet from* BONTEMPS *and, with the wedge unexorcized, drives it home with two mighty blows.*

GRANDIER'S *scream echoes in the garden where* JEANNE *sits alone.*]

JEANNE: Is it only in the very depths that one finds God? Look at me.

First I wanted to come to Him in innocence. It was not enough. Then there was the lying and play-acting. The guilt, the humiliation. It was not enough. There were the antics done for the dirty eyes of priests. The squalor. It was not enough. Down, down further.

[*The sound of hammering.* GRANDIER'S *voice:*]

GRANDIER: God. God. God. Don't abandon me. Don't let this pain make me forget You.

JEANNE: Down. Down. Into idiot oblivion. No thought. No feeling. Nothing. Is God here?

[*The upper room.* DE LAUBARDEMONT *comes forward.*]

LAUBARDEMONT: Take him out. It's no good.

[BARRÉ, RANGIER, *and* BONTEMPS *lift* GRANDIER *from the box and seat him on a stool.* BONTEMPS *covers Grandier's shattered legs with a rug.* GRANDIER *stares down at himself.*]

GRANDIER: Attendite et videte si est dolor sicut dolor meus.

[JEANNE *gets up.*]

JEANNE: Where are You? Where are You?

[JEANNE *goes from the garden.*
BARRÉ *and* RANGIER *have come down into the lower room.*]

ADAM: Any good?

BARRÉ: No.

MANNOURY: No confession?

BARRÉ: No.

ADAM: I say!

BARRÉ: Perfectly good reason.

MANNOURY: What?

BARRÉ: He called on God to give him strength. His god is the devil and did so. Made him insensible to pain. We'll get nowhere like this.

ADAM: Insensible to pain? What were all those screams?

BARRÉ: A mockery.

[BARRÉ, MIGNON, *and* RANGIER *go down into the street.*]

[*The upper room.*]

GRANDIER: Take no notice of these tears. They're only weakness.

LAUBARDEMONT: Remorse?

GRANDIER: No.

LAUBARDEMONT: Confess.

GRANDIER: No. There are two things a man should never be asked to do in front of other men. Perform with a woman, and suffer pain. You people know how to bring hell on earth for someone like me. Make it all public.

LAUBARDEMONT: That is vanity, Father.

GRANDIER: Is it? I don't think so. A man is a private thing. He belongs to himself. Those two most intimate experiences, love and pain, have nothing to do with the mob. How can they concern it? For the mob can feel neither.

LAUBARDEMONT: The mob is made up of Christian souls. Six thousand of them are waiting for you in the market place. Tell me, do you love the Church?

GRANDIER: With all my heart.

LAUBARDEMONT: Do you want to see it grow more powerful, more benevolent, until it embraces every human soul on this earth?

GRANDIER: That would be my wish.

LAUBARDEMONT: Then help us to achieve this great purpose. Go to the market place a penitent man. Confess, and by confessing, proclaim to these thousands that you have returned to the Church's arms. By going to the stake unrepentant you do God a disservice. You give hope to the sceptics and unbelievers. You make them glad. Such an act can mine the very foundations of the Church. Think. You are no longer important. Are you any longer important?

GRANDIER: No.

LAUBARDEMONT: Then make a last supreme gesture for the Catholic faith.

[Silence. DE LAUBARDEMONT eagerly leans forward. Then GRANDIER looks up. His face is drawn in an agonized smile.]

GRANDIER: This is sophistry, Laubardemont, and you're too intelligent not to know it. Pay me the same compliment.

LAUBARDEMONT: You can laugh? Now?

GRANDIER: Yes. Because I know more about it than you.

LAUBARDEMONT: When I tell you, Grandier –

GRANDIER: Don't persist. I can destroy you. At least in argument. Keep your illusions, Mister Commissioner. You'll need them all to deal with the men who will come after me.

LAUBARDEMONT: Confess.

GRANDIER: No.

LAUBARDEMONT: Confess.

GRANDIER: No.

LAUBARDEMONT: Sign.

GRANDIER: No.

[DE LAUBARDEMONT *goes to the door. He calls down the stairs.*]

LAUBARDEMONT: Let me have the guard here!

A street.

[*A crowd is staring into the distance. The people are quiet, shifting, uneasy, withheld.* BARRÉ, RANGIER, *and* MIGNON *come towards them.* RANGIER *and* MIGNON *are scattering holy water and intoning exorcisms.* BARRÉ *moves along the crowd, taking men and women by the arm, speaking to them individually.*]

BARRÉ: My dear children, you are about to witness the passage of a wicked and unrepentant man to hell. I beg of you – you, sir – take the sight to your heart. Let it be a lesson that will stay with you – my good woman – all your life. Watch this infamous magician who has trafficked with devils and ask yourself – my child – is this what a man comes to when he scorns God?

[*A drum.* GRANDIER *comes into sight. He is seated on a chair which has been lashed to a kind of litter, and is carried by four soldiers. He wears a shirt impregnated with sulphur, a vivid yellow, and there is a rope round his neck. His broken legs dangle. He is a ridiculous, hairless, shattered doll. The* CLERK *walks beside him.* DE LAUBARDEMONT *and soldiers follow.*]

Saint Ursula's Convent.

[*The procession comes to the convent door and stops. The* CLERK *puts a two-pound taper into Grandier's hand.*]

LAUBARDEMONT: You must get down here.

GRANDIER: What is this place?

LAUBARDEMONT: It is the Convent of Saint Ursula. A place you have defiled.

[*A* SOLDIER *lifts* GRANDIER *from the litter like a child, and puts him on the ground.*]

LAUBARDEMONT: Do what must be done.

GRANDIER: In this strange and unknown place I ask pardon of God, the King and Justice. I beg that I may – [*He falls forward on his face: cries out*] Deus meus, miserere mei Deus!

[*The convent door opens and from the dark entrance come* JEANNE, GABRIELLE, CLAIRE, *and* LOUISE.]

LAUBARDEMONT: Ask pardon of this Prioress, and these good Sisters.

GRANDIER: Who are these women?

LAUBARDEMONT: They are the people you have wronged. Ask their forgiveness.

GRANDIER: I have done no such thing. I can only ask that God will forgive them.

[*Utter silence as* GRANDIER *and* JEANNE *stare at each other.*]

JEANNE: They always spoke of your beauty. Now I see it with my own eyes and I know it to be true.

GRANDIER: Look at this thing which I am, and learn the meaning of love.

[*The drum.* GRANDIER *is lifted back on to the litter. The procession moves on into the distance.*

A great bell. Voices:]

Dies irae, dies illa, solvet saeclum in favilla, teste David cum Sybilla.

Quantus tremor est futurus, quando judex est venturus, cuncta stricte discussurus!

[JEANNE, *alone, comes forward. Darkness.*]

The streets of Loudun. Night.

[*The town seems to be on fire. Distant buildings are silhouetted against a harsh red sky. A church door gapes like a sulphurous mouth. Armed men with banners cross a bridge. A man is climbing a ladder, waving into the distance in hopeless distress.*

The crowd (which watched Grandier into the distance) has broken up and is rushing, hysterical, screaming, laughing, through the streets.

JEANNE *wanders on alone.*

MANNOURY *and* ADAM.]

MANNOURY: Very odd, you know.

ADAM: What?

MANNOURY: That business of human fat being rendered down by heat to the consistency of candle wax and then igniting with a flame of such exquisite colour.

ADAM: Rum business, altogether.

MANNOURY: Interesting, though. I'd say, Adam, if there's any aesthetic appeal in your work as a chemist it lies in that direction. Wouldn't you?

ADAM: Maybe.

[*They go.*

BARRÉ, MIGNON, *and* RANGIER.]

BARRÉ: He's in hell. Be sure of it.

MIGNON: Tonight he roasts.

BARRÉ: Unrepentant, frightful man!

RANGIER: You know, I saw his women sitting there, watching. One was in tears, it's true. But she was watching. Never turned away.

BARRÉ: Devils. All devils. What's the matter with you?

MIGNON: I don't feel very well.

BARRÉ [*hitting him on the back*]: Smoke got down you, I expect.

MIGNON: I think I'll go to bed now, if you don't mind.

BARRÉ: We're all going to get to our beds, Mignon. How long we shall be allowed to lie there depends on friend Satan. We vanquished him and brought peace to this place today. But you can be sure that even now he is creeping back. Ah, my dear friends, men of our kind will never lack employment.

[*They go.*

PHILLIPE TRINCANT. *She is monstrously pregnant, and lumbers forward leading the* OLD MAN *by the hand.*]

PHILLIPE: Come along home, dear husband. You must try to walk a little quicker. What? [*The* OLD MAN *whispers to her.*] Watching all

203

this today has made you quite excited. [*He whispers again.*] Yes, you shall do whatever you like. And I'll do all I can for you. Wipe your mouth. We've many happy years ahead together. What? Yes, of course there's a way. I'll turn and turn about for you. Jesus, I will. I'll show you tricks. So come home, darling.

[PHILLIPE *and the* OLD MAN *go.*

D'ARMAGNAC *and* DE CERISAY. *They are drunk.*]

D'ARMAGNAC: We shouldn't be doing this, De Cerisay. We are the rational, forward-looking men of our age. We should be taking a stand.

DE CERISAY: Quite right.

D'ARMAGNAC: About something or other. I'm not quite sure what. Why is the air full of insects tonight? What was I saying?

DE CERISAY: We should take a stand.

D'ARMAGNAC: And assert ourselves.

DE CERISAY: What about?

D'ARMAGNAC: What we believe.

DE CERISAY: And what do we believe?

D'ARMAGNAC: Ask me tomorrow. Am I mad? Were they fornicating in the street up there? And what did that old woman have in the basket? Human remains? Why was that animal leading a man on a rope? What is the strange, sweet smell that hangs over the place? And that musician crucified upon the harp. What does it all mean, De Cerisay? As rational men we should be able to explain it.

DE CERISAY: I can't.

D'ARMAGNAC: Neither can I. So take me home.

[*They go.*

JEANNE'S *wandering through the streets has brought her to the* SEWERMAN.]

SEWERMAN: When it was done they shovelled him to the north, the south, the east, and the west.

JEANNE: Do you know who I am?

SEWERMAN: Yes, madam, I know.

[*Some of the crowd are passing. They are fighting among themselves for some objects which are passed from hand to hand.*]

JEANNE: What are they doing?

SEWERMAN: It's bits of the body they're after.

JEANNE: As relics?

SEWERMAN: Don't try to comfort yourself. No, they want them as charms. There's a difference, you know. [*He snatches a charred bone from one of the men.*] They don't want to adore this. They want it to cure their constipation or their headache, to have it bring back their virility or their wife. They want it for love or hate. [*He holds out the bone.*] Do you want it for anything?

[JEANNE *shakes her head. The crowd has gone.* THE SEWERMAN *goes.*

JEANNE *alone. She cries out in her own voice:*]

JEANNE: Grandier! Grandier!

[*Silence.*]

CURTAIN

HENRY LIVINGS

Nil Carborundum

First presented by the Royal Shakespeare Theatre, by arrangement with the New Arts Theatre, at the Arts Theatre on 12 April 1962 with the following cast:

WARRANT OFFICER KEIGHLY	Arthur Lovegrove
WARRANT OFFICER MCKENDRICK	John Rae
S.A.C. ALBERT MEAKIN	Nicol Williamson
MR HIGGINS	George Tovey
NEVILLE, A/C 2 HARRISON	James Booth
TAFFY, A/C 2 JONES	Terry Palmer
SERGEANT BULL	Arthur Mullard
WING COMMANDER HOWARD	Graham Crowden
THE ADJUTANT	Terence Knapp
MARGIT	Margery Withers
JOHN	Ken Parry
JUNE MEAKIN	Kate Pinchy
MESS WAITER	Charles Lewson
PILOT OFFICER FEATHER	Edward Fox
WARRANT OFFICER CLAPP	Ray Mort
S.P. SERGEANT FAIRCLOUGH	Phillip Newman
S.P. CORPORAL	Kenn Warren
AIRMAN	Harry Dickman
NO. 1 COMMANDO	Kenneth Farrington
NO. 2 COMMANDO	Ilario Pedro
NO. 3 COMMANDO	Timothy West
CORPORAL JERRY	Peter Anderson
AIRMAN	Gawn Grainger
GROUP CAPTAIN LYONS	Paul Dawkins

Directed by Anthony Page
Designed by Michael Knight

CHARACTERS

S.A.C. ALBERT MEAKIN is twenty-three, married, randy, with a girlish energy about him ... swift and efficient without strength, he's also dishonest and very selfish. He is dirty in his person. Wears his beret in the kitchen as if to signify that the best part of his time is spent elsewhere: uniform shirt and tie, cook's jacket and apron, greasy uniform trousers sharply creased. He speaks fast and slovenly in a hectic Leeds accent to which he gives a sneering adenoidal overtone all his own. His infrequent efforts at friendly intercourse are charming because he is so selfish he expects others to be equally indifferent to him. He doesn't shave regularly, and the sparse fair bristles on his cheek make his already scrofulous complexion seems even more so.

NEVILLE (A/C 2 HARRISON), twenty-two. He mistakenly broke his course as an agricultural student and is now living through the remainder of his period of service with cheerful obstinacy. He is heavy-footed though not heavily built. Long thick hair in a D.A. He is cockily cheerful and a bit of a clown. Intelligent, resilient, and rarely aggressive. The occasional eccentricity he shows is the result of the pressure of military discipline and the only effect it has had on him.

TAFFY (A/C 2 JONES) is a great lump. He's eighteen and he comes from Swansea. A face like a fiery sun and the disposition of a happy and careless child. His hair stands up like a blacking brush. He is nearly illiterate, reads American funnies with hypnotized concentration and loves the sound and roll of the spoken word. He's a monumental mason by trade and it's a bloody shame he ever joined. He's a useless waiter, but willing and kind even to those who torment him.

WARRANT OFFICER MCKENDRICK, the Catering Officer, is a tough old bird, probably in his last posting before retiring. His hair is white, and his peeky little face looks young by contrast. He speaks quietly and seldom, with an elegant and pure Scots accent. His eyes are shrewd and self-mocking, and he likes his own way well enough to wait for it ... which is what he normally has to do.

WARRANT OFFICER KEIGHLY, the Station Warrant Officer (N.C.O. in charge of discipline on the camp) is an enormous old lardy gourmand. He was once a butcher and he's been learning steadily and greedily about food ever since. Flat feet, vast paunch, small white hands, and a great round cropped grey bullet of a head. He has a genial disposition, is a sensible disciplinarian and a careful administrator. He once saw R.S.M. Britton in a film and it made a permanent impression on him; but luckily he openly enjoys the joke of himself in the role of the sadistic N.C.O.

SERGEANT BULL looks like a boxer with his heavy stocky frame. His life is a tragic waste and he knows it. He drinks constantly and is dangerous in his drink. Whatever he could have been or has been, he is at zero now: in command of a section of one, supervising the packing of parachutes that are never unpacked.

THE ADJUTANT is an earnest and intelligent young administrative officer, with a minimum of professional interest in war and a maximum of schoolboy vulnerability on the subject. Good-looking, open-faced, clean-cut. If he were in his father's business or a bank he would not be an ass, but he isn't and here he seems an ass.

THE C.O. Wing Commander Howard was a bomber hero during the war. He is now nothing but mis-spent aggression: a louring un-happy man, blackavised and a heavy drinker. He drives his car wildly and has crashed the few paltry planes he could get his hands on since he's commanded this station. He's a fighter, not a soldier, and not a bit grateful for the Adjutant's administrative attention.

MR HIGGINS, the civilian steward, was born of Flemish parents in the East End of London; he couldn't be more British, but his career as a *commis* in France and then as waiter and on to more responsible jobs in England has transformed his cockney shine to a cosmopolitan polish. It would be easy to suppose that he is a foreigner: the waiters with whom he's spent most of his life were French, and like them he speaks Cockney without the grammatical mistakes or slovenly pronunciation. He abuses power unmerci-fully on the pretext that he is passing on priceless standards. He is secretive and nobody really knows his history, but hardly anybody fails to realize he's phoney.

MARGIT is grossly fat, about fifty. 'Have your fun while you're young' she was telling herself fuzzily as a succession of airmen looted her last traces of bloom. She is nervous, tremulous, garrulous, soft, and cruelly abused by the blind man she companions.

JOHN, the blind man, is a malicious old rogue with a gentle calm face, like you might imagine a saint to look.

JUNE MEAKIN (Albert's wife) is pretty and bewildered ... not at all used to being married.

WARRANT OFFICER CLAPP, a smiling young man.

The S.P. Sergeant (SERGEANT FAIRCLOUGH) was only ever really happy in the East. He has a yellow malarial complexion and a malignant disposition. He is honest, upright, and wishes he were in the S.I.B. or somewhere he could visit his righteousness more savagely on the heads of defaulters.

GROUPIE (GROUP CAPTAIN LYONS, I/C the R.A.F. Regiment Commando Force) is a hairy forty-five-year-old schoolboy. It doesn't worry him that there aren't any of his kind of wars left. It was always a chap-to-chap business with him, and you can always meet chaps. He sold vacuum cleaners door to door in 1939, and suddenly somebody made him a gentleman.

S.P. CORPORAL, dull and large.

2ND SERGEANTS' MESS WAITER.

CORPORAL JERRY, and other AIRMEN who man the Bren on the larder roof.

PILOT OFFICERS FEATHER AND BEESTON.

Regiment Commando Airmen: PILOT OFFICER, CORPORAL, FOUR AIRMEN.

ACT ONE

[*A small cinema screen shows the words:* 'Flashback ... the Glass-house', *and through the play will indicate briefly the changes of scene and time. A scrim represents a row of huts. Three strands of barbed wire stretch tautly across the Proscenium Arch. The downstage area is littered with useless military equipment ... tank-tyres, rusty tracks, ragged uniforms and flying jackets, shredded blankets, a propellor, etc. Down right is a built piece, open on our side, a Guardroom. We can see the head and red cap of a military policeman on duty at the desk. Down left is another built piece, an Office. We hear a deadening and sinister orchestration of military noises. Hoarse voices yap rhythmically:* 'Right-right-right-right-right-ha! Right-right-ha! Right-right-hin!'*

Individuals and small groups marching rapidly. Whistles blow harshly. All this pattern of noise is interrupted at irregular intervals by dead, absolute, and still silence.

Above the Guardroom a small armoured air-force police van draws up. The back door opens and an R.A.F. service policeman descends pulling after him by handcuffs a blue-uniformed but badgeless prisoner. They are both marking time at a sharp marching pace. Still marching, raising his knees high, the prisoner turns and his kitbag is hurled from the van into his arms. Another S.P. descends from the van and one S.P. before and one behind, the three march across to the office. The rear S.P. banging his knees into the thighs of the prisoner and kicking his heels and screaming hoarsely into his ear: 'Right-right-right ...' *until* 'Hin!' *to halt him before the desk in the Office.*

Silence.

The words on the screen jumble and re-form to 'Kcabhsalf ... Eht Pmac', *and the prisoner and escort reverse their actions exactly until they are back in the van and the door is closed ... accompanied by the reversed prison noises.*

The scrim rises to reveal a third built piece centre: the Sergeants' Mess. A small kitchen with back-to-back stove and central chimney. On the]

right Store Room and coal hole, on the left wash-up, Steward's Office
... a door ... crockery, and Mess Hall. During the time that anyone
in the Kitchen has to look out of the window ... as now ... a window
is lowered for them to look out of.
In the Kitchen are Station Warrant Officer Keighly ... large, glut-
tonous, and wheezy, Mr Higgins, the civilian steward ... neat, prim,
and phoney, Warrant Officer McKendrick ... a dry old bird, Senior
Aircraftman Albert Meakin, a scrofulous crook, all gazing stolidly out.
In the Mess Hall is Taffy ... a great red-faced loon, clearing up after
breakfast.
In the Guardroom the M.P. changes hats for a white one so that he is
now an S.P.
The door of the van re-opens and the prisoner and escort emerge back-
wards and back briskly across.
The words on the screen re-jumble slowly to 'Flashback ...' which
fades as soon as the prisoner and escort have crossed, and then to 'The
Camp' which fades slowly in its turn as the scheme gets under way.
The prisoner and escort cross back again to the van, the right way round.
The barbed wire is reeled in tautly to one side and is not seen again
until it is needed during Act Three. Mr Keighly peers into a large pan
which is rattling its lid on the stove.]

MR KEIGHLY: Ah, duff. [*Goes back to look out of the window.*] A hard
life, the Air Force, Mr McKendrick.

MR MCKENDRICK: Aye. Ninety days' detention is a lot for mis-
appropriating two pork pies and a bottle of booze, even if it was
from the Officers' Mess.

MR KEIGHLY: I was speaking of my own hardship. That pimply
rogue who's just been marched off for a richly merited spell of ill-
treatment was the best cook on the station.

ALBERT: Yer, a smashing cook.

MR KEIGHLY [*bawling*]: You shut your gob Meakin! ... in fact the
only cook the Sergeants' Mess has *had*, in *years*. You're all pitying
him, I dare say. You seem to have lost sight of the fact that the
pork pies weighed seven pounds apiece and the champagne was a
magnum. It's me that's to be pitied, I'll wither.

MR MCKENDRICK: There's been altogether too much thieving, Mr
Keighly.

MR KEIGHLY [*with loud wondering sarcasm*]: You're absolutely right, Mr McKendrick. Too much thieving. And too little cooking. And it's to be put an end to. I intend to grind out wickedness and cruelty to Station Warrant Officers, and grind in a holy and bowel-watering fear of bad cooking. And I don't care if certain airmen [*he means Albert*] disappear altogether in the process.

[A/C NEVILLE HARRISON *approaches the Kitchen, carrying a box of rations on his head. He is in whites, his hat squashed and folded into a sort of Pandit Nehru cap which he wears well forward. He is a cocky figure and sings cheerfully.*]

NEVILLE [*sings*]:

This is my story, this is my song . . .

MR MCKENDRICK: Here's your new assistant.

NEVILLE [*sings*]:

I've been in this Air Force . . . too frigging long.

They won't let me murder for my country's good

And this one-handed sex-life's more use to a spud.

MR KEIGHLY: He'd better be good.

MR HIGGINS [*bustling away suddenly to his office, where he sits facing the open door, drumming his fingers and hoping for something good to happen to him*]: I shall see him later, Albert, my boy.

[ALBERT *ignores him and begins to work noisily, collecting dirty pans from breakfast and dumping them in the sink.* NEVILLE *comes in to the kitchen door. He catches Albert's eye and jerks his head to indicate the Store-room door.*]

NEVILLE: This where you want the rations?

ALBERT: You the new cook?

NEVILLE [*to McKendrick*]: Morning sir.

MR MCKENDRICK [*pleased*]: Morning Harrison.

MR KEIGHLY: Morning bobbagee. Why weren't you on parade?

NEVILLE: Morning sir. I was.

MR KEIGHLY: Not with that haircut you wasn't.

NEVILLE: I tuck it up under my hat. [*He goes into the larder to stow the stores.*]

MR KEIGHLY: I shall have to watch out for that. Must look very interesting. Like a plucked hen. [*Roars*] Can you cook, bobbagee?

NEVILLE [*shouts from the larder*]: Yes sir!

[*Keighly gives McKendrick a quizzical look and they both go into the Mess Hall.*]

MCKENDRICK: Will you be making a cup of tea, Albert?

ALBERT: Yes sir.

[ALBERT *continues to work noisily and ostentatiously. He takes prepared veg. from the bench to the stove and pours boiling water from the kettle on them, riddles the fire, etc.*

NEVILLE *stands and watches the performance with close interest which finally disconcerts Albert and he tails off into silence. He looks at Neville.* NEVILLE *listens to the rattle of the lid on the duff, looks at Albert, then turns and replies to the pot as if it was giving out messages in morse. Then he turns calmly to Albert.*]

NEVILLE: What'll I do then?

ALBERT [*a bit nonplussed, but gaining momentum*]: You clean and then do tea. I'm mucking off after this but I'll see you right for tea first. We work it between us here. Tomorrow you do breakfast and . . .

NEVILLE: What was he called the fellow that got ninety days?

ALBERT: Er . . . Harry. Tomorrow you do breakfast and finish early. All right?

NEVILLE [*pitches into the pans*]: Sure.

ALBERT: Just one thing now you're here: you don't want to take no notice whatsoever of Mistriggins.

NEVILLE: Higgins?

ALBERT: The civvy steward. He thinks he owns the Sergeants' Mess, well he doesn't. I'm in charge here, and you and me can work it between us.

[NEVILLE *gets on with the pans,* ALBERT *watches him uneasily. Meanwhile* TAFFY *is strolling out of the Mess Hall; out of the corner of his eye he sees Higgins, who stiffens at the sight of his prey, and he accelerates past the door of Higgins's office.*]

HIGGINS: Jones.

[TAFFY *starts industriously to lay a tray for two.* HIGGINS *comes to his door.*]

Jones, what are you doing now? Mr Keighly and Mr McKendrick want some tea.

TAFFY: Yes, Mr Higgins, I'm getting it.

HIGGINS: Well do it, do it.

TAFFY: That's just what I am doing.

HIGGINS: Hurry if you please, they are waiting for their tea.

[HIGGINS *returns abruptly to his office.* TAFFY *finishes laying the tray.*]

ALBERT: My name's Bert, what's yours?

NEVILLE: Neville Harrison.

ALBERT: That's a funny name, isn't it?

NEVILLE: Suits me.

ALBERT: No, I never heard of anybody being called Neville before.

NEVILLE: Neville Chamberlain.

ALBERT: Oh yer.

[TAFFY *comes into the kitchen.*]

TAFFY: Oh hello Nev. You working here now then? Perhaps we shall have some decent grub after all this time. Morning S.A.C. Meakin Bert.

ALBERT: Gerrout this kitchen, Taffy.

TAFFY: Oh now don't be like that, Bert. I brought you two cups here for Mr Keighly and Mr McKendrick's tea and I could just fancy a cup myself. Only no arsenic in mine if you please.

Old Higgins is acting a bit funny this morning, in' he? He's sitting in his office like Lord God Napoleon.

ALBERT: What's fresh about that?

TAFFY: Should have heard the way he was on at me to get tea for them two; I wouldn't ha' minded only that's what I was doing.

ALBERT: Oh muck off, Taffy, you're everlasting blethering.

TAFFY: Not till I get that tea. It's more than my life's worth to go back in there without no tea.

ALBERT: Well the kettle's empty.

TAFFY: Oh blimey crikey, let me fill it then. Excuse me Neville. [*Takes the kettle from the stove and fills it at the sink.*]

[HIGGINS *opens the kitchen door.*]

HIGGINS [*to Taffy*]: Go back in the mess now.

TAFFY: Oh blimey crikey. [*Drops the kettle in the sink.*]

[ALBERT *pushes the door closed as* TAFFY *goes out and puts the kettle on the stove.* HIGGINS *opens the door again and* TAFFY *shouts despairingly over Higgins's shoulder:*]

You'll bear witness it was no fault of mine, won't you?

[HIGGINS *taps Neville on the shoulder and gives him a peremptory signal to follow him into his office.* NEVILLE *watches him go and closes the door again.*]

ALBERT: Take no notice. He's trying it on. He's got no authority whatsoever over you. Don't half lead them waiters a dance though. Here give us that tin for my roast potatoes.

[HIGGINS *opens the door again.* NEVILLE *glances up and lets the tin fall back into the water.* HIGGINS *is trying to appear easy under trying circumstances.*]

HIGGINS: Neville, my boy, one moment please, I should like to have a word with you.

NEVILLE: Oh yes?

ALBERT [*fishing out the roast tray*]: Excuse me Mistriggins.

NEVILLE: Thing is I'm a bit busy just now.

HIGGINS [*relieved that Neville bothers to find an excuse at all*]: It's all right, it's all right. Don't disturb yourself.

NEVILLE: There's all these pans, and then there's the tops and the floor.

HIGGINS: Good boy, I'm glad to see you're clean.

ALBERT: Is there a pan for me gravy water, Nev? [*Fishes out a large pot.*] It's all right, it only wants rinsing.

HIGGINS: I just wanted to say I never interfere in the kitchen, that's none of my business.

[ALBERT *spits on the fire and crashes more coal on.*]

NEVILLE: Very nice of you to say so.

HIGGINS [*with an uncertain smile*]: But of course I like to see everything nice. . . .

ALBERT: Oh and there's another thing Nev, when you're cleaning. You look after the fire. You don't want coal on your hands when you're cooking.

HIGGINS: There's no reason why we shouldn't all get on very well with each other. We all have our jobs to do, and if we work together the customers will be happy, and we shall be happy. Co-operation. . .

[*The loud and terrible voice of* KEIGHLY *from the Mess Hall fills the air.*]

KEIGHLY: What about that friggin cup of tea Meakin you idle man!
Jones!!

[TAFFY *skids back into the kitchen.*]

TAFFY: Yes sir, I'm just goin'.

KEIGHLY: Get your hair cut!

TAFFY: Three bags full. That rotten kettle on yet, Bert?

ALBERT: That other one's being boiling for half an hour.

TAFFY: Oh blimey crikey, I'm a desperate man.

[TAFFY *fills the tea pot and is hurtling off back with the trayful.*]

ALBERT: Gerrus a cup out of it after Taffy, d'you hear me?

TAFFY: O.K.

NEVILLE [*meets Taffy with two cups*]: Here you are.

TAFFY [*frantic*]: No, no, no, Neville please! Let me by there's a good
boy. Oh hell.

[*He lays the tray down and fills the two cups for Neville, dashes back
to refill the pot, and then dashes out.* ALBERT *puts sugar and milk in
the cups.*]

HIGGINS: Well I'll see you later Neville, my boy. Any time you want
to see me or discuss a menu or anything, come to my room here.

[HIGGINS *goes back to his room.* ALBERT *barely lets him get out
before:*]

ALBERT: Him and his 'room'. Took him six months to get in there.
They kep cracking on they'd lost the key, but in the end they had
to give in and he sits in there hoping someone'll come in and make
him feel big. He usually has to shout for a waiter in the end. I never
take no notice. Harry, him what's just been court-martialled, he
used to sing: 'And we'll all go round to Higgins's room, Higgins's
room's a piggery is Higgins's room.' Huh. Made me laugh.

HIGGINS [*impassive at the kitchen door*]: There's just one thing I wanted
to ask you Neville my boy; can you make pancakes?

ALBERT: Now we're norravin pancakes when I've already made duff
Mistriggins. Besides we haven't got the pan for 'em.

NEVILLE [*puzzled*]: Yes, I can make pancakes.

HIGGINS [*going hastily and with dignity, so as to have the last word*]:
Good. One day we must have pancakes.

ALBERT [*bitterly*]: That's another thing with him. Pancakes. He's only
the friggin' steward here you know.

[NEVILLE *carries on with the cleaning and* ALBERT *with the cooking. Meanwhile in the Mess Hall* SERGEANT BULL, *thick-necked and red-eyed, is looking out of the window at a lonely and shabby erk who mooches by. The two warrant officers have their tea before them and* TAFFY *is hovering by the green baize curtain which covers the doorway to the Kitchen.*]

BULL: Look at that idle man.

KEIGHLY: Who sergeant?

BULL: My section. Old here's-a-penny-bail-yourself-out-Jack the parachute packer. Humph.

[KEIGHLY *laughs indulgently.*]

MCKENDRICK: There are no parachutes for him to pack are there?

BULL [*turns on him aggressively*]: He could be filling in chitties. Get out Jones.

TAFFY: I got to be somewhere, Sergeant.

BULL [*closer*]: I'd want proof of that.

TAFFY [*shakily*]: Cup of tea, Sergeant?

[*He sees the look in Bull's eye. Goes through to the Kitchen.*]

ALBERT: Gerrout this kitchen, Taffy!

TAFFY: Oh blimey crikey Bert.

HIGGINS: Jones! Come here!

[TAFFY *goes into Higgins's room. He re-appears with a message in a little while.* NEVILLE *is cleaning the floor by now and* ALBERT *is in the store room sorting the rations.*]

KEIGHLY: He'd better be good this new lad, Jock.

MCKENDRICK: He's not bad at all. I try to keep one good cook in each mess, all other things being equal. That burglarious young cretin that's just gone was one of the best and Neville was the best in the Airmen's Mess.

KEIGHLY: It took you long enough to find him out, cretin or not.

MCKENDRICK: You never know what's going on inside a man's head.

KEIGHLY: It's not much trouble to find out what goes on inside the Station Ration Stores.

MCKENDRICK: You don't think they do it while I'm there? Ach, they're aye borrowing rations from one another . . . especially from the Airmen's Mess. Had an S.I.B. man in there.

KEIGHLY: Rogues and vagabonds.

MCKENDRICK: The S.I.B.?

KEIGHLY: Both of them. Police and cooks. What a nefarious crew. You maybe don't know what goes on inside their heads; but I can tell you, its knavery.

MCKENDRICK: Anyway Harrison's not bad at all.

KEIGHLY: If I wasn't weakened by the diet I'd have murdered that walking tin-opener S.A.C. Meakin for some of his atrocities before this.

MCKENDRICK: Excuse me, sir, but I'm not responsible for the quality of my cooks. I can only try to get the best out of the material that I have.

KEIGHLY: Don't you get academic with me, Mr McKendrick. I'll tell you what you're responsible for and that's feeding *me*, and you're not doing too well. [*He gets up to go.*] So think on, Jock. Orderly Sergeant tonight, Sar'nt Bull. [*Going.*]

BULL: What about the booze-up in the Mess?

KEIGHLY: I had thought of that. [*He goes.*]

[*Meanwhile* NEVILLE *is scrubbing the passage outside the larder door. He pushes open the door so as to scrub under, the door is pushed to from inside.* NEVILLE *pushes it open again and carries on, having scrubbed under, down the corridor.*

ALBERT *appears hastily in the door and goes along to the kitchen as* NEVILLE *gets up and comes back the same way.* ALBERT *addresses the kitchen at large.*]

ALBERT: I wish you wouldn't do that, you know.

NEVILLE: You what?

ALBERT [*spins round*]: I wish you wouldn't keep doing that, you know.

NEVILLE: What?

ALBERT: Som'dy kept opening that door.

NEVILLE: Sorry, Bert, you should have said.

ALBERT: That's my responsibility, rations. I look after them.

NEVILLE: All right.

ALBERT: Like, me being an S.A.C. I'm in charge; so I have to have the key of the Ration Store, don't I? I was just checking them, you don't want to bother your head about them.

NEVILLE: You're going on about it a bit, aren't you?

ALBERT: You've got to get these things straight for a start. Because it's me that's responsible to McKendrick for the amount of rations.

NEVILLE [*slightly louder*]: I said you're going on about it a bit.

ALBERT: Well som'dy kept pushing open that door, and I didn't want no misapprehensions. [*Hastily*] Keep an eye on dinner for us, will you, while I go and have a word with McKendrick?

NEVILLE: Aye.

[ALBERT *goes through to the Mess Hall. After checking the various pots* NEVILLE *goes to the door of the Ration Stores and tries it. It is locked. He stands thoughtfully with his back to the door, drumming his fingers on it. After a second he goes back into the kitchen.* ALBERT *speaks to McKendrick in the Mess Hall.*]

ALBERT: Excuse me, sir, I been thinking, with this new bloke coming, I can have my leave, can't I?

MCKENDRICK: I'm afraid with these manouvres coming off . . .

ALBERT: Thot's just what I mean, sir . . . I shall have to get it in quick, shan't I?

MCKENDRICK: Oh I see. Yes. I don't want Harrison on his own till he knows the kitchen.

ALBERT: I'm entitled to my leave, aren't I, sir?

MCKENDRICK: Oh yes you are. Oh Harrison's a good lad. He'll manage I dare say. Let me have your application then.

ALBERT: Here it is all ready, sir.

MCKENDRICK: All right, Meakin, I'll attend to it.

ALBERT: Thank you very much, sir.

[ALBERT *goes back into the kitchen and is soon locked in the Ration Stores again.*

The C.O. *enters the office reading a directive from Bomber Command that gives him no pleasure. The* ADJUTANT, *fresh-faced and young, follows.*]

C.O. [*reads*]: 'It is assumed, for the purpose of the Surprise Exercise, that the Home Counties have been dislocated by ground-to-ground nuclear missiles. All units are acting independently pro tem. A flight of R.A.F. Regiment from Command will represent a marauding commando unit. They will try to take over R.A.F. Geldon as part of a plan to prepare for enemy landings on a larger scale. It is assumed that the strip is in working order and therefore useful to either side.' That's a dirty crack. 'Blanks will be issued to Bren teams.' It is assumed that somebody can fire 'em. Groupie says he'll buy us champagne for the Mess if his commando captures the station. I loathe the blasted stuff.

ADJUTANT: They won't, sir.

C.O.: What do you know about it, you wet-eared erk!

ADJUTANT: I say, sir.

C.O.: What do you know about war, or fighting! I don't suppose you've ever been drunk in your life!

ADJUTANT: I think that's a bit uncalled for.

C.O.: Have you!

ADJUTANT: Well no. Not actually *drunk* . . .

C.O.: Uncalled for? You sound like a parcels agent.

ADJUTANT: I don't think you can deny that I know my job.

C.O.: It's me that'll be called for. Job? Oh yes, but is your job worth knowing?

ADJUTANT: It's not a great deal different from yours, sir.

C.O. [*with a trace of humour*]: If I'm on drinking form it's identical. Book-keeping. [*Points to his wings.*] There was a time when what I did counted. We were proud of it. Now I'm despised for my incompetence in a job I detest.

ADJUTANT: I'm glad to do as much as I can, sir.

C.O.: Aren't you bloody just. Look at this letter. That's what they think of me. Fifteen years ago I wanted to die, and it would have been a good death; now all I can do is go rotten slowly. And Groupie with his champagne for the Mess. . . .

ADJUTANT: Oh come, sir, that's just the Group Captain's fun.

C.O.: I know Groupie. I know what his fun is: shooting holes in people. He's a murderous thick-headed lout. He wasn't good enough for flying! And now he's telling me. I'll show him. Him and his heel-banging shitehawk soldiers.

I'll get an S.I.B. man to come down and go over security with a nit-comb. I'll put a bomb under Keighly and frighten some blood round those drooping corpses. Can any of them do anything except eat?

ADJUTANT: We've had weapon-training, sir.

C.O. [*nearly going melancholy mad, reads*]: 'Personnel on R.A.F.

Geldon will wear white flashes as a distinguishing mark; the attacking force, red. Umpires will wear yellow armbands.' It's the sheer absolute bloody fantasy that gives me heartburn: 'The Home Counties have been dislocated by ground-to-ground nuclear missiles ... Umpires will wear yellow armbands.' It's in the same letter! [*He goes for the door.*]

ADJUTANT: Yes sir?

C.O.: Don't you see? The yellow armbands would be seriously faded by the nuclear flash.

ADJUTANT [*unnerved*]: Yes sir? Shall I get on to Command for a Special Investigation Branch man, sir?

C.O.: Yes, yes. And see if you can't get them to throw in a psychiatrist or a bottle of Alka Seltzers.

ADJUTANT: Now I don't know what to do when you talk like this, sir.

C.O.: Get an S.I.B. man!! [*Pause.*] Carpet eating can be fun.

[*The* C.O. *goes out and the* ADJUTANT *phones.* TAFFY *has started preparing the Mess Hall for dinner and* HIGGINS *is fussing about. He sees that the door to the kitchen is open.*]

HIGGINS [*to Neville*]: I don't like to see the door of the kitchen left open all the time, Neville my boy.

NEVILLE [*grinning*]: Well you don't have to look.

HIGGINS [*with a humourless but polite smile*]: You always smile and laugh, Neville. I shouldn't like to see you come to harm.

NEVILLE [*moving away about his business*]: If I do it'll be my own fault and nobody else's.

HIGGINS: Now, now, Neville, don't get me wrong. I mean it what I say. You know this last boy what had your place got a very serious sentence for stealing rations?

NEVILLE [*attentive now*]: Oh yes?

HIGGINS: Of course you know.

NEVILLE: And he didn't do it?

HIGGINS [*secretive smile*]: I think you know what I mean. Whether he did it or he didn't do it he got into trouble, didn't he?

NEVILLE: Oh yes?

HIGGINS: Now, now don't be playful. You can do a lot of things wrong perhaps, if you're a bad boy, and not get caught. But there's some people who like things to go wrong with others, because then nobody's looking for *their* badness.

NEVILLE: That's complicated.

HIGGINS: Don't get put on, Neville my boy. Careful nobody grinds you down. You and me, I'm sure we can work together here; but not everybody is only interested in just the work. And the other people, they're not interested in your welfare very much.

NEVILLE: It's a hard world, Mr Higgins.

HIGGINS: You get into any trouble, Nev my boy, you tell me.

NEVILLE: You'd be glad to know?

[ALBERT *saunters in at the other door.* HIGGINS *goes discreetly.*]

ALBERT: What was he on about? Stirring, I'll bet. You want to watch him.

NEVILLE: Watch everybody it seems like.

ALBERT: Yer. Even the potatoes got eyes here. Huh. Hey, Nev, dinner's on and everything, and I've trayed up tea in the larder and I'll bring it out for you. All right if I get off now? You only got just serving, leave the pans and I'll gerrin early tomorrow.

NEVILLE: Sure Bert. You get off now.

ALBERT: Only you see it's a bit different for me living out. You being on the camp like you're here anyway, aren't you?

NEVILLE: That's right, isn't it?

ALBERT: Thanks a lot. And don't do *nothing* for breakfast, right?

NEVILLE: All right.

ALBERT: Thanks a lot. I'll see you right here, don't worry. I'll do the same for you any time.

[ALBERT *goes off to get ready.* MCKENDRICK *looks in from the Mess Hall.*]

MCKENDRICK: Where's Meakin, Neville?

NEVILLE [*elaborately*]: Oh I er . . . He's not here at the moment.

MCKENDRICK: So I see. Where's he gone? He doesn't finish duty till two.

NEVILLE: I think he went across to H.Q., sir.

[NEVILLE *looks at his watch.* MCKENDRICK *looks at his watch.*]

MCKENDRICK: Neville, as a matter of interest, what were you in civilian life?

NEVILLE: Agricultural student, sir.

MCKENDRICK: I shouldn't have thought there was any sphere of life where an intelligent lad couldn't learn to lie skilfully.

NEVILLE: Pardon, sir?

MCKENDRICK [*with a fine degree of sarcasm*]: Tell Meakin I'd like a word with him when he comes back.

NEVILLE: Yes sir, I'll remember.

MCKENDRICK: Neville, you're a hard-working fellow, and you'll come to no harm with me on that account; as soon as Meakin's had his leave . . .

[NEVILLE *looks up;* MCKENDRICK *takes note.*]

Aye, I'd a feeling that might be a piece of news for you.

Well I'm not a wet-nurse, and I think you'll find your own way of dealing with anyone that puts on you; but don't put your trust in a man just because he hasn't got a rank . . . nor mistrust an N.C.O. automatically. D'you understand me?

[MCKENDRICK *goes without waiting for a reply, looking very pleased with himself.* NEVILLE *watches him go solemnly.* ALBERT *returns ready to go and carrying trays of food ready for tea.*]

ALBERT: What did McKendrick want?

NEVILLE: I told him you'd gone across to H.Q.

ALBERT: What for? Oh, oh yer . . . thanks. Didn't want him poking about, did I? With me getting ready to go eh? What did he want?

NEVILLE: Eh? Oh he just said compliments on the breakfast.

ALBERT: First time I ever heard of him doing that. All right if I get off now?

NEVILLE: Sure Bert, you get off home.

ALBERT: Thanks a lot, Nev, I'll do the same for you any time.

[*The screen shows* 'The Red Lion . . . That night'. *The scene changes to a narrow high-backed settle. A blind man,* JOHN, *malicious old man with a gentle voice and saintly face, and* MARGIT, *his companion, fat and wobbly, sit with glasses in their hands.*]

MARGIT: Look who's coming, John, it's Albert and June. Oh aren't they lovely.

JOHN: I know.

[JUNE MEAKIN, *pretty and cheap like a celluloid doll, comes in with Albert. He has a carrier bag.*]

Hallo Albert and June. [*Gives Margit money.*] Here you are, Margit, get us another.

[MARGIT *goes.*]

How are you Albert?

ALBERT [*shuffles along the carrier bag*]: All Officers' Mess stuff.

JOHN: Bless you, Bert lad, bless you.

[MARGIT *comes back with two drinks.* JOHN *handles the change.*]

MARGIT: Aye, God bless you, lad.

JOHN: You haven't got them a drink, Margit?

MARGIT: Oh bless them I never thought.

JOHN: Daft enough for ought.

[MARGIT *takes back the change and goes again.*]

ALBERT: [*to June*]: New bloke came today.

JOHN: Oh did he?

JUNE: You'll be glad of that. Is he nice?

MARGIT: Here you are, darlings.

[ALBERT *and* JUNE *take the bottles and glasses and pour them out.*]

Look at them, it's lovely to see them, so young.

JOHN: You never said a truer word, Margit.

ALBERT [*edgy, trying to get on with his conversation with June*]: Smashing bloke. That's how I come to get off after this.

JUNE: Oh Bert, are you sure you should?

ALBERT: He was glad to do it for us.

MARGIT [*to John, re. Albert*]: Is he a pilot then, John?

JOHN: No, no, he's a cook.

MARGIT: Well bless 'em all, I say.

JOHN: That's right, Margit.

ALBERT: I've fixed up my leave, I'll be away early tomorrow.

JOHN: Leave? You're not going on leave, lad?

JUNE: I thought you said there was going to be some surprise manoeuvres?

ALBERT: Well that's just why, isn't it? I've got to get them in quick.

MARGIT: Our boys. Them as starts wars ought to fight 'em I say. They little think what it costs.

JOHN: Yes, yes, Margit.

MARGIT: They take our lovely boys.

JOHN: He says he's going on leave.

ALBERT [*to June*]: Me and Nev'll work it between us. He's a good feller. I like him, you know, gerron wi' him.

MARGIT: Get their faces burned off them or else their legs shattered.

ALBERT: I wish you'd shurrup, missis.

MARGIT: Now then don't take on, lad.

JOHN: Howd thy peace, Margit, else I s'all lam thee.

MARGIT [*whimpering*]: Oh John you wouldn't.

JOHN [*to Albert*]: When does your leave start?

ALBERT: Tomorrow.

JOHN: Tomorrow! But whatever shall I do?

ALBERT: Shut your face.

JOHN [*hastily*]: Margit, show Mrs Meakin where the ladies is, she doesn't know.

JUNE: Eh?

JOHN: She's shifting about I can tell.

JUNE [*hotly*]: I am not shifting about!

ALBERT [*quietly*]: Away you go. Business.

JUNE [*flustered*]: Well, why didn't you say?

JOHN: Margit!

MARGIT: Don't bully me, John, please.

[*The two women go.*]

JOHN: You're not going to let me down, Albert lad. You couldn't do that.

ALBERT: Of course I'm not. I've got a friggin kitbag full of stuff if you want to know. But I'm not trundling that out until I know how soft this new lad is.

I'll make sure his record is well smudged before I let him in on my capers.

JOHN: You can't be too careful. I can tell you now Harry was all set to shop you before he was caught and sent up over them pork pies. You better watch it when he gets out.

ALBERT: I knew I daresn't trust him. I felt it in my bones.

JOHN: I wonder where he's feeling it now?

ALBERT: Never you mind. That's my business. I'll have that stuff over the wire tomorrow early, before he gets into the kitchen. And pick it up before tomorrow night.

JOHN: A kitbag full! Oh Albert you're a lovely lad. God bless you. Bring it round to our house.

ALBERT [*significantly*]: Ten pounds worth.

JOHN [*closing up*]: Well we'll say that when we've sold it, shall we?

ALBERT: I'm talking about what you've had already and haven't settled yet. Don't think that just because som'dy got nicked that you're going to save yourself his share.

JOHN: Nay Bert, it fetched nowhere near ten pound.

ALBERT: I'll have it now, and cash tomorrow night. I've worked on a barrow, you don't have to tell me how much things cost.

JOHN: I couldn't get to the bookies today. Things aren't easy.

ALBERT: Ten pounds mister, I'm not waiting on no bookies.

JOHN: Oh where'd I get ten pound from Albert lad?

ALBERT: From selling my stuff what I brought you.

JOHN: By you're hard man to deal wi'.

ALBERT: I'll be hard on your head wi' that stick of yours if you don't stop messing.

JOHN: See here's the girls back.

ALBERT: Come on with it, you bony old bastard.

JOHN: Just watch your step, young fellermelad. I can soon stir things up for you. At the camp. I'll soon shop you, with the S.I.B. and all, I'll soon shop you.

ALBERT [*vicious*]: Right.

[*The women return.*]

MARGIT: See them there still chatting. It's nice for him you know.

ALBERT: Come on June, we're going.

JUNE: What, already?

ALBERT: I've some accounts to settle.

MARGIT: What a shame. John they're going.

JOHN: You're not going yet, nay then. Margit, gerrus all another.

MARGIT: You haven't supped what you've got yet.

JOHN: Shorts. Shorts for everyone. Go on Albert, you'll have just the one. Sit down lad.

ALBERT [*sits*]: I am sitting down.

JOHN: Good lad . . . Margit . . .

ALBERT [*forestalling Margit . . . testing John*]: She's already gone.

JOHN: Nay she hasn't, not bart money.

[*He gives Margit some money. Turns away from Albert and fishes surreptitiously in an inside pocket for some notes.* MARGIT *goes for the drinks.*]

ALBERT: I have me suspicions about him. Too friggin fly by half.

JOHN: Here you are, Albert, have this for yourself.

[*Presses notes into Albert's hand.* ALBERT *pockets them swiftly and ungraciously.*]

JUNE: Ooh, what is it, Albert?

ALBERT: Business.

JUNE: You and your 'bloomin' business. I'm gerrin a bit sick of it. I felt proper soft when we got outside just now and I didn't want to go anywhere. I had to borrow a penny and all.

[MARGIT *brings the drinks.*]

JOHN: All right now, Bert?

ALBERT [*nods*]: Cheers.

MARGIT: Cheers everybody. Well this is nice, isn't it? Quite a jubilee.

ALBERT [*to June*]: I shall be going to work early tomorrow morning.

MARGIT: Oh lovely boys. Up in the clouds. They think it's not fighting when the boys are up there, but when there's blood on the joystick it's fighting all right.

ALBERT: Will you belt up, grandma!

MARGIT: Oh.

CURTAIN

ACT TWO

[*The screen indicates that it is dawn the next day on the camp. In the Sergeants' Mess kitchen breakfast things are laid out on the working surface: bacon trayed-up neatly, tray of eggs, tea tin, sugar, a big pan of porridge on the stove. The kettle is on, and* NEVILLE *is working the twiddler to make the fire burn up. He puts on a large frying-pan and puts a tray of bacon in the oven. He amuses himself by clucking like a hen as he works . . . probably by association with the eggs.*

In the Mess Hall there are signs that a violent party has taken place during the night. The tables and chairs are in odd groups and the floor is untidy. Glasses have been washed, and the bar shutter is down. KEIGHLY *sits contemplating a gin bottle. One or two sergeants doze in chairs or against the wall. One light burns. Outside the camp is still and grey. We hear* TAFFY'S *voice . . . full and soaring . . . and then begin to make out the words of his song:*]

TAFFY [*sings*]:

> My father was an L.A.C.
> And I'm an AC2
> He died with Pontius Pilate's boys
> In 1942
> Dressed in blue
> Same to you
> He'd a hole in his head with no brains in
> And I wish I was that way too.

[TAFFY *pokes his head into the kitchen. He wears his greatcoat with a red and black armband showing he's on fire picket, battle dress as before, with the bottoms of his pyjamas showing underneath.*]

TAFFY: Morning Nev, you're up early.

NEVILLE: Morning Taffy. Happy?

TAFFY: I have had better moments. Mind if I come in and have a warm? I'm on fire-picket and I haven't had a smell of one all night, the service is terrible. Brrr. Roll on demob. [*Plants himself in front of the stove.*]

NEVILLE: You'd be warmer if you were working, fetch us a bucket of coal.

TAFFY: Oh Nev, don't be mis'rable, you know I'm allergic to work, it gives me a temperature. That kettle on for tea?

NEVILLE: There's the bucket.

TAFFY: Here, you seen Sergeant Bull about? He's supposed to be Orderly Sergeant and we ain't seen him this morning at all.

NEVILLE: It's early yet.

TAFFY: Should 'a' been up. They had a party in there last night and he was in and out. I hope he didn't come to no good. It must be terrible to behold in there this morning. I'm glad I aren't on today.

[TAFFY *hears Keighly and one of the sergeants stirring in the Mess and slips discreetly away.*

NEVILLE *is busy and clucks away happily until the two N.C.O.s are in the kitchen. They have both been drinking all night and are cheerful and proud.*]

SERGEANT: Morning cookie. Innit terrible when you're the only one sober and everyone else's pig-drunk?

KEIGHLY [*bellowing after the fleeing figure of Taffy*]: Get your hair cut, Jones! Any tea in that pot bobbagee?

NEVILLE: No sir.

KEIGHLY: Who was it had that chicken in here just now?

NEVILLE: I wouldn't do any such thing.

[*This strikes* KEIGHLY *as a tremendous joke and he reels out wheezing with laughter. The* SERGEANT *follows him tittering uncontrollably.*

NEVILLE *is now all set for breakfast except for the fire which refuses to draw up and boil the kettle.*

ALBERT *comes in from the outer door and goes straight to the larder and unlocks it. He has a kitbag folded under his arm. He is taken aback when he sees Neville in so early, and goes quietly to the kitchen door and watches him hectoring the kettle.*]

I'll have you on a 252 before you can say feather-duster! Failure to comply with the order of a *su-perior*! Mutiny! Dumb bloody insolence! Stand up! I'll have you in the guardroom so fast your feet won't touch the ground! [*Paces up and down.*] Boil you horrible kettle, boil! [*Grabs the kettle and rushes to the sink, empties it out.*] *Dishonourable discharge!*

[*Refills it from the hot tap and puts it back on the stove. Starts his clucking again.* ALBERT *shrugs and moves back to the larder. As he reaches the door it opens and there emerges a truly appalling sight. It is* SERGEANT BULL, *stiff drunk, who has been eating heaven knows how many eggs. He has a tray covered with eggshells in his hand and stares glassily at Albert as he sucks yet another. He is daubed with shells and their contents.* BULL *turns unsteadily and goes thoughtlessly back into the larder.* ALBERT *shuts the door on him.*]

ALBERT: Snookered. [*Goes to the kitchen. Panicked*] Hey Nev! Have you looked in the larder?

NEVILLE: Morning Bert. No, not yet.

ALBERT: Som'dy's in the muck I don't know who.

NEVILLE: Why? What's wrong?

ALBERT: I come in early to see if you was all right; I just happened to open the larder door ... chance in a million ... I'll swear I locked it and took both keys. No, we'd better say you had it.

NEVILLE: Why?

ALBERT: Because there's not supposed to be two keys out, this one should have been in the guardroom. Just a minute though, it *was* locked, and there *was* two keys in the guardroom. I've never liked that system, you don't never want to trust them S.P.s.

NEVILLE: What was locked?

ALBERT: The larder door.

NEVILLE: Of course it was, you left all the rations out yesterday.

ALBERT: Yes, that's right, you can swear to that can't you? No, you had the key.

NEVILLE: Did I heck. Why?

ALBERT: What d'you mean why? I told you. Som'dy's in the muck here and it's not going to be me.

NEVILLE: So it's forced to be me?

ALBERT: Don't you try to switch it on to me, I wasn't even friggin here! I'm going on leave today and that's flat.

NEVILLE: This is all very interesting. I'd like to hear all about it some time.

ALBERT: Look, there's no need for us to fall out. There's only two of us here, so nobody can call us liars. You had the key and you locked up. No *I* had the key; there that clears you. I'll say that and you back me up and swear you had the key in your pocket. You're only new here so they won't say nothing to you.

NEVILLE: When you've finished talking morse I'd like to hear more about this leave of yours.

ALBERT: Oh to hell with my leave.

NEVILLE: That's what I say.

ALBERT: There's more important things.

NEVILLE: You may be right there.

ALBERT: We've got to get *him* out.

[NEVILLE *looks at Albert and then along to the larder where he points.*]

NEVILLE: Who?

ALBERT: That friggin parachute-packing beer-barrel, Sergeant Bull. He's in the larder.

[NEVILLE *goes coolly along to the larder, looks in, walks back.*]

NEVILLE: So this is the hole you've been inviting me to fall into.

ALBERT: Oh belt up Nev. . . .

NEVILLE: Just a minute, he's supposed to be Orderly Sergeant.

ALBERT: Well poor old him. There's going to be some sorting out here Nev. We're not carrying this one. I'll have a word with Sergeant Bull.

NEVILLE: I should say he'd very likely sort *you* out Albert.

ALBERT: Hey if he's Orderly Sergeant that's how he got access to the keys! We're all right Nev; we're in the clear.

NEVILLE: I don't think I was ever anything else, was I Bert?

ALBERT [*tolerantly*]: What? Negligence with R.A.F. stores?

NEVILLE: No but didn't you tell me you were solely responsible for the rations? I wasn't to bother me head? You being an S.A.C.?

ALBERT: Oh that was just me making it easier for you. You don't think a court martial'd take that attitude? Don't worry Nev, I'll see you right.

[NEVILLE *is staring out of the window, weighing a big rolling-pin in his hand.*]

In a way, Nev, I'm quite glad that this has happened.

NEVILLE: Yes?

ALBERT: No I don't mean like you having a hot moment. But you see now that you've got me to back you up. They're all after you here, because anybody can make a mistake some time. . . .

NEVILLE [*not interrupting*]: After me?

ALBERT: No I mean anybody. I mean you all feel guilty because nobody's perfect.

NEVILLE [*he is looking at Albert keenly and sardonically, as if wondering whether he's going to lam him with the pin*]: I don't feel a bit guilty, Albert. I didn't do anything remember?

ALBERT: Ach you're not listening. You don't know what it's all about. You'll never make an airman in a thousand years.

[NEVILLE *takes a large potato out of a pan of water on the table. He lays it on the table-top near Albert.* ALBERT *looks on mystified. Suddenly* NEVILLE *hits the potato with the rolling pin, squashing it.* ALBERT *starts back out of the way . . . far too late if the blow had been for him.*]

Hey you want to bloody watch what you're doing! That could have been my friggin hand just then. What's the idea? You want to hurt som'dy or sunthin'?

NEVILLE [*grinning*]: What about Bull?

ALBERT [*he has a shake on*]: I told you. I'll shop him.

[BULL *is in the doorway, morose and belligerent.*]

BULL: Meakin, make me a cup of tea, or I'll smash your head in.

ALBERT: It's not me on duty, sergeant.

[BULL *lurches forward.* ALBERT *gets on with it.* NEVILLE *whips off the tea towel he wears round his middle over his apron and douses it with cold water.*]

NEVILLE: Come here, sergeant.

[BULL *goes meekly over and* NEVILLE *starts to clean him up.*]

You've got about two minutes to get to the guardroom.

BULL: Lerrem wait. 'm gonna change m'uniform.

NEVILLE: Don't be a clod. The troops'll be half asleep and the N.C.O.s'll all have been boozing like you, and I don't suppose the duty officer would have the neck to comment if you turned up in a busby.

BULL: Don't ever get like me bobbagee.

NEVILLE [*giving him a cold compress with the towel*]: You shouldn't have joined if you can't take a joke.

BULL: When d'you get out?

NEVILLE: Six months. August. You?

BULL: Never. Not fit for anything else. D'you think I'd be any good in civvy street? [*This is not a rhetorical question – he wants to know.*]

NEVILLE: Boozers always get good references.

[BULL *is steadier and tidier now. He goes to Albert and takes the mug of tea from his hand and goes.*]

BULL: It'd better have plenty of sugar in it.

ALBERT: Don't you worry Nev, I'll have him.

NEVILLE: I should get in some sprinting practice before you start on him.

ALBERT: Huh. What I'd like to know is what we do for eggs for a week.

NEVILLE: I shall keep these two trays for batters and that, and take off eggs altogether.

ALBERT: They won't stand for that.

NEVILLE: They will when they find out how they went. Anyway that's not your worry, since I hear you're away today.

ALBERT: Oh yer.

NEVILLE: How long for, just as a matter of interest? I mean it had crossed your mind I might like to know how long I'd be working two shifts a day and no breaks?

ALBERT: No need to get bitter and twisted about it Nev. You get your leave, just the same as me. Only I've fourteen days still to come. . . .

NEVILLE: Fourteen days? You'll be glad of that.

ALBERT: You bet I am. And so's my missis I can tell you. Actually it's only ten, but I missed my forty-eight when Harry was on the court martial and before you came.

NEVILLE: That's still only twelve days the way I count.

ALBERT: Aye, but there's my week-end off as well isn't there. I didn't want to say anything really until I were sure. I only put in for it yes'day.

[NEVILLE *takes out another potato and lays it by Albert.* ALBERT *moves away.*]

I'll give you a hand wi' breakfast and then start on wi' cleaning eh? They'll all be in early, what with the parade and boozing all night.

[*The screen indicates:* 'The Airstrip' *and the scene changes. A civil*

airline windsock flutters limply. An elaborate flagstaff centre. MR
KEIGHLY *addresses several hoarse and unintelligible shouts at
us:*]

KEIGHLY: Ar-ay! Ar-ay hin!

[*Stereophonic noise of troop coming to attention.*]

Ar-ay rai . . . hese! [*Shuffle.*]

Aye-ee funt!

[ADJUTANT *enters and stands to attention.* KEIGHLY *marches to
report to him.*]

Parade present and correct, sir!

[*They salute.*]

ADJUTANT: Thank you Mr Keighly. Parade! Pa-rade stand-at-
ease!

[*Noise of boots.*]

Fall in the supernumary officers.

[*Junior officers enter.*]

Pa-rade, shun! [*Noise of boots.*]

Pa-rade right, dress! [*Shuffle.*]

Eyes, front!

Pa-rade stand-at, ease! [*Noise of boots.*]

[C.O. *enters.* ADJUTANT *about-turns to him.*]

Pa-rade, shun! [*Noise of boots.*]

Parade present sir.

C.O.: Parade, stand-at ease!

[*Noise of boots.* C.O. *about-turns to face flag.*]

General salute! Atten-shun!

[*The flag is broken as all salute it. It is upside down and the S.P.
hastily runs it right down and up again the right way round.*
C.O. *about-turns to Adjutant.*]

C.O.: At ease parade.

[ADJUTANT *about-turns to Keighly.*]

ADJUTANT: At ease Mr Keighly.

[KEIGHLY *about-turns to face us. Supernumary officers about-turn.*]

KEIGHLY: Ar-ay! Aray andar-hi!

C.O.: Men! I expect you've all seen Station orders already, and know
that we are to take part in a surprise exercise, and you will know
what dispositions have already been made.

Nobody, neither the attacking force nor we the defenders, knows when this is to take place. But it is our duty in the normal course of things to be prepared for war and attack, at any time.

Now this station has a fine record in history as well I know, since I had the honour and privilege of serving here as a pilot in 1944 when it was first set up as a base for night-bomber forays. And more recently when I returned in peacetime to take up command we have had the honour to hold at various times the table-tennis shield for Bomber Command, the Inter-Services Squash Challenge Cup, and a special mention in the Command Mess-Hall Competition. So I can tell you we're pretty well thought of at Command H.Q.

And I can tell you something else: when this exercise is over, we are going to be held in even greater respect. Because we are going to win! We are going to roll them back, if they come in their thousands!

I want you to look on this exercise as a serious and vital task; consider that in time of war this sort of thing is deadly earnest, the only way of saving our way of life, and the very lives of our loved ones, from a ruthless invader.

When the moment comes, men, stand your ground. The security of the station and of everything it is our sworn duty to defend, depend on everyone of us standing firm, until the umpire gives the order to section commanders to withdraw.

[*He stares at us for a moment with the distressed look of a man who is about to be sick.*]

Thank you, Mr Keighly. Carry on.

KEIGHLY [*a slight huskiness in the voice*]: Pa-ray! Paray hin! Paray will marroff ay flights . . . pa-ray ra-ay hin!!

[*All salute and* MR KEIGHLY *joins the group round the C.O. and they walk off.*

In the Sergeants' Mess kitchen NEVILLE *is clearing up after breakfast.* ALBERT *emerges cautiously from the back door with his kitbag, now stuffed with loot.*]

ALBERT: I'm not trusting *him* that's one thing for sure. Friggin nutter.

[*After a quick look round he goes to where the perimeter wire would*

be and pushes the kitbag under. Marching feet approach and we hear
them being dismissed by flights. Airmen begin to be seen about their
tasks. ALBERT *hastily drags some debris over the kitbag and goes back*
into the kitchen.]

There's just one thing Nev; I wonder if I was to get tea all ready,
would you come in later on this afternoon and just serve it up for
us? And then I could get away to a good start.

NEVILLE [*after a second's pause*]: Sure.

ALBERT: Thanks a lot Nev. I'll do the same for you any time, you
know that.

NEVILLE: That's all right.

[KEIGHLY *comes in through the Mess Hall.*]

ALBERT: Morning sir.

KEIGHLY [*a bit hard*]: Morning Meakin. [*Now with a shout*] Morning
Bobbagee!

NEVILLE [*shouting back*]: Morning sir!

KEIGHLY: What I should like to know, Meakin, is what happened
to you this morning on parade?

ALBERT: Nothing, sir.

KEIGHLY: Well it might have done if you'd been there mightn't it?
[*To Neville*] That kettle on, Bobbagee?

[NEVILLE *puts it on*, KEIGHLY *turns back to Albert.*]

Well? Never mind standing there thinking up excuses I want no
excuses.

ALBERT: I was on duty, sir.

KEIGHLY: Look, Meakin, I'm giving you a personal and specific
order to be on parade tomorrow morning, or I'll have you with
your cap off before you can say knife.

ALBERT [*his face twitching*]: Yes sir.

KEIGHLY: I'll not be defied, so think on.

[KEIGHLY *goes back into the Mess Hall.*]

ALBERT: He's got some hopes; I'll be a few mile off here tomorrow
morning. He's got no authority whatsoever to order us on parade
you know. Not while we're on duty.

[NEVILLE *is working away*, ALBERT *isn't doing a bat, he just*
follows Neville around . . . . talk, talk, talk.]

You notice he daresn't have a go at you, he knows. Mr McKendrick could have us in the guardroom just as quick as him if we *went* on parade.

Defecation of duty.

Take that kettle off the fire to hell wi' 'im. We get no rations for making spare cups of tea all day. I expect they had you everlasting parading in the Airmen's Mess?

NEVILLE: It's so long since I paraded nobody recognizes me in uniform.

ALBERT [*this stops him for a second but he steams on*]: You got to work the system Nev. You can commit friggin murder so long as you sign a chitty for it. Next time he comes moaning about his friggin parades one of us'll *go*. And take friggin hours getting back. And he can friggin whistle for his cup of tea I'll be *too busy*; because me mate's on parade.

[NEVILLE *has made the tea. A waiter comes in with a laid tray.* NEVILLE *pours out two mugs and refills the pot.* MCKENDRICK *and* BULL *have wandered into the Mess Hall to Keighly.* NEVILLE *hands a mug to Albert, who is still in spate.*]

Oh, thanks. [*To the waiter*] You can tell the S.W.O. with my compliments we don't get rations for spare cups of tea [*To Neville*] I was a fool, I should have told him about Bull and them eggs.

[*The* WAITER *puts the tray in front of the two W.O.s.* BULL *is by the window, and goes back to the wash-up.*]

KEIGHLY [*to McKendrick*]: Can you cover it up?

MCKENDRICK: I can.

KEIGHLY [*to Bull*]: You, you blockhead, you'll go out and buy three dozen eggs this morning.

BULL: I'm orderly sergeant, I can't.

KEIGHLY: You'll do as I tell you. Am I S.W.O. of this station or just a hole in the wall? How much are three dozen eggs?

MCKENDRICK: I'll get some, don't worry.

KEIGHLY: How much are they?

MCKENDRICK: Let him put a pound in the mess fund and I'll cover it up.

KEIGHLY: I should think you will! What about the men?

MCKENDRICK: Harrison you can trust. I found the young fool out covering up for Meakin yesterday. Meakin slipping off early and leaving Harrison to finish his shift for him. Harrison'll never see anyone in the muck.

KEIGHLY: *I'll* deal with Meakin.

MCKENDRICK: It won't be necessary. He can't do much by himself. Besides he's going on leave today.

KEIGHLY: Makes a mockery of good order and discipline. Too fly by half. I'll have the guardroom watch he doesn't slip off early any more.

BULL: I'll watch him.

KEIGHLY: You watch yourself, sergeant! Anyway you won't be there. You'll be out buying eggs.

MCKENDRICK: I buy the eggs on this station.

KEIGHLY: Talking of eggs, can we trust Higgins to keep quiet?

[HIGGINS *is standing outside the baize curtain, affecting interest in something else. The* WAITER *keeps his distance.*]

MCKENDRICK: You can. Mainly because he doesn't know ... and secondly because his job's in it.

[HIGGINS *turns towards the kitchen, pained and prim, as if there were somebody watching him ... which there is: himself. He enters the kitchen.*]

HIGGINS: Now boys, who's doing tea?

ALBERT [*looks up sharply*]: Why d'you ask that Mistriggins?

HIGGINS: Albert, I should like a word with you. [*Turns and goes into his room*]

ALBERT: All right. [*Follows him.*]

HIGGINS [*to the waiter*]: Have you taken away the tea tray?

WAITER: No, Mr Higgins, I was waiting.

HIGGINS: Go and take away the tea things if you please and I want to see you laying the tables for luncheon.

[*The* WAITER *goes.* HIGGINS *turns to go into his room, but* ALBERT *stays in the wash-up, so* HIGGINS *has to.*]

ALBERT: Now then Mistriggins, what's all this about?

HIGGINS: I simply wanted to discuss the menu with you, Albert. [*He's beginning to feel like Talleyrand.*]

ALBERT: Now we've no eggs for pancakes Mistriggins.

HIGGINS: Well you should have. I shall speak to Mr McKendrick for you.

ALBERT [*a bit bitter*]: I shouldn't bother.

HIGGINS: Oh it's no bother at all. If you've used up all the eggs ...

[*He waits to be told what he knows already but Albert's waiting for a subtle attack on his afternoon off.*]

How are you getting on with the new boy?

ALBERT: All right.

HIGGINS: I'm very glad you got somebody like him under you. So what have you got for luncheon?

ALBERT: Chops. Two each.

HIGGINS: ... and tea?

ALBERT: Finney Haddock I expect, I haven't made up my mind.

HIGGINS: Good. Very good.

[ALBERT *goes.* HIGGINS *follows him after a second. As* HIGGINS *closes the door behind him* MCKENDRICK, *coming from the Mess Hall, re-opens it.*]

Albert, I'll tell you what is very nice with haddock and that's a poached egg on the top of it.

[*Everyone in the kitchen turns to look at McKendrick in the doorway.*]

MCKENDRICK [*cold*]: Meakin, you'll be doing tea today I imagine, since you weren't here yesterday afternoon?

ALBERT: Well actually, sir, I'd like to do a swap with him, so I can get away just that bit early, if that's all right with you, sir.

[*Pause.*]

I mean it's usual, isn't it, sir?

MCKENDRICK: It is not all right with me. Anything else?

[*He looks round briefly and then goes off out.* HIGGINS *holds the door for him.*]

HIGGINS: I don't like unfortunate incidents in the kitchen, Albert.

[*Goes.*]

ALBERT: He friggin knows about them friggin eggs I'll swear. And McKendrick knows about me nicking off yes'day. What a mess. I'll be glad when I'm on leave. I tell you once they get tabs on you they'll grind you out of existence.

NEVILLE: Who will?

ALBERT: Them. Anybody. Even Mistriggins. It's worse than blackmail because you daresn't even let them start to threaten you. I'd like to know who's stirring it for us.

NEVILLE: You. Not me.

ALBERT: That's worra said.

NEVILLE: You should be used to threats by now anyway. How long have you been in?

ALBERT: Five year. You don't know it yet. I'm telling you. There's threats and threats: like when Keighly starts shooting off about 'get your hair cut' that's just him fancying himself R.S.M. Britten; he doesn't hardly look at your hair. No, it's what behind it all, the Glasshouse and you by yourself with the M.P.s and their big boots.

NEVILLE: Well if you weren't so devious about everything you'd get on better for a start. You didn't *have* to lie to me for instance, about your leave, did you? And you could have come straight out about the eggs to them. It's my opinion you'd prefer to have them threatening over your head.

ALBERT: Don't you call me a liar. I've never told one lie since you come here. Here it's since you come here people have started getting at me. It's you, is it?

NEVILLE: It isn't.

ALBERT: Well you watch it that's all if it is you.

NEVILLE [*getting a bit funny*]: It isn't.

ALBERT [*shifting his gaze moodily*]: I'll be here till friggin six o'clock near on.

NEVILLE: If it was me trying to fix you you'd know it; I don't fight if I can't win.

Anyway you're the one that's been giving off all the heehaw about the system. Work yourself out of this one: you're supposed to know all the rules.

ALBERT: All right, forget it, that's enough. You're not interested in my problems, so now we know. You're fireproof, all right.

NEVILLE: You poor festering waif.

ALBERT: I said all right, didn't I? Why can't you drop it?

NEVILLE: You're like a lot of mice in a wheel. Because I say nowt and keep my head down you all scutter round tweeting at me to come and join us. 'Dreamland, where men are men, and you get a chitty to prove it.'

ALBERT: Who's tweeting?

NEVILLE: Every flamer . . . except Taffy, and he's too dense to have any malice in him. Even the blanket corporal said watch it because I've got six more blankets than I should have.

ALBERT: So they've all been stirring it for us have they?

NEVILLE: If you'll just put your business activities out of your head for a moment I'll tell you something.

ALBERT [*very sharp*]: What you mean 'business activities'?

NEVILLE [*slowly and distinctly*]: I don't give a tuppenny fart for your soldiering, your stirring, your Queen's Regulations, your skiving and your bull. I want out. I've learnt sense my dad could have told me for nothing if I'd listened . . . he's the longest established deserter in the British Legion bowls team . . . and I want a job where it's a good thing if you *do* it, not one where you're more use idle. I'm going to sell plastic novelties.

ALBERT: Oh. [*Relieved*] Oh, for a minute I thought you was on about . . . I mean, well it's daft really, but I thought you thought I was like, you know, nicking rations or sumthin'. Huh.

Oh well, if you're a yellow-bellied pacifist why didn't you say? You didn't have to join did you? Anyway what if there's a war?

NEVILLE: Who said anything about a war?

ALBERT: You'll have to fight then.

NEVILLE: The forces have nothing to do with fighting!

ALBERT: Oh I give up, you're crackers.

NEVILLE [*ignoring him*]: It's an organization for knocking the guts out of the gutless. 'A fine fighting force' . . . you know who that means? *Us*. You and me, spelt US.

It means a bunch of healthy unemployables polishing the missiles, making sure they point the right way, until somebody gets bilious and hysterical enough to want them set off and no questions. And if the lot round here are any measure mate, it won't be long now.

ALBERT: Well, what's wrong wi' that? Got to have wars haven't you? It's human nature to fight. The bad's got to come out.

NEVILLE: You call that fighting? You want to come round our street.

[*Through the outer door to the kitchen comes a smiling and rosy young warrant officer, W.O. CLAPP.*]

CLAPP: Morning. You the cook here?

NEVILLE [*after Albert doesn't answer*]: Yes. Me and him.

CLAPP: Like the job? I said did you like the job?

[KEIGHLY, MCKENDRICK, *and* HIGGINS *come through from the Mess. They have heard some rumour about a new W.O.*]

NEVILLE: I've only been here two days.

CLAPP [*to Albert particularly*]: And what about you? Do you like the job? What's your name?

ALBERT: Meakin.

CLAPP: S.A.C. Meakin. That's right, isn't it? The other one got ninety days, didn't he? That's more than you've got if you carry on, isn't it?

ALBERT: Me?

CLAPP: You'll do. It has to be somebody.

KEIGHLY: What's going on here?

CLAPP: That's just what I was wondering, sir. I'm getting some very funny answers to my questions.

KEIGHLY: What're you doing asking questions in the first place?

CLAPP [*earnestly*]: There's nothing funny going on here, is there, sir?

KEIGHLY: Not to my knowledge. Anyway who are you? What's your business?

CLAPP: Warrant Officer Clapp, sir. [*To McKendrick*] You're the catering officer?

MCKENDRICK: I am.

CLAPP: How d'you do. Warrant Officers Keighly and McKendrick, S.A.C. Meakin, A/C Harrison . . . and Mr Higgins. Now I know everybody don't I? Lucky I found you all together. Of course when I say *know* . . . you get to know someone bit by bit, don't you? You watch, and you get little hints, people come and give you little hints. I love my job, [*to Albert*] d'you like your job? [*To everyone*] Everyone should be in a job they like. And fit. Is it all right if I have lunch here?

HIGGINS: Yes, sir.

[CLAPP *smiles all round and goes out the way he came.*]

KEIGHLY: Insulting young bastard, I'll break him. I'll find out about him and break him. Now, everybody in this room, listen!

ALBERT: He was S.I.B., sir! Don't trust him, he's got shifty eyes!

KEIGHLY: Shut your gob, Meakin. Now I won't go into the various difficulties we're coping with here, except to say I'm backing you all up to the hilt to get things straight. This is *internal*. Nobody's perfect. But by the gods, if any words, if half a syllable, reaches the ears of any outsider, of any damaging information, the man with the mouth will be in the glasshouse until he thinks he's a tomato.

[*The phone rings in the Mess.*]

Don't answer it!

No, answer it [MCKENDRICK *goes.*] if you please. If it's for me I'm on my way. No. Find out who it is first.

[MCKENDRICK *has picked up the phone and answered. It is the Adjutant ringing from the office.*]

ADJUTANT: Sergeants' Mess? I want the Station Warrant Officer.

[KEIGHLY *and* HIGGINS *are coming out of the kitchen and* MCKEND-RICK *meets them and delivers his message.* KEIGHLY *goes to the phone.*]

ADJUTANT: Mr Keighly, have you seen a strange Warrant Officer on the camp.

KEIGHLY: They're all strange, sir, some are stranger than others, but if you mean the one calling himself Warrant Officer Clapp he beats all.

ADJUTANT: That's the one. For goodness' sake hold him, stop him, bring him back to the guardroom.

KEIGHLY: Certainly, sir, with pleasure. Had you any particular charge in mind?

ADJUTANT: Stop waffling, Mr Keighly, this is deadly serious.

KEIGHLY: I agree with you, sir.

ADJUTANT: Agree with me! D'you realize that man's been sent here to test security and he's just walked straight in? Get him. The C.O.'s got in his car and I swear he'll run him down the mood he's in, unless you get there first. He's nearly out of his mind because it was he that asked for a security check in the first place.

[HIGGINS *has gone back into his room.* MCKENDRICK *looks at Keighly.*]

MCKENDRICK: Are you all right?

KEIGHLY: I'm getting old for this game.

MCKENDRICK: Take it easy.

KEIGHLY: What did I say just now in the kitchen? Nothing that could be brought home?

MCKENDRICK: You just threatened hellfire and detention all round.

KEIGHLY: Nothing about why?

MCKENDRICK: Don't worry, just relax.

KEIGHLY: You're right. I'll just stroll, very slowly, to the guard-room. Have a chat about that Warrant Officer with Sergeant Fairclough.

MCKENDRICK: Don't you worry about him.

KEIGHLY: Oh, I'm not. D'you think you could check if the M.O.'s on camp?

MCKENDRICK: Ach come off it. You're not going to die.

KEIGHLY: I don't think I am Jock. But somebody might, mightn't they? You never know your luck. Somebody might.

[KEIGHLY *goes out with slow dignity.* HIGGINS *emerges, putting on his raincoat. He goes into the kitchen.*]

HIGGINS: What'd you think of that boys? Special investigation branch coming here. I've had an idea to slip down to the village for a few eggs, Albert. Make some nice pancakes, just for us three.

[HIGGINS *goes happily out of the back door.*]

NEVILLE: Hard to tell who the battle's with really, isn't it?

ALBERT: I friggin know who it's with.

NEVILLE [*going up close; genial*]: Ah, but do you know who's going to win?

CURTAIN

ACT THREE

[*The screen indicates that it is ten to six the same evening. . . . The camp. Dusk. The camp is still. In the guardroom* WARRANT OFFICER CLAPP *is seated comfortably, leafing through some personal records from a large briefcase, examining the faces in the photographs.*

SERGEANT FAIRCLOUGH, *N.C.O. I/C Service Police, a malignant and upright man, is pacing in an affectation of confidence and military probity. An* S.P. CORPORAL *dozes behind the desk.*

We hear NEVILLE'S *voice in the stillness, in a cod-indian wail:*]

NEVILLE [*off*]:

> Sixteen annahs make one rupee
> Seventeen annahs one buckshee
> Sergeant-major hollow-ground razor
> Queen Victoria very good man
> Ah cha boogaree damn and slag the bobbagee.

[CLAPP *selects a record and holds it out for comment from* SERGEANT FAIRCLOUGH. FAIRCLOUGH *betrays his nervousness by darting instantly to Clapp's elbow.*]

CLAPP: That one?

FAIRCLOUGH: The provo. Flying Officer Gunn. Hot on discipline.

CLAPP: Not much scope for him here, eh?

FAIRCLOUGH [*with a weak grin*]: Well, the C.O.'s not what you might call predictable. Sometimes it's tricky for any of us concerned with discipline to know whether he'll back us up or not. You can't get that fine edge on your pounces that you might wish.

CLAPP: Man late off leave and you don't know whether it's twenty-eight days C.B., a caution, or a rollocking for the police?

FAIRCLOUGH: Something like that.

[CLAPP *goes on leafing.*]

CLAPP: Even that approach can work. I hear that in the Glasshouse now they're much more psychological than they were. It's been known for a screw to go in the chokeys and give a few screams all by himself, just to tone up the holy terror in the lads' bellies. [*Chuckles.*]

FAIRCLOUGH [*chancing a bit of humour*]: You know if I followed the C.O.'s wishes I'd have you under close guard in case you're part of this surprise exercise 'Shatter', and you've come to infiltrate us.

CLAPP [*not looking up*]: Was that a joke?

FAIRCLOUGH: Not all that funny perhaps.

[CLAPP *holds out another record.* FAIRCLOUGH *looks at it and then at Clapp without speaking.* CLAPP *looks up.*]

CLAPP: That one?

[FAIRCLOUGH *looks again and back without speaking.* CLAPP *looks for himself.*]

You don't know him?

FAIRCLOUGH: That's my record.

[CLAPP *compares the record and Fairclough with a genial amazement. Laughs merrily.*]

CLAPP: I don't know: I'll get somebody off this station before I've finished. It's all very well for your C.O. to pick up a phone and say 'complete security check' . . . . I'm the one who ends up responsible you know.

[CLAPP *goes back cheerfully to his records, showing one or two to Fairclough. We hear* NEVILLE'S *voice again, and then he appears, still in whites, strolling across the camp.*]

NEVILLE:

> Seven long year you slag my daughter
> Now you go to blighty sa'b
> May the ship on which you sail
> Sink to the bottom of the pahnee sa'b
> Ah cha boogaree damn and slag the bobbagee.

[*In the office a phone begins to ring. A whistle is blown and an* S.P. *hauls down the flag with a crack and a rattle.* NEVILLE *hesitates and then disappears rapidly as a voice bellows:*]

FAIRCLOUGH: You there stand still! Airman! Stand still till the flag's down! [*To Clapp*] Harrison. A/C Harrison. Sergeants' Mess cook. [*Meanwhile an* AIRMAN *in full kit comes into the guardroom and hands a pass to the* CORPORAL *who writes in a ledger. The phone continues to ring unanswered in the office.*]

CORPORAL [*slowly as he writes*]: Leave finishes on ... [*checks 295*] 1800 hours, 18th ... that's all right airman.

FAIRCLOUGH: Where've you been?

AIRMAN: Command H.Q. I've just been posted here. I'll need a billet.

FAIRCLOUGH: Oh? Very interesting. Where's your 1250? [*To Clapp*] Have you got anything Mr Clapp? Sir?

[CLAPP *glances down at his papers without really looking and shakes his head with a kind smile, looking at the airman.* FAIRCLOUGH *turns back to the airman.*]

Of course you wouldn't have anything to do with Exercise 'Shatter'? [*Looking at identity card ... the airman's blue 1250*] Trade ... R.A.F. Regiment. That's interesting. Where's your shoulder flashes airman? You notice he's got no shoulder flashes corporal. You notice that, sir? [*Back to the airman*] What time does it start then? Come on, you know what I'm talking about: Exercise 'Shatter'.

AIRMAN: I wouldn't know.

SERGEANT FAIRCLOUGH [*hard*]: You wouldn't know what?

AIRMAN [*mumbles, humiliated*]: I wouldn't know, sergeant.

FAIRCLOUGH: I think I'd like to have a chat with you about what you wouldn't know airman.

[*Much of this is for the benefit of Clapp, who takes very little notice, but sits benignly watching everything like a deaf old auntie.*]

We have some very nice long chats in this guardroom, don't we corporal?

[*The* CORPORAL *grins.*]

We're specialists.

[*Almost kindly to the airman:*] Stand up airman.

[*The airman stiffens.*]

Now if you'll just step through.

[ALBERT *has come in hastily for his leave pass.*]

CORPORAL [*to Sergeant*]: Meakin.

SERGEANT: What d'you want, Meakin?

[CLAPP *gets up and strolls to the door to look out.*]

ALBERT: My leave pass, sergeant.

FAIRCLOUGH: What time?

ALBERT: 1800 hours.

FAIRCLOUGH: It's not 1800 hours yet by one minute.

ALBERT: I mean after duty.

FAIRCLOUGH: Which?

ALBERT: 1800 hours and after duty I think it says. I've finished work, sergeant.

FAIRCLOUGH: What's that you've got in your side-pack, Meakin?

ALBERT: Nothing. After duty.

FAIRCLOUGH: I mean I haven't got my side-pack, sergeant.

[FAIRCLOUGH *turns to look at the airman. The* CORPORAL *looks through a rack for Meakin's pass. The phone stops ringing in the office. There is a slight pause, then:*]

You can sit down here.

[*The guardroom phone rings.* FAIRCLOUGH *picks it up.*]

Hello, guardroom R.A.F. Geldon. Yes. Yes. Very good, sir. He'll be at the Officers' Mess. Hello PBX? Put this call through to the Officers' Mess and give me the Duty Corporal. Hallo. Sergeant Fairclough speaking. Alert all sections for Exercise 'Shatter'. You heard me. Beginning 1800 hours tonight. Don't tell me what time it is I know. [*Rings off.*] You heard that corporal? You can tear our friend Meakin's 295 up for him, Exercise 'Shatter' is on.

ALBERT: But sergeant my pass says after duty, and the exercise hasn't even begun.

FAIRCLOUGH: Don't talk back to me. All leave is automatically cancelled as per Station Orders. Every man will be needed. [*To the airman*] Now then my laddo, we'll have a bit of a check about you. [*He takes down a bundle of orders from its nail and starts to leaf through.*] Postings postings postings.

[ALBERT *can't get out of the guardroom for* CLAPP, *who stands in the doorway.*]

ALBERT: Excuse me, sir. [*No move.*] Excuse me . . . it's that I have to get out now, sir. . . .

[*The clock clicks up to six o'clock. A clatter of boots, and a Bren team hurries by.* FAIRCLOUGH *looks out at them.*]

FAIRCLOUGH: That's very good, those men. Very quick turn out.

ALBERT: Excuse me.

FAIRCLOUGH: Meakin! What section should you be at?

ALBERT: Sarnts' Mess sergeant, only its . . .

FAIRCLOUGH: Get there then! Don't idle!

[ALBERT *squeezes himself desperately past Clapp.* CLAPP *moves out and away with his briefcase.*

The AIRMAN *rises, takes out a small flour bag, and brings it down smartly on the* CORPORAL'S *head. The* CORPORAL'S *hat is well down and there's flour everywhere. The police look at him, stunned.*]

AIRMAN: That's you finished anyway. I've just blown you and the guardroom to high heaven. Fetch an umpire.

FAIRCLOUGH: You just stay where you are, airman.

AIRMAN: And you're dead, work your way out of that one.

CORPORAL: If we're dead so is he, sarge!

FAIRCLOUGH: Aha! Just a minute! The exercise hasn't begun yet! That's something you didn't know Montgomery isn't it? That clock's eight minutes fast and it's only just past six by it now.

AIRMAN: You rotten liar!

FAIRCLOUGH: You call me a liar airman and I'll soon think up a few particularly horrible charges for you. Watch him, corporal. [*On phone*] Hallo PBX, give me a time-check will you? Sergeant Fairclough. [*Holds the receiver out to the airman.*]

AIRMAN: Er . . . hallo? Thank you. Yer, thank you . . .

FAIRCLOUGH: Nignog thinks it's a real person speaking. All right airman that'll do, you can't go on chattering to the talking clock all night. Is Greenwich Mean Time good enough for you? Because I'm afraid our sundial is out of order. I could go and get you a dandelion off the strip except I'd be worried about the blankets in the cells tonight.

AIRMAN: You can't capture me, sergeant! The exercise hasn't begun yet.

FAIRCLOUGH: Then you'll just have to wait here until it does, won't you?

AIRMAN: But you can't hold me for nothing!

FAIRCLOUGH: I'll think of something if you really insist.

[*A commando of R.A.F. Regiment airmen has been gathering outside the wire, which is now pulled up taut. They have rifles, flourbags, webbing and small packs, denims, rubber boots, faces blacked-up, red flashes behind dulled cap-badges. All very dramatic.*

A PILOT OFFICER *in similar order approaches at a crouching run.*]

PILOT OFFICER: Hello, men.

COMMANDOS: Evening, sir.

PILOT OFFICER: Good show. Ah there you are, corporal. [*Looks towards the camp.*] They're quick off the mark anyway. But I don't think much of their dispositions.

[*In the camp there is a certain amount of activity, among which a Bren is being mounted on the larder roof of the Sergeants' Mess, and a small searchlight.*]

Seems to be a cookhouse there. Some asses are installing a Bren on the roof ... ah! And a searchlight. Interesting. You'll have something to sharpen your teeth on this side.

[*A thunderflash is set off somewhere. None of the men stirs. But several airmen scuttle across the camp.*]

If you get into a rough-house, don't leave any marks, you've all got rubbers on. [*Sees Harry.*] Oh, that you Harry?

HARRY: Yes sir.

PILOT OFFICER: [*to Corporal*]: Watch that Bashi Bazook there doesn't kill anybody, corporal.

Get an umpire before you sort that Bren out. Infiltration attacks begin at 1810 hours, and every unit sticks to its own zero. O.K.? Just keep 'em busy. Don't go rushing in till your zero, then give 'em hell. O.K.? Check watches: 1805 hours check? My goodness I must be off. There's Corporal Lloyd's infiltration due to begin. Gosh. [*He scoots off like a crab.*] Good luck.

CORPORAL: Thank you, sir. Good luck. [*To the men*] You heard what he said? Keep 'em busy. You first Harry, you're on your own.

[*One of the commandoes begins to wriggle towards the camp. We hear the thunderous roar of a passing car and TAFFY dodges nervously on. He carries two rifles and has a white flash in his beret. Troops trot by trailing rifles.*]

TAFFY: Hey Nev! Nev!

NEVILLE [*enters, watching the troops with considerable interest*]: What's up with everyone?

TAFFY: Here I brought you your rifle from the billet.

NEVILLE: Why?

TAFFY: Didn't you know there's a war on? Mr McKendrick says

will you be ready with egg and chips for the sergeants during the night. And tea. And pay special attention to the needs of the mess waiter he says.

NEVILLE: Soldiers?

TAFFY: That's right, Nev boyo. Here you are [*the rifle*]. That there little hole at the end is where the bullets come out as I remember. I've an idea the C.O. knows there's a war on too ... we nearly had our first casualty just now, missed me by inches as I was coming up the road. Brings out the whole drama of battle when you drive fast don't it? Only I don't think I'm a hero, because I skipped out of the way pretty quick.

[ALBERT *comes mooching by on his way to the Mess.*]

'Do unto others as you would be done by yourself', tha's what they say don't they? Well how'd you cope with a fellow like our C.O. who ain't bothered whether it's him or another who gets battered into little pieces? I think he's an anti-social element and irreligious into the bargain. Perhaps I ought to shoot him with one o'my imaginary bullets and let him imagine he's dead. Oh hello Bert you better get yourself a gun or you won't make a realistic target for the enemy.

[ALBERT *lours. He and* NEVILLE *move into the kitchen to escape Taffy's barrage of chatter.*]

Well I'll be seeing you lads. Me and the others have got to fall into line and be shot at.

[TAFFY *pauses briefly and we hear the clicking of rifle bolts that fills the air like crickets.*]

Just listen to them rifles clicking. Sinister innit? But don't worry chaps, they're ours.

[*A thunderflash goes off close by.*]

That's them bloody rotten umpires. I seen 'em sneaking about with them fireworks. I prefer the enemy. I mean you can't even surrender to an umpire can you? Bye now. [TAFFY *goes.*]

ALBERT [*following Neville into the kitchen*]: Rotten farce. It wouldn't be so bad even if we had blanks for the friggin rifles. I suppose you realize that's my leave gone for a burton?

NEVILLE: Don't worry Bert, it'll soon be done. You can get away the minute it's over.

ALBERT: That's what you think. [*Almost hysterical*] They tore up my friggin pass in the guardroom!

[*The* ADJUTANT *goes by with a walkie-talkie.*]

ADJUTANT: Able to M.G. Able to M.G. Do not sortie. Do not sortie. Maintain patrols, maintain patrols. Out. [*Sees Albert.*] You there! Where's your rifle?

ALBERT [*picks up Neville's*]: Gorrit here, sir.

ADJUTANT [*going*]: Carry on.

ALBERT [*to Neville*]: I'll just have a look outside.

[ALBERT *goes to the outer door.*]

PILOT OFFICER: You there! Report to H.Q. for patrol duty!

ALBERT: I am on duty, sir.

PILOT OFFICER: Who's section?

ALBERT: I'll just get my rifle, sir.

PILOT OFFICER: That's better. Report to H.Q.

[ALBERT *goes back into the kitchen.*]

ALBERT: Hey Nev, what you doing? I'll give you a hand. If I keep moving nobody can have me creeping about in the cold.

NEVILLE: You can chip some potatoes for me.

ALBERT: All right.

[ALBERT *goes along to the larder door. He puts on the light. One of the Bren team on the roof leans down to the window and calls:*]

AIRMAN: Hey ! Hey!

[ALBERT *shoots out and back into the kitchen.*]

ALBERT: Nev, there's some frigger in there.

[NEVILLE *is putting the chip pan on the stove. He goes to look in the larder. Looks at Albert and then goes back to his work.*]

Friggin gremlins.

AIRMAN: Hey!

[*The* AIRMAN *on the roof dangles down the flex of the searchlight with a large plug on the end of it, so as to tap on the window.*

ALBERT *hesitates and then walks boldly into the larder, shutting the door.*

The AIRMAN *taps on the window.*

ALBERT *scrabbles at the door frantically and then reappears. He looks up and down the corridor.*

The AIRMAN *taps on the window again and* ALBERT *swings round.*]

He sees the dangling plug and goes to the window and leans out to look up.]

AIRMAN: Hey!

ALBERT: You want to watch who you're friggin messin' about you do.

AIRMAN: Find a power point and shove that in, will you? Plug it in. And listen, are you going to be there all night?

ALBERT: You'll get shot by your own men, tapping on windows. All night? More like all week. You read Station Orders? They cancelled my leave just because imagery missiles have supposed to have fallen on England. Good luck to 'em I say. It's friggin indefinite!

AIRMAN: All right, all right. [*To the others on the roof*] Bloody pacifist here we've got. [*Back down to Albert*] Look I'm not the Air Ministry d'you mind? All I want to know is are you going to be there?

ALBERT: What I want to know is what's missiles for if we have to have all this?

AIRMAN: Now don't go on about it, just listen: plug it in.

[*The searchlight blazes as* ALBERT *plugs it in.*]

Switch it off! Cor. Now are you listening? When I give two taps with my boot, you switch it on, all right? Take no notice of us tramping about. Two clear taps like this:

[*He taps. The searchlight blazes.*]

Not now you thickheaded misbegotten zombie! Switch it off! Switch it off!

[*Off it goes again.*]

Make the place look like Blackpool. *When* I signal. Cor.

[ALBERT *leans out again.*]

ALBERT: Hey you don't think they'll attack this side, do you?

AIRMAN: I'm sure they will.

ALBERT: But they can't.

AIRMAN: You could go and tell them that, they'll be somewhere out there.

[ALBERT *comes out of the larder and goes to the back door. With great caution he goes to the wire. The* CORPORAL *on the roof, who is scanning with night glasses, could see him if he looked down; the parapet of the roof shields him from the view of anyone else on the roof.*

The commando airman HARRY *reaches the wire a little way along and begins to sever the wire. As it sags* ALBERT *looks along and sees Harry. He looks back to where his loot is hidden and is filled with dread.* ALBERT *turns to wave to the Corporal on the roof to warn him.* HARRY *sees the movement and half rises. After a second's hesitation during which he debates going through the wire now,* HARRY *stands on his side, presents his rifle, and begins a terrifying screaming charge along the wire at Albert. The* CORPORAL *on the roof wakes up. Albert is rooted with terror until the Bren gives a burst, ineffective because of the parapet. This galvanizes* ALBERT *just as Harry is on him, Albert on the other side of the wire, and he legs it wildly along the wire with* HARRY *yelling behind him. He doubles back and flies in the other direction. As he passes the Mess the second time he realizes that that way lies safety and he bolts inside.* HARRY *hurls a flour bag which explodes on the parapet. In the resulting white cloud the Bren is lifted on to the parapet and gives another burst. Umpires come running and a patrol armed with rifles. Officers shout orders and umpires shout to countermand them. Several airmen go through the gap in the wire and others give them what would be a highly lethal covering fire.* NEVILLE *gazes out of the kitchen at the battle.* HARRY *quickly joins his companions out of the way.*]

ALBERT: Nev. Nev! They're attacking! Don't just friggin stand there!

NEVILLE: It's interesting.

ALBERT: But we can't just let them! [*Seizes Nev's rifle.*]

NEVILLE: What are you panicking about?

[*The* C.O. *is in the office talking into a walkie-talkie on the desk. The* ADJUTANT *approaches the Sergeants' Mess battle.*]

ADJUTANT: I've called up Green, sir, and Blue is coping. We should contain them here, sir. Main Gate is coping.

[*The* C.O. *is clearly saying something quietly unkind.*]

ALBERT: There's that rotten nit again with his chatterbox. Look at them milling about. They're all over the place!

NEVILLE: So? Anyway those are ours. I thought you were going to cut me some chips?

ALBERT: Chips at a time like this? The whole world's gone mad. I don't know what to do. It's not happening, it's a nightmare.

Somebody'd have told us if this was really going to happen. One thing I'm not stopping here. Fat lot of good you'd be in a war.

NEVILLE: Don't say that Bertie lad. I'd fight to the last breath to avoid fighting to my last breath. Can't you just see it? You and Queen's Regulations just a shadow on the concrete, and me and I.G. Farben sitting down to a triumphal tea of radioactive toast. The winners!

ALBERT: You don't seem to think anything's worth defending. You're a coward! I'm sorry Nev, I didn't mean to say that.

NEVILLE: You are in a state, aren't you?

ALBERT: They're going through the wire!

[*The Regiment Commandos have moved right away so as to evade pursuit. The* CORPORAL *examines the scene.*]

COMMANDO CORPORAL: Oh very good Harry. You should be promoted Air Commodore. Oh dear, oh dear. That bloke thought he had the Light Brigade behind him! Well lads I think that was the most successful attack since the brass band captured Amsterdam. There's about a hundred men on this side of the camp.

ADJUTANT [*on walkie-talkie*]: Blue is sortie-ing sir. Blue is sortie-ing.

C.O. [*jumps up to full tether of the headphone lead and sits again*]: Well get them back! Get them back! Great heavens the main gate is under heavy attack. There's so many umpires there they can't see the enemy! Who's the officer responsible?

ADJUTANT: Pilot Officers Feather and Beeston, sir.

C.O.: Tell 'em I'll feather and beeston them! Crimpyhaired weteared brainless pair of runts. Tell them that!

ADJUTANT: Yes sir. Feather and Beeston, sir.

[*The two officers in charge hear their names and approach.*]

C.O.: Leave a guard on the wire. Patrol. And the rest of 'em double, double, double to main gate. Out. Repeat out.

ADJUTANT: Yes, sir and out. [*To the two P/Os*] A detachment to guard the break in the wire. Green Flight to patrol. Blue Flight to report to main gate at the double. Covering fire for Yellow from the airstrip perimeter. Stand by to reinforce main gate. Dismiss. And don't go near the C.O. for a while. For about a month.

[*The two officers whistle up their troops.* TAFFY *is detailed to guard the gap in the wire. As the troops move off, the Adjutant is left. He notices* W.O. CLAPP, *an incongruous figure with his briefcase, standing quietly as the men bustle by. The* ADJUTANT *approaches him, puzzled.* CLAPP *smiles, changes hands with his case, and salutes smartly. The* ADJUTANT *can't think of anything to say, salutes vaguely, and goes.* CLAPP *seems to be admiring the view.*]

ALBERT: Thank goodness they're going. Hey Taffy! The others are going off.

TAFFY: Hush, I'm on guard.

ALBERT: Yeh, but the others are going off.

TAFFY [*coming closer*]: Isn't that just like them. Any chance of a cup of tea, Neville, I'm parched. What was it happened just now?

NEVILLE: Two hundred howling fuzzie wuzzies just went for Bert here.

TAFFY: No kidding? D'you think I'd better step inside?

ALBERT: Dark isn't it now?

TAFFY: By aye. They could be creeping up out there again.

ALBERT: [*edgy again*]: I don't know what they want to keep attacking the Sergeants' Mess for.

TAFFY: Well they got to ain't they? It's a war.

ALBERT: What good'll it do them if they capture us and everything? What good's the Sergeants' Mess to anybody?

TAFFY: Trouble with you Albert Meakin, you don't trust your superior officers. You haven't a proper sense of discipline. You're a soldier now, and you got to rely on your properly constituted officers to land you in the muck else where are you?

It's obvious to me that the Sergeants' Mess is an important objective. Once they got that our men will be reduced to an indisciplined rabble and they can go home then can't they? And as the C.O. was saying to me that's the last thing *we* want innit Jones bach? Them criminal aggressors out there want to get it over and home to their beds. Only the umpires won't have that: they know when everything's supposed to happen. They was very bitter about this battle we just had, and was all for sending us away. Said there wasn't supposed to be no attack at all.

ALBERT: Friggin farce. Hear that Nev?

TAFFY: Anyway we're all right for a bit. Not an umpire in sight. The enemy'll just have to creep about out there for a bit.

ALBERT: I wish you'd shurrup about them blokes creeping about.

TAFFY [*moving off*]: I'll be back by.

[JOHN, *the blind man, and* MARGIT, *stand a little way off the wire outside.* ALBERT *goes to the back door and calls after Taffy.*]

ALBERT: Hey Taff.

[TAFFY *looks round.* ALBERT *checks that there's no one about before he speaks. Sees Clapp and goes straight back in.* CLAPP *moves away.*]

Bet you're fed up, eh Nev? Bet you just fancied a night off in the village. Few beers and pick up a kitbag bird, eh?

[NEVILLE *watches Albert.*]

My leave going I know how you feel. That's why I was so sharp just now, my leave, nothing else. Sorry, Nev. Tell you what, if you fancy slipping out for a while, there's that hole in the wire. Taffy won't say nothing and I can cover up easy.

[NEVILLE *goes suspiciously to the back door and looks round outside. All he can make out is Taffy. He comes back and gets the peeled potatoes from the larder and goes back into the kitchen. Takes out a potato and lays it by Albert on the table.* ALBERT *moves away.*]

Is he still there then? I thought he'd gone.

[NEVILLE *picks up the potato and a rolling pin and moves up to Albert.*]

NEVILLE: Is who still where?

ALBERT: I don't understand you, Neville, you get right funny sometimes. Wonder what's going on outside.

[ALBERT *goes out to the back. He's just peering round to where Clapp was when* MARGIT *calls softly.*]

MARGIT: Albert. Albert darling.

[ALBERT *goes hastily to the wire.*]

I hope you don't mind me coming like this, but he's such a funny old man.

ALBERT: Where is he?

[MARGIT *points to where John leans on his white stick.* ALBERT *glances to the Corporal on the roof and round about.*]

MARGIT: He's not far off.

ALBERT: You'll get me into trouble.

MARGIT: That's just what I said. But once he wants something ... He wouldn't even ask properly like you should, at the front gate.

I know I used to, during the war, to find out if some feller'd been posted or what had happened to him. Lovely boys they were.

ALBERT: There's an exercise on. The camp's closed.

MARGIT: There you are, I expect he knew. But he never tells me anything. You'd think he would. I'm his eyes you know ... at night, when he won't bring the dog out.

ALBERT: I wish you'd stop blethering.

MARGIT: Oh am I talking too much again? John says I always do. It's nerves you know. And I've hardly got my breath.

ALBERT: Shurrup and gerron with it.

MARGIT: All right. Well, *he* says, and I'm sure I don't know what he means, he says: tell Albert I'm here waiting and no messing. Those were his very words. Look he's standing there. You'd think he could see to look at him wouldn't you? Any reply?

[*The* CORPORAL *on the roo leans down to speak to Albert.*]

CORPORAL: What d'you think you're on, airman?

MARGIT: No. He said there wouldn't be. I must be off now else I'll be getting you put in that glasshouse poor lamb. God bless.

CORPORAL: Airman!

[MARGIT *goes trotting off, and she and John withdraw.* ALBERT *goes back into the kitchen, to the indignation of the Corporal.* CLAPP *appears outside the wire. He walks softly across to one of the commandos who is watching the camp intently. Crouches beside him. The commando starts and lashes out with the stock of his rifle.* CLAPP *brushes the blow away skilfully with his briefcase.*]

CLAPP: Careful how you go, airman. Seen two old people, one with a white stick, up near the wire.

COMMANDO [*wary*]: Yes.

CLAPP: Yes, so have I. That's a funny thing, isn't it? You'd wonder what to make of it. Where are they now?

[*The* AIRMAN *indicates the way they took and* CLAPP *goes off that way.* ALBERT *reappears at the back door.* TAFFY *is idling by.*]

ALBERT: Can you see anything, Taffy?

TAFFY: Not a damn thing.

ALBERT: Hey Taff, will you do us a favour?

TAFFY: Will I hell, S.A.C. Meakin.

ALBERT: No, seriously: I want to slip down to Geldon to see the missis. She's expecting me.

[TAFFY *makes no reply.*]

You'd be no good in a war, would you? You just don't care. You're not even looking.

TAFFY: I'm quite jumpy enough with imagining the enemy, thank you, without actually seeing them. If there's one he won't attack by himself, and if there's two that's me finished anyway, innit?

ALBERT: Look! There!

TAFFY [*immediately on his guard*]: Where? Where?

ALBERT [*derisive*]: That made you jump.

TAFFY: So would you if I was to shout in your earhole.

ALBERT [*he's had a cunning thought*]: There they go. Them tyres.

[*Points farther away down the wire.* TAFFY *looks and takes a step with his rifle at the ready.*]

Go on, I'll get an umpire.

TAFFY [*tense*]: Yes, you get an umpire. You ain't kidding me, are you Bert?

ALBERT: Can't you see them?

TAFFY: I don't know, first smell of blood and all my savage instincts ... [*Alarmed*] How many?

ALBERT [*adjusting*]: Just one.

TAFFY: Get an umpire, Bert. I'm going in.

[TAFFY *considers going outside the wire, then goes inside, very cautious. Trips slightly and recovers.* ALBERT *looks at the roof. The* CORPORAL *has taken notice and is following Taffy's progress.* ALBERT *slips through the gap and begins to creep away with his kitbag.*

The commandos are getting restive.]

COMMANDO: It's as soft as cowflop this side, Jack. We could do it at a fast run. One guard, and that Bren on the roof.

COMMANDO CORPORAL: And what about the searchlight, professor?

COMMANDO: We'd be there before they woke up.

COMMANDO CORPORAL: We attack when orders say we do.

COMMANDO: Well I want a smoke.

COMMANDO CORPORAL: Cor. You'd be a great help in a war. A smoke he says.

COMMANDO: There'll be a war all right if you keep the lads here much longer.

[*Gazes moodily at the camp. Sees Albert wriggling along, inching the kitbag before him.*]

Hey!

COMMANDO CORPORAL: What's the matter?

COMMANDO: There's somebody out there.

COMMANDO CORPORAL: Keep your heads down.

COMMANDO: I'll have him, Jack. Let me have him.

COMMANDO CORPORAL: Counter-attack. There might be hundreds of them crawling about out there. If we stop to deal with any of them we might miss our zero.

Listen: we're going through them. We're an infiltration unit and that's what we're going to do. With a bit of luck we'll go straight through them, and they'll think we're their own men if they see us at all. We can flop down in some of that rubbish close up to the wire and wait five minutes. If we're spotted by that Bren crew I shall give the order to charge. Come on.

[*They advance, spreading out and crouching. A commando pitches straight over Albert winding him. The others reach cover close to the wire.*

On the roof the CORPORAL *gestures for the searchlight to be switched on and an* AIRMAN *taps on the roof with his boot.* NEVILLE, *who has been cutting chips, goes to the larder and looks in. Tap, tap again.*]

CORPORAL: Light Jerry.

[*The* AIRMAN *taps again.*]

Come on Jerry, let's have that light.

[JERRY *taps again.*

The COMMANDO *holds the butt of his rifle in Albert's face.*]

COMMANDO: One squeak buster, and you get it. Cripes.

[*He reassures himself that Albert is alive. On the roof* JERRY *taps again.*]

CORPORAL: Look, will you cut out that Fred Astaire stuff and get this light on!

[*Inside the larder* NEVILLE *switches on the light.*]

Put that light out!

[NEVILLE *switches off the light and leans out at the window.*]

JERRY: Hey, hey! Light!

NEVILLE: I have done.

JERRY: Put the light on.

NEVILLE: You just said switch it off.

[NEVILLE *switches on the larder light.*]

JERRY: No, not that one. Switch it off. The *light*. [*Desperately to the others*] They've changed the bloke.

[NEVILLE *switches off the larder light. The* COMMANDO *who fell over Albert comes forward.* ALBERT *starts to crawl away.*]

Now, switch the light on!

NEVILLE [*looking out of the window*]: Are you trying to make a charlie out of Neville?

[*The* GUNNER *hoists the Bren on to the parapet and fires a burst.*

ALBERT *throws caution to the winds and flies with his kitbag.*]

JERRY [*frantic*]: The light! The light! The other one!!

CORPORAL: For god's sake light! For pity's sake!

JERRY: The power point!

[*The Bren fires once more. With a wild yell the* COMMANDO CORPORAL *dives through the gap in the wire. The rest of the commandos follow him screaming. The searchlight beam shoots vertically up and someone dives on it. We hear distant commands and clattering boots. Thunderflashes go off. The* C.O. *hurtles into the office to the walkie-talkie. Umpires come running. The commandos swarm into the mess and on to the roof.*]

C.O.: Adge! H.Q. calling Adge. A for apple come in! Where is that firing? Where is that firing? Over.

[*A* COMMANDO *belts the Bren gunner smartly over the head with a flourbag and gets the team off the roof. He turns the search-light to illuminate the rest of the camp. Men begin to file into the Sergeants' Mess Hall as prisoners, face to the wall, hands on heads.*

A COMMANDO *goes into the kitchen.*]

COMMANDO: You're my prisoner, cookie.

NEVILLE [*puts a ladle into the fat*]: Like to see this fat sizzle?

[*The* COMMANDO *makes a move and then dodges with a yell as* NEVILLE *coolly whangs a ladle full of hot fat at him. In the Mess Hall one* COMMANDO *is left in charge of the prisoners, among whom by now is* SERGEANT BULL. *As the* GUARD *comes near enough* BULL *takes a wild drunken swing at him. The* GUARD *brings up his rifle to protect himself and catches Bull on the jaw. Down he goes and they crowd anxiously round him. In the kitchen* TAFFY *marches in to find a* COMMANDO *with his back to him.*]

TAFFY: All right hands up everybody I'm a hero.

[*The* COMMANDO CORPORAL *has come through from the Mess Hall.*]

COMMANDO CORPORAL: You shut your face. Get through there with the rest of the prisoners the pair of you. [*To his own man*] Don't just stand there mack, bustle them.

COMMANDO: Look out, Jack!

[*The* CORPORAL *dodges back as* NEVILLE *dips the ladle in the fat and holds it ready.*]

NEVILLE: Away and shoot some sergeants if you want to make yourself useful; don't come bothering me.

COMMANDO: He's crackers, Jack. He nearly had me with that fat. [*Points to the stain where the fat hit the wall.*]

COMMANDO CORPORAL: You're dangerous airman. I shall bang in a report about you.

[*The* CORPORAL *turns back to the Mess and beckons the commando to follow him. They begin to marshal the other prisoners. The* ADJUTANT, *still with his walkie-talkie, is brought in.*]

ADJUTANT [*on walkie-talkie*]: I'm sorry I didn't get that last message, sir, I've been captured. The enemy is infiltrating our lines from main gate. I think we've bought it, sir. I'm worried about casualties, sir, Sergeant Bull's jaw seems to be broken.

C.O.: What's that? Repeat message. Repeat message. Over.

[*The* CORPORAL *gently relieves Adjutant of the radio and it is stacked with the prisoners' rifles in the middle of the Hall.*]

What's happened to Green Flight, Adge? Double them up to the Sergeants' mess and report back. You must contact them.

[*The* c.o. *looks up as* GROUPIE, *an enormous hearty thick-set man, bursts into the office flanked by two commandos with sten-guns. He has a bottle of champagne.*]

Look here Groupie your men are completely out of hand.

[*The camp is quietening down. Prisoners file out of the Mess. Occasional clickings and bangs and the clangour of an ambulance bell, whistles and distant orders.*]

GROUPIE: Hellow Howard. Got glasses? You've lost.

c.o.: Yes very clever Groupie, but you've got to stop this nonsense or there'll be a massacre. One of my sergeants has had his jaw broken.

GROUPIE: Good heavens! Give me that thing, you shouldn't have it anyway.

[*He turns the radio round and pulls the cans off the C.O.'s head . He doesn't put them on himself, just shouts into the mike.* TAFFY *is in the wash-up, peering cautiously after the departing prisoners.*]

Listen you! [*Nothing.*] Listen you! Over. [*To the C.O.*] Who's supposed to be on the other end.

c.o.: My adjutant. He's been captured.

GROUPIE: You're going to pieces, Howard. Any other day of the week you'd have been delighted to lose that rabbit. [*On radio*] This is Group Captain Lyons speaking from H.Q. R.A.F. Geldon. All R.A.F. Geldon troops still active to surrender at H.Q. Over. [*Nothing. To the C.O.*] Deaf as well as stupid. I'd better go down there and see what's happening. Come on, the exercise'll be good for the liver.

[*They leave the office.* TAFFY *comes back into the kitchen.*]

TAFFY: Pocket of resistance, that's what we was Nev boyo. We oughter be mentioned in dispatches. Those chips look smashing, where's the vinegar?

NEVILLE: Clean that grease off the wall for us, Taffy.

TAFFY: They couldn't capture us could they, Nev? Bet we won't even get a medal. Unsung heroes. D'you think I ought to go and give them back our guns now that the fighting and the tumult's died and Sergeant Bull's safe in the sick bay? I'm glad he's out of the way anyway; there's a lot to be said for having a war once in a while.

NEVILLE: Clean that grease off the wall for us Taffy, and you can have a plate of hot chips.

TAFFY [*going about it*]: Ooooh ... with vinegar on them eh, Nev?

[ALBERT, *bedraggled and miserable, is creeping back into camp.*]

NEVILLE: Aye but sharp.

TAFFY: And a cup of tea eh, Nev?

[*The grease isn't easy to get off.*]

Couldn't I have a plate of chips first, just to give me strength to carry on, eh? And a cup of tea?

ALBERT [*in the door*]: We get no rations for gash cups of tea, Taffy. Gerrout.

[NEVILLE *and* TAFFY *look at Albert, who pours himself a cup of tea and puts on a small frying-pan. Finally:*]

TAFFY: We been fighting the enemy, Bert, who you been fighting?

ALBERT [*to no one in particular*]: Som'dy's going to suffer for tonight's work. [*Breaks eggs into the pan.*] Ouf! Even the friggin eggs are turning on me. [*Goes round to the other stove behind and dumps them in.*] Dump them on the other fire, seeing it's out.

[*Comes back and puts two more eggs on.* NEVILLE *gives Taffy a plate of chips.* TAFFY *gazes with rapture at Albert's eggs.*]

Pooh, smell them eggs. Perhaps I should have rinsed the pan. Look at that rotten gannet. [*To Taffy*] Don't stand there drooling Taffy gerrout.

[TAFFY *moves behind the stove out of sight.*]

Worse nor a spaniel dog.

I've had a rollicking from the S.W.O.

I've had me leave pass tore up.

I just happened to slip out the back there and I got walked on.

[*There is a muffled explosion from the other stove.*]

They still at it?

[NEVILLE *goes round to look.*]

NEVILLE: No, it's them bad eggs you put in the other stove. Must be still alight.

[TAFFY *appears round the other way. His face is sooty and his chips are covered with soot.*]

TAFFY: You dirty beggar Meakin.

ALBERT: You can talk you've got soot all over your face.

NEVILLE [*he has picked up a rusty old cookhouse triangle*]: Come, come lads, where's that merry sparkle? Fall in for the investiture.

[*He places himself between them to make a rank. They are reluctant to join in, but do so half-heartedly.*]

Me-en hi! In recognition of our courage and fortitude in battle we have been awarded the N.A.A.F.I. medal gongs all round chaps. [*Bangs the triangle.*] Hi! N.A.A.F.I. No ambition and frigg-all interest.

[*Sings*]

We don't want to fight, but by jingo if we do

We'll be known to all the nations as the mighty precious few.

Me-en hi! Anda-ar he! Me-en hi! Anda-ar he!

[*Steps out of the rank and repeats the same orders.*]

Me-en hi! Anda-ar he! Me-en hi! Anda-ar he!

TAGGY: Oh give over, Nev. What the hell you on about?

NEVILLE: I was just wondering which felt dafter . . . in among you or out here looking at you.

ALBERT [*reluctant smile*]: Huh, you're a laugh Nev. I never know how to take you.

[KEIGHLY *looks into the kitchen.*]

KEIGHLY: Straighten yourselves up. C.O.'s inspection.

[*He looks at Taffy, who faces him still with the plateful of soot and chips in his hand.*]

You forgot the ketchup.

[KEIGHLY *goes.* TAFFY *gets rid of the mess.* ALBERT *seizes a broom and begins to clean up frantically.*]

ALBERT: It's not enough we get trampled on and shot at and charged at oh no . . . we have to have a friggin inspection as well. I ask you, right in the middle of an exercise!

[*The* C.O. *comes in with* KEIGHLY.]

KEIGHLY: Sar'nt Mess Kitchen hi!

C.O.: Easy. [*Rubs his hands.*] Looks nice and cosy in here, cookie [*he means Neville*], after that shambles out there. That tea, I see?

[NEVILLE *gives him Bert's mug and pours out one each for Keighly and himself.*]

Much damage here cookie?

TAFFY: We had a minor engagement, sir, and emerged triumphant.

c.o.: Who the devil's that baboon?

TAFFY: Waiter here, sir.

c.o. [*not much enlightened*]: Oh.

TAFFY [*eager*]: We fought them off single-handed.

c.o. [*with a strange look*]: Hear that, Mr Keighly? Pity there weren't a few more like him. [*To Albert*] You the other waiter here? Good show.

ALBERT: I'm the Senior Aircraftman here, sir. Cook. Should be on leave now, sir. [*This with a polite smile suggesting that he doesn't really blame the C.O. personally.*]

c.o.: Oh well that sort of thing can't be helped.

ALBERT: I lost my leave, sir.

c.o.: You on duty here?

    [w.o. CLAPP *approaches the camp. He has his briefcase, and Albert's kitbag, still full.*]

ALBERT: Yes, sir.

c.o.: Where are your whites?

ALBERT: Not on duty *here*, sir. On duty. Patrolling the wire.

c.o.: Oh? Why aren't you at H.Q. with the others?

ALBERT: I was attacked, sir, by the enemy. Got kicked.

c.o.: Got kicked? Where?

ALBERT: In them fields, sir, out there.

c.o.: Fields? I gave no order to sortie. Who's your section commander?

ALBERT [*his mind beginning to race*]: Sergeant Bull, sir.

c.o.: Sergeant Bull? He's the Orderly Sergeant. He hasn't got a section.

ALBERT: I mean Mr McKendrick, sir. I was on duty here.

c.o.: On duty here? Where are your whites?

    [CLAPP *comes into the kitchen and stands by the door.*]

One way or another this man's lying, Mr Keighly. Put him on a charge. [*He goes.*]

ALBERT [*after the C.O.*]: But I'm on duty, sir! And I should be on leave!

KEIGHLY: Report yourself to the guardroom, S.A.C. Meakin.

CLAPP: I'll walk up with him, sir. It'll be company. [*Smiles at Albert.*]

ALBERT [*babbling*]: Thank you very much, sir. I'd be glad to have a talk with you. I've been worried about the amount of rations missing from my stores.

CLAPP: That's nice, isn't it, Mr Keighly? [*Gives Albert the kitbag.*] Here you'd better carry this. You might want it. It is yours, isn't it?

ALBERT: Yes sir, I think so. I was just wondering who I lent it to.

KEIGHLY: Move, airman!

ALBERT [*hysterical by now*]: But I'm on guard, sir!

KEIGHLY [*slowly*]: The exercise is over, airman.

[ALBERT *follows Keighly out shakily.* CLAPP *goes last. The window comes down and* NEVILLE *and* TAFFY *come forward to look out of it. The orchestration of glasshouse sounds that began the play starts up.* ALBERT *crosses the stage to the guardroom with Clapp behind him pressing the pace increasingly.*]

CURTAIN